An Economic Theory
of Democracy

An Economic
Theory of
Democracy

ANTHONY DOWNS

HARPER & ROW   PUBLISHERS   NEW YORK

To

My Mother and Father

Contents

PART III

SPECIFIC EFFECTS OF INFORMATION COSTS

PART IV

DERIVATIVE IMPLICATIONS AND HYPOTHESES

Acknowledgments

Like all supposedly original works, this study owes a great deal of its content to the thoughts and efforts of persons other than the author. I would especially like to thank Kenneth Arrow for all the hours he devoted to guiding and correcting my thinking and for the many excellent ideas he contributed. I would also like to thank Robert A. Dahl and Melvin W. Reder, both of whom read the manuscript and made many suggestions that I have incorporated. In addition, my gratitude goes to Dorothy Wynne, who corrected several errors in the first draft of Chapter 10; to Julius Margolis, whose interest and patience in early discussions of the topic encouraged me to embark on this study; and to Mrs. Carolyn Young and James Smith, who handled the extensive labors of typing and editing the final draft. Finally, I would like to thank the Office of Naval Research for the grant that made this study possible. Naturally, whatever errors remain herein must be counted as part of my own original contribution.

ANTHONY DOWNS

Stanford University
May, 1956

Foreword

This book seeks to elucidate its subject—the governing of democratic states—by making intelligible the party politics of democracies. That was the proper point at which to attack the intellectual problem the author chose for himself, or so it seems to me. It is a fact that competitive party systems are a conspicuous feature of virtually all those nations the non-Communist world thinks of as democratic. It is an even more important fact that what is involved in governing, and in the competition to control the offices of government, amounts to very much the same thing. Fundamentally, governing means getting people to do things, or getting them to refrain from doing things. Those who have the formal authority to govern, if they are to govern actually, must seek to find out who is with them and who is against them. In modern democratic states these intelligence and propaganda operations *are* party politics, or mainly that. A theory of democracy that fails to take account of this fact is of little help in giving us an appreciation of the kinds of actions we may expect of democratic government.

Having given party politics a central place in his thought about democracy, Downs treats it very differently than do other students of politics. His entire effort is to *account for* what parties and voters do. His explanations are systematically related to, and deducible from, precisely stated assumptions about the motivations that attend the decisions of voters and parties and the environment in which they act. He is consciously concerned with economy in explanation, that is, with attempting to account for phenomena in terms of a very limited number of facts and postulates. He is concerned also with the central features of party politics in *any* democratic state, not with that in the United States or any other single country. Downs' book does not in any sense make obsolete the careful and impressively documented descriptions of partisan activities that characterize the best previous work in the field. It is rather a starting point for ordering and assigning significance to the findings of a great deal of past and future research.

Downs assumes that political parties and voters act rationally in the pursuit of certain clearly specified goals—it is this assumption, in fact, that gives his theory its explanatory power. Most of us are such uncritical children of Freud that to say, "He did that because he decided it was the best way to get what he wanted," is apt to strike us as not very profound. Yet, just as firms that do not engage in the rational pursuit of profit are apt to cease to be firms, so politicians who do not pursue votes in a rational manner are apt to cease to be politicians. The behavior of voters may be ignorant but that is not equivalent to its being irrational. The usefulness of assuming rationality on the part of political actors, quite obviously, must be rigorously tested against experience, but its claims to usefulness ought to be clear from what Downs has done with that assumption.

I cannot say, even in this Foreword, that Anthony Downs' *An Economic Theory of Democracy* is a book without faults. I can say quite sincerely that there are few books that have had so great an impact on my thinking, or that I would like so much to have written. Some years from now I shall be surprised if Downs' work is not recognized as the starting point of a highly important development in the study of politics; its influence is already considerable and continues to grow.

STANLEY KELLEY, JR.

Princeton, N.J.
May, 1965

Part I

Basic Structure of the Model

1

Introduction

THROUGHOUT the world, governments dominate the economic scene. Their spending determines whether full employment prevails; their taxes influence countless decisions; their policies control international trade; and their domestic regulations extend into almost every economic act.

Yet the role of government in the world of economic theory is not at all commensurate with this dominance. True, in each separate field of economics, recent thought has fruitfully concentrated upon the impact of government on private decision-making, or the share of government in economic aggregates. But little progress has been made toward a generalized yet realistic behavior rule for a rational government similar to the rules traditionally used for rational consumers and producers. As a result, government has not been successfully integrated with private decision-makers in a general equilibrium theory.

This thesis is an attempt to provide such a behavior rule for democratic government and to trace its implications. In pursuing these ends, we do not pretend to solve all the problems which have been frustrating analysis in this field. However, we hope to start toward a solution of some and to formulate a reasonable evasion of others which are intrinsically insoluble.

3

I. THE MEANING OF RATIONALITY IN THE MODEL

A. THE CONCEPT OF RATIONALITY IN ECONOMIC THEORY

Economic theorists have nearly always looked at decisions as though they were made by rational minds. Some such simplification is necessary for the prediction of behavior, because decisions made at random, or without any relation to each other, do not fall into any pattern. Yet only if human actions form some pattern can they ever be forecast or the relations between them subject to analysis. Therefore economists must assume an ordering of behavior takes place.

There is no *a priori* reason to suppose that this ordering is rational, i.e., reasonably directed toward the achievement of conscious goals. Nevertheless, economic theory has been erected upon the supposition that conscious rationality prevails, in spite of acid assertions to the contrary by men like Thorstein Veblen and John Maurice Clark. Since our model is *ex definitione* one concerning rational behavior, we also make this assumption.[1]

As a result, the traditional methods of prediction and analysis are applicable in our model. If a theorist knows the ends of some decision-maker, he can predict what actions will be taken to achieve them as follows: (1) he calculates the most reasonable way for the decision-maker to reach his goals, and (2) he assumes this way will actually be chosen because the decision-maker is rational.

Economic analysis thus consists of two major steps: discovery of the ends a decision-maker is pursuing, and analysis of which means of attaining them are most reasonable, i.e., require the least input of scarce resources. In carrying out the first step, theorists have generally tried to reduce the ends of each economic agent to a single goal, so that one most efficient way to attain it can be found. If

---

[1] See footnote 3, p. 5. Our definition of *rationality* includes the assumption that men pursue their own interests directly without disguising them, except in one specific instance discussed in Chapter 3. For an analysis of when rational men conceal their preferences, see Kenneth J. Arrow, *Social Choice and Individual Values* (New York: John Wiley & Sons, Inc., 1951), p. 7. Like Arrow, we exclude the "pleasures of the game" aspects of choice-making from our study except for a few specific comments.

multiple goals are allowed, means appropriate to one may block attainment of another; hence no unique course can be charted for a rational decision-maker to follow. To avoid this impasse, theorists posit that firms maximize profits and consumers maximize utility. Any other goals which either possess are considered deviations that qualify the rational course toward the main goal.

In such analysis, the term *rational* is never applied to an agent's ends, but only to his means.[2] This follows from the definition of *rational* as efficient, i.e., maximizing output for a given input, or minimizing input for a given output. Thus, whenever economists refer to a "rational man" they are not designating a man whose thought processes consist exclusively of logical propositions, or a man without prejudices, or a man whose emotions are inoperative. In normal usage all of these could be considered rational men. But the economic definition refers solely to a man who moves toward his goals in a way which, to the best of his knowledge, uses the least possible input of scarce resources per unit of valued output.

To clarify this definition, let us consider an example of behavior which is rational only in the economic sense. Assume that a monk has consciously selected as his goal the achievement of a state of mystical contemplation of God.[3] In order to attain his goal, he must purge his mind of all logical thoughts and conscious goal-seeking. Economically speaking, this purging is quite rational, even though it would be considered irrational, or at least nonrational, by any of the noneconomic definitions of rationality.

[2] We are assuming throughout this study that ends can be separated from means in the mind of the decision-maker. Although it can be argued that goals will be modified by the processes used to attain them, some separation of ends from means must be allowed or all behavior becomes disorganized and pointless. Consequently, we assume that every decision-maker evaluates the alternatives facing him by their relation to his ends, even if these ends are temporary or are themselves means toward some ultimate end. For a discussion of this problem, see William J. Baumol, *Welfare Economics and the Theory of the State* (London: Longmans, Green and Co., 1952), p. 121 n.

[3] Consciously selected goals need not be (1) continuously held in awareness while they are being pursued or (2) purely a matter of free choice. The first point is proved by the example given. The second can be shown by the fact that men consciously seek to obtain food, though their underlying desire to eat is intrinsic to their natures. Thus conscious selection may at times be limited to specifically carrying out basically unconscious drives.

Economic rationality can also be formally defined in another manner. A rational man is one who behaves as follows: (1) he can always make a decision when confronted with a range of alternatives; (2) he ranks all the alternatives facing him in order of his preference in such a way that each is either preferred to, indifferent to, or inferior to each other; (3) his preference ranking is transitive; (4) he always chooses from among the possible alternatives that which ranks highest in his preference ordering; and (5) he always makes the same decision each time he is confronted with the same alternatives.[4] All rational decision-makers in our model—including political parties, interest groups, and governments—exhibit the same qualities.

Rationality thus defined refers to processes of action, not to their ends or even to their success at reaching desired ends. It is notorious that rational planning sometimes produces results greatly inferior to those obtained by sheer luck. In the long run, we naturally expect a rational man to outperform an irrational man, *ceteris paribus*, because random factors cancel and efficiency triumphs over inefficiency. Nevertheless, since behavior in our model cannot be tested by its results, we apply the terms *rational* or *irrational* only to processes of action, i.e., to means. Of course, some intermediate ends are themselves means to ultimate goals. The rationality of the former we can judge, but evaluation of the latter is beyond our scope.

B. THE NARROW CONCEPT OF RATIONALITY IN THE PRESENT STUDY

However, even though we cannot decide whether a decision-maker's ends are rational, we must know what they are before we can decide what behavior is rational for him. Furthermore, in designating these ends, we must avoid the tautological conclusion that every man's behavior is always rational because (1) it is aimed at some end and (2) its returns must have outweighed its costs in his eyes or he would not have undertaken it.

To escape this pitfall, we focus our attention only upon the economic and political goals of each individual or group in the model.

---

[4] These conditions are drawn from the analysis in Chapters 1 and 2 of Arrow, *op. cit.*

Admittedly, separation of these goals from the many others which men pursue is quite arbitrary. For example, a corporation executive may work for a higher income because he enjoys working as well as to gain more purchasing power; hence, viewing the latter as his only real motive is erroneous as well as arbitrary. Nevertheless, this is a study of economic and political rationality, not of psychology. Therefore, even though psychological considerations have a legitimate and significant place in both economics and political science, we by-pass them entirely except for a brief mention in Chapter 2.

Our approach to elections illustrates how this narrow definition of rationality works. The political function of elections in a democracy, we assume, is to select a government. Therefore rational behavior in connection with elections is behavior oriented toward this end and no other. Let us assume a certain man prefers party A for political reasons, but his wife has a tantrum whenever he fails to vote for party B. It is perfectly rational *personally* for this man to vote for party B if preventing his wife's tantrums is more important to him than having A win instead of B. Nevertheless, in our model such behavior is considered irrational because it employs a political device for a nonpolitical purpose.

Thus we do not take into consideration the whole personality of each individual when we discuss what behavior is rational for him. We do not allow for the rich diversity of ends served by each of his acts, the complexity of his motives, the way in which every part of his life is intimately related to his emotional needs. Rather we borrow from traditional economic theory the idea of the rational consumer. Corresponding to the infamous *homo economicus* which Veblen and others have excoriated, our *homo politicus* is the "average man" in the electorate, the "rational citizen" of our model democracy.

Because we allow this political man to be uncertain about the future, he will not appear to be as much of a calculating-machine-brained character as was the utilitarians' economic man. Nevertheless, he remains an abstraction from the real fullness of the human personality. We assume that he approaches every situation with one eye on the gains to be had, the other eye on costs, a delicate ability to balance them, and a strong desire to follow wherever rationality leads him.

Undoubtedly, the fact that our model world is inhabited by such artificial men limits the comparability of behavior in it to behavior in the real world. In the latter, some men *do* cast votes to please their wives—and vice versa—rather than to express their political preferences. And such behavior is often highly rational in terms of the domestic situations in which it occurs. Empirical studies are almost unanimous in their conclusion that adjustment in primary groups is far more crucial to nearly every individual than more remote considerations of economic or political welfare.[5]

Nevertheless, we must assume men orient their behavior chiefly toward the latter in our world; otherwise all analysis of either economics or politics turns into a mere adjunct of primary-group sociology. However, nearly all primary groups are strongly influenced by general economic and political conditions; hence we may provisionally regard the peculiarities of each such group as counterbalanced by opposite peculiarities of other primary groups. Therefore when we define rationality in terms of general conditions alone, we are not distorting reality as greatly as it might at first appear.

The exact nature of the economic and political ends from which we derive our descriptions of rational behavior will be revealed in the specific structure of our model. But before we consider that structure, we must clarify one more aspect of what we mean by rationality: how can we distinguish between the mistakes of rational men and the normal behavior of irrational ones? If rationality really means efficiency, are inefficient men always irrational, or can rational men also act inefficiently?

C. IRRATIONALITY AND THE BASIC FUNCTION OF POLITICAL RATIONALITY

To distinguish clearly between rational errors and irrational behavior is not an easy task. Our first inclination is to declare that a mistaken rational man at least intends to strike an accurate balance

---

[5] For a summary of such studies, see Elihu Katz and Paul F. Lazarsfeld, *Personal Influence* (Glencoe, Illinois: The Free Press, 1955), part one.

between costs and returns; whereas an irrational man deliberately fails to do so. But numerous cases of unconscious neurosis belie this criterion. Even hopeless psychotics often behave with perfect rationality, given their warped perception of reality. Therefore, intention is an inadequate distinction.

For our limited purposes in this model, correctability is a much better means of telling errors from irrational behavior. A rational man who is systematically making some mistake will cease to do so if (1) he discovers what the mistake is and (2) the cost of eliminating it is smaller than the benefits therefrom. Under the same conditions, an irrational man will fail to rectify his errors because he has some nonlogical propensity to repeat them. His actions are not primarily motivated by a desire to attain his overt ends efficiently; hence he fails to do so even when he can.

There are two objections to this method of distinguishing error from irrationality. The first is that it often requires hypothetical testing, since erroneous rational men do not always discover their mistakes. If a man continues to make mistakes, how can we tell whether he is irrational or merely lacks information? In such cases, are we not driven back to judging his intentions, which we have just shown to be useless indicators?

This objection strikes at a basic difficulty in the social sciences by attacking the inability of these sciences to prove all their assertions experimentally. Undoubtedly it weakens our argument. However, if we yield to it completely, we must refrain from making any statements whatever about many vital issues in all the social sciences. To avoid such paralysis we hypothesize whenever it is absolutely necessary, recognizing the limitations of doing so.

The second objection is similar to a point we have already discussed. It states that behavior which is irrational according to our definition is highly rational in the psychic economy of the individual's personality. Neurotic behavior is often a necessary means of relieving tensions which spring from conflicts buried deep within the unconscious.[6] But we are studying rational political behavior,

[6] See Karen Horney, *The Neurotic Personality of Our Time* (New York: W. W. Norton & Company, Inc., 1937), *passim*.

not psychology or the psychology of political behavior. Therefore if a man exhibits political behavior which does not help him attain his political goals efficiently, we feel justified in labeling him politically irrational, no matter how necessary to his psychic adjustments this behavior may be.

The reason we are trying to distinguish so carefully between rational errors and irrational acts is that we wish simultaneously (1) to point out how the cost of information can lead rational men to make systematic errors in politics and (2) to avoid any discussion of political irrationality. Our desire to by-pass political irrationality springs from (1) the complexity of the subject, (2) its incompatibility with our model of purely rational behavior, and (3) the fact that it is an empirical phenomenon which cannot be dealt with by deductive logic alone but also requires actual investigation beyond the scope of this study.

There is only one point at which irrationality needs to be discussed in connection with our model. If a significant section of any body politic becomes irrational in its behavior, a difficult problem is posed for the man who does not. How should he act? What is the best course for a rational man in an irrational world?

The answer depends upon whether the irrationality he faces involves predictable patterns of behavior. If so, rational action is still possible for him. And because almost no society can survive for long if no one in it is efficiently pursuing his goals, there is usually some kind of predictability in the political system. Citizens who behave irrationally do so partly because someone who stands to gain thereby urges them on. For example, a party which perennially makes false promises can gain votes if it convinces voters to believe its lies. It is rational for this party to encourage voters to behave irrationally. Tensions of this type often exist, but as long as someone's rationality prevails, behavior can still be predicted.

Thus, to cope with seemingly irrational behavior, the rational man must try to discern the underlying pattern of rationality; he must discover whose ends this behavior is actually serving and what those ends are. Then he can decide, in view of his own ends, how he should react to this behavior. Only when no pattern can be discovered and all acts are unpredictable—i.e., when chaos prevails—is there no rational course for a man who knows his own goals.

Therefore rational behavior requires a predictable social order. Just as the rational producer must be able to make reasonably accurate forecasts of his demand and costs if he is to invest intelligently, so the rational man in politics must be able roughly to predict the behavior of other citizens and of the government. Some ambiguity is inevitable, but whenever uncertainty increases greatly, rationality becomes difficult.

Because government provides the framework of order upon which the rest of society is built, political rationality has a function much more fundamental than the mere elimination of waste in governing. Rational behavior is impossible without the ordered stability which government furnishes. But government will continue to furnish such stability only so long as the political system functions efficiently, i.e., so long as it is rational. Thus political rationality is the *sine qua non* of all forms of rational behavior.

Of course, political rationality need not operate democratically, as it does in our model. As long as uncertainty is diminished and stable order introduced and maintained, rational action is possible, even if tyranny prevails. Furthermore, political rationality need not be perfect, since most political systems operate tolerably well without being purged of every inefficiency. Nevertheless, a high degree of political rationality is necessary in every large-sized society if it is to solve its problems successfully.

II. THE STRUCTURE OF THE MODEL

Our model is based on the assumption that every government seeks to maximize political support. We further assume that the government exists in a democratic society where periodic elections are held, that its primary goal is reëlection, and that election is the goal of those parties now out of power. At each election, the party which receives the most votes (though not necessarily a majority) controls the entire government until the next election, with no intermediate votes either by the people as a whole or by a parliament.

The governing party thus has unlimited freedom of action, within the bounds of the constitution.

The most important of these bounds is that the government—i.e., the governing party—cannot hamper the operations of other political parties in society.[7] It cannot restrict their freedom of speech, or their ability to campaign vigorously, or the freedom of any citizen to speak out against any party. Nor can it alter the timing of elections, which recur at fixed intervals.[8]

Economically, however, there are no limits to its power. It can nationalize everything, or hand everything over to private parties, or strike any balance between these extremes. It can impose any taxes and carry out any spending it desires. The only restraint upon it is that of maintaining political freedom; therefore it must not vitiate its opponents by economic policies aimed specifically at injuring them. Also it must economically uphold the voting rights of its citizens.[9]

Some political theorists may object that this government seems to have little connection with the state it is supposed to run. Sociol-

[7] Throughout this thesis we use the term *government* in the European sense; i.e., it always refers to the *governing party* unless otherwise noted.

[8] Although elections recur at fixed intervals in our model, they could just as easily recur at any time *within* fixed time limits, with the exact date set by the incumbent party, as in the British political system. Thus our stricture is stronger than necessary; we make it so only to eliminate the timing of elections from the area of party strategy. Alteration of this axiom to resemble the British system would affect none of our conclusions.

[9] It can be argued that government must not destroy private property rights if it is to guarantee political freedom for its citizens, since they must remain independent of its control. However, *private property* in this sense does not mean an ownership claim over the means of production, but a legally protected share of their output. If a citizen knows his income depends upon fulfillment of certain well-defined tasks connected with his job, and that the law protects him from income losses resulting from any actions unconnected with that job, he is free to follow his own political inclinations, regardless of whether he works for the state or a private firm. He owns his job, and as long as he carries out its duties, he cannot be deprived of it without due process of law. Examples of this are seniority rights in unions and status grades in the civil service. We would agree that the government must not abolish *both* this kind of private property and private ownership of the means of production if political freedom is to exist; therefore government's economic power has some limits. Furthermore, since all private property depends upon a legal system independent of politics, one of the elements of our model's constitution must be such a system.

ogists might further object that reëlection *per se* is of no value to anyone; therefore some deeper motives must lie behind it. We will deal with both of these criticisms in Chapter 2. Meanwhile, let us assume that every government's goal is to be reëlected, whether the government be that of a nation, a province, or a municipality.[10]

Having given government a purpose, we can discover the most efficient means it can employ to achieve that purpose. In other words, we can construct a model showing how a rational government behaves in the kind of democratic state we outlined above. However, we first need to know more about the world in which our model government is to function.

This world differs from the usual general-equilibrium world because it contains uncertainty. True, in order to study the basic logic of decision-making in our political economy, we will assume perfect knowledge in Chapters 3 and 4. However, these chapters are only preliminary to the later analysis of behavior when uncertainty prevails.

Our reason for stressing uncertainty is that, in our opinion, it is a basic force affecting all human activity, particularly economic activity. Coping with uncertainty is a major function of nearly every significant institution in society; therefore it shapes the nature of each. A prime example is money, which Lord Keynes and others have shown to be a response to uncertainty, a link between the present and a not-definitely-known future.[11] It would be absurd to study money only in a certain world and hope to discover its essence —in fact, the attempt to do so led to inherent contradictions.

Similarly, though we can find out something about how rational governments operate by analyzing them in a "certain" world, we learn much more by facing uncertainty and the problems it creates. Many of these problems are related to the cost of obtaining informa-

[10] Our main concern is with the national government throughout this thesis. However, much of the reasoning also applies to the other types.

[11] See John Maynard Keynes, *The General Theory of Employment, Interest, and Money* (New York: Harcourt, Brace and Company, 1936), ch. 17. For a lucid explanation of this chapter, see Abba P. Lerner, "The Essential Properties of Interest and Money," *Quarterly Journal of Economics*, LXVI (1952), 172–193.

tion. Therefore we devote several chapters to examining how this cost affects rational political behavior.

We hope that our study will be of interest to students of democracy as well as to economists. Few of our conclusions are new; in fact, some have been specifically stated by Walter Lippmann in his brilliant trilogy on the relation between public opinion and democratic government.[12] However, our attempt to trace what rational men will do, both as citizens and in government, is novel as far as we know. It tends to prove logically contentions that Lippmann and others have reached by observing politics empirically.

Thus our model could be described as a study of political rationality from an economic point of view. By comparing the picture of rational behavior which emerges from this study with what is known about actual political behavior, the reader should be able to draw some interesting conclusions about the operation of democratic politics.

III. THE RELATION OF OUR MODEL TO PREVIOUS ECONOMIC MODELS OF GOVERNMENT

Most economic treatments of government concern its policies in particular fields, such as monetary control, maintenance of employment, price stabilization, regulation of monopolies, and international trade. The few analyses of government activities as a whole are mostly normative; i.e., they deduce the type of actions which a government *should* undertake from some basic ethical principle about its proper function.

Our analysis is likewise deductive, since it posits a basic rule and draws conclusions therefrom. However, it is also positive, because we try to describe what *will* happen under certain conditions, not what *should* happen. Nevertheless, we shall briefly show how it is related to several normative ideas advanced by other economists, and how it attempts to solve certain problems they have raised.

[12] Walter Lippmann, *Public Opinion* (New York: The Macmillan Company, 1922), *The Phantom Public* (New York: Harcourt, Brace and Company, 1925), and *Essays in the Public Philosophy* (Boston: Little, Brown and Company, 1955).

A. THE PROBLEM OF FALSE PERSONIFICATION VS. OVER-INDIVIDUALISM

In an article on "The Pure Theory of Government Finance," James Buchanan suggested two mutually exclusive ways to view decision-making by the state.[13] The first is to consider the state a separate person with its own ends not necessarily related to the ends of individuals. It acts to maximize its own welfare or utility by manipulating government spending and taxation so that the marginal gain from further spending is equal to the marginal loss from further taxing. These gains and losses are social—felt by the personality of the state. They are not the gains and losses of individuals in some aggregated form.

Though this "organismic" approach is intellectually neat, it has no substantive content, as Buchanan points out. No one knows what the welfare function of the state-as-a-person looks like, nor can anyone ever find out. Therefore it is useless as a guide to practical decisions.

Buchanan's second approach considers only individuals as having end structures. The state has no welfare function of its own; it is merely a means by which individuals can satisfy some of their wants collectively. For example, the state has a monopoly of certain services, but instead of trying to maximize profits, it seeks only to cover costs in the long run. Individuals buy services from it and pay it only for those services they receive. Thus a basic *quid pro quo* benefit principle underlies the functioning of the state and establishes limits on what it does.[14]

At first glance, this voluntaristic view of the state does not square with its use of coercion in collecting taxes. If taxes are merely *quid pro quo* payments for services rendered, why must citizens be forced

---

[13] James Buchanan, "The Pure Theory of Government Finance: A Suggested Approach," *Journal of Political Economy*, LVII (December, 1949), 496–505.

[14] These two approaches have been elaborated in greater detail by Edward C. Banfield, who distinguishes between two types of "unitary" view of the state and three types of "individualistic" view. His analysis does bring Buchanan's ideas closer to reality, but it does not alter the basic dichotomy which we are discussing. See "Note on the Conceptual Scheme," in Martin Meyerson and Edward C. Banfield, *Politics, Planning, and the Public Interest* (Glencoe, Ill.: The Free Press, 1955), pp. 322–329.

to pay them? Paul Samuelson has answered this question by arguing that in this model world the state undertakes only those activities providing indivisible benefits.[15] Since every man enjoys the benefits of every government act, no matter who pays for it, each man is motivated to evade paying himself. However, he will be willing to pay his share of the cost—since he does receive benefits for it—if all others also bear their shares. All citizens agree to be coerced, since each individual's gain more than offsets his part of the cost, and benefits are provided which otherwise could not be had. The voluntaristic nature of the state is thus not contradicted by its use of coercion.[16]

Julius Margolis has strongly attacked this conception of the state as entirely unrealistic.[17] He points out that almost no activities undertaken by the state produce purely indivisible benefits. Even national defense, the classic example of indivisible benefits, aids some people more than others, and the marginal expenditure on it may actually harm some citizens. Most other government actions produce clearly divisible benefits; e.g., the more citizens B through Z use government-built roads, the more crowded these roads become, and the less utility citizen A gets from using them. The fact that government carries out such activities instead of private firms cannot be explained by Samuelson's criterion. His model, says Margolis, limits the state to so few actions that it cannot reasonably be accepted even as a normative theory of government activity. We agree.

[15] Paul A. Samuelson, "The Pure Theory of Public Expenditures," *Review of Economics and Statistics,* XXXVI (November, 1954), 387–389. Samuelson states also that the government will make direct transfer payments (taxes plus expenditures) to satisfy "the ethical observer." However, these transfers do not involve any resource-exhausting government activities; hence they are irrelevant to our discussion of such activities.

[16] A similar approach is used by William J. Baumol, *op. cit.,* and is stated and criticized by Richard A. Musgrave in "The Voluntary Exchange Theory of Public Economy," *Quarterly Journal of Economics,* LIII (1939). These analyses are enough like Samuelson's so that we need not treat them separately.

[17] Julius Margolis, "A Comment on the Pure Theory of Public Expenditures," *Review of Economics and Statistics,* XXXVII (November, 1955), 347–349. Samuelson's reply concedes some of the points made by Margolis and clarifies the nature of "public" and "private" goods. See Paul A. Samuelson, "Diagrammatic Exposition of a Theory of Public Expenditure," *Review of Economics and Statistics,* XXXVII (November, 1955), 355–356.

Our own criticism of the Buchanan-Samuelson approach is that it poses a false dichotomy between two views, one of which is totally false and the other of which expresses only part of the truth. On one hand, the organismic view of government is untrue because it is based upon a mythical entity: a state which is a thing apart from individual men. On the other hand, the individualistic view is incomplete because it does not take coalitions into consideration.

As we shall see in Chapter 2, when a small group of men acting in coalition runs the apparatus of the state, we can reasonably speak of the government as a decision-maker separate from individual citizens at large. Thus we avoid both false personification of a mental construct and an over individualistic view of society. However, we are still faced with the problem of discovering a relationship between the ends of individuals at large and the ends of the coalition which does not restrict government to providing indivisible benefits. Our model attempts to describe such a relationship.

B. THE SOCIAL-WELFARE-FUNCTION PROBLEM

Exactly the same problem has long been the center of controversy in the new welfare economics, where Abram Bergson's "social welfare function" was advanced as a solution to it.[18] Having rejected cardinal utility and psychological interpersonal comparisons, Bergson attempted to substitute for them an abstract rule for the derivation of social ends from individual ends. He called this rule the "social welfare function."

This amorphous entity has been the target of two major criticisms. One is that it does not remove the necessity of weighting each individual's desires in the process of arriving at a collective end structure. Yet any such weighting is in fact an interpersonal comparison of welfare; it serves the same function as the assumption that all men are of equal ethical value in Pigou's earlier analysis. Thus, using a social welfare function does not solve the problem of

[18] Abram Bergson (Burk), "A Reformulation of Certain Aspects of Welfare Economics," *Quarterly Journal of Economics*, LII (February, 1938), 314–344.

how to make interpersonal comparisons, as Bergson himself admitted.[19]

The second criticism has been stated by Kenneth Arrow and will be analyzed in detail in Chapter 4.[20] To put it briefly, Arrow has shown that if most choice situations involve more than two alternatives, and if the preferences of individuals are sufficiently diverse, no unique and transitive general welfare function can be constructed unless some part of society dictates to the rest. This argument demolished what was left of Bergson's social welfare function and dissolved the relationship between individual and social ends which it had tried to establish.

Welfare economics was therefore pushed back into the emasculated state it had earlier entered by rejecting two postulates: cardinal utility and interpersonal welfare comparisons. These axioms had been thrown out because the first was unnecessary and both were based upon an empirically false psychological view of man. But without them or others to replace them, few significant policy statements can be made.

Our model attempts to forge a positive relationship between individual and social end structures by means of a political device. Because each adult citizen has one vote, his welfare preferences are weighted in the eyes of the government, which is interested only in his vote, not his welfare. Thus in answer to the first criticism raised against Bergson, we admit openly that we are adopting an ethical principle—equality of franchise. We are making it a part of politics, where we believe social ethics should be dealt with. In short, we are returning to *political economy*.

However, this does not eliminate Arrow's contention that rational social action is sometimes impossible. Our defense against this attack consists essentially of a double evasion. We try to show the following: (1) Arrow's criticism is not always relevant, and (2) even when it is relevant, its impact is often limited to much narrower

---

[19] See Tibor Scitovsky, "The State of Welfare Economics," *American Economic Review*, XLI (1951), 303–315.

[20] Kenneth J. Arrow, *op. cit., passim.*

areas of choice than one might suppose. These arguments will be presented in Chapter 4.

Although our model is related to the basic welfare-economics problem which Bergson tried to solve, it is not a normative model. We cannot use it to argue that society is better off in state A than in state B or that government should do X but not Y. The only normative element it contains is implicit in the assumption that every adult citizen has one and only one vote. Actually, even though an ethical judgment must be the ultimate justification for this assumption, we incorporate it into our model simply as a factual parameter, not a normative one. Therefore the relationship we construct between individual and government ends is one that we believe will exist under certain conditions, not one that should exist because it fulfills some ideal set of requirements.

C. TECHNICAL PROBLEMS

Many normative approaches to government decision-making feature such devices as referenda on every decision, perfect knowledge by the government of every citizen's preference structure, and precise calculation and payment of compensation. These devices undoubtedly play a legitimate role in theoretical analysis; we occasionally use them ourselves. However, most of our study is concerned with what would actually happen if men in our fairly realistic world behaved rationally. Therefore we cannot rely on procedures which the division of labor renders impractical, as it does all three of those mentioned above.

On the other hand, our analysis suffers from the same generality that plagues the traditional theories of consumer and firm behavior. We cannot fill in the details of our vote function any more than J. R. Hicks filled in the details of the indifference maps or production functions in *Value and Capital*.[21] To do so is the task of politicians, consumers and businessmen respectively. Abstract analysts

[21] J. R. Hicks, *Value and Capital*, Second Edition (Oxford: Clarendon Press, 1950), Chs. I, VI, and VII.

like ourselves can only show how these details fit into the general scheme of things.

IV. SUMMARY

Although governments are of crucial importance in every economy, economic theory has produced no satisfactory behavior rule for them comparable to the rules it uses to predict the actions of consumers and firms. Our thesis attempts to provide such a rule by positing that democratic governments act rationally to maximize political support.

By *rational* action, we mean action which is efficiently designed to achieve the consciously selected political or economic ends of the actor. In our model, government pursues its goal under three conditions: a democratic political structure which allows opposition parties to exist, an atmosphere of varying degrees of uncertainty, and an electorate of rational voters.

Our model bears a definite relation to previous economic models of government, though ours is positive and most others are normative. Buchanan posed a dichotomy between organismic and individualistic conceptions of the state; we try to avoid both extremes. Samuelson and Baumol argued that the state can efficiently undertake only straight income transfers and actions with indivisible benefits; we try to show that it has many other legitimate roles. Bergson tried to establish relations between individual and social ends by means of a purely ethical postulate; we adopt an ethical axiom in political form. Arrow proved that no such relations could be established rationally without dictation; we try to show how his dilemma can be circumvented.

We attempt these tasks by means of a model which is realistic and yet does not fill in the details of the relationships within it. In short, we wish to discover what form of political behavior is rational for the government and citizens of a democracy.

2

Party Motivation and the
Function of Government
in Society

Introduction

THEORETICAL models should be tested primarily
by the accuracy of their predictions rather than by the reality of their
assumptions.[1] Nevertheless, if our model is to be internally consistent,
the government in it must be at least theoretically able to carry out
the social functions of government.[2] In the present chapter we
will attempt to show how and why the governing party discharges
these functions even though its motive for acting is unrelated to
them.

[1] For an excellent statement of this viewpoint, see Milton Friedman, "The
Methodology of Positive Economics," *Essays in Positive Economics* (Chicago:
University of Chicago Press, 1953).
[2] In this chapter the word *government* refers to the institution rather than the
governing party. However, we return to using the latter meaning in all subsequent
chapters.

I. THE CONCEPT OF DEMOCRATIC GOVERNMENT IN THE MODEL

A. THE NATURE OF GOVERNMENT

The definition of government used in this study is borrowed from Robert A. Dahl and Charles E. Lindblom, who wrote:

Governments [are] . . . organizations that have a sufficient monopoly of control to enforce an orderly settlement of disputes with other organizations in the area. . . . Whoever controls government usually has the "last word" on a question; whoever controls government can enforce decisions on other organizations in the area.[3]

As Dahl and Lindblom point out, "All short definitions of government are inherently ambiguous."[4] Nevertheless, their definition succeeds in differentiating government from other social agencies without precisely circumscribing its powers. Hence this definition is ideal for our model, since the government therein has very broad powers, as explained in Chapter 1.

But what is the government supposed to do with these powers? What is government's proper role in the division of labor? Clearly, these questions are vital in the real world of politics. However, no one can answer them without specifying an ethical relationship between government and the rest of society. And since such specification is normative instead of positive, it lies outside the purview of our study. As far as this study is concerned, it is permissible for government to do anything whatever that does not violate the constitutional limits described in Chapter 1.

In the real world, governments in fact do almost everything which an organization conceivably can. However, not every government does the same thing as every other, so it is fruitless to describe the functions of government by listing a set of typical activities. Some governments would not perform all of them, and nearly every one of them would be performed by some nongovernment agencies. There-

---

[3] Robert A. Dahl and Charles E. Lindblom, *Politics, Economics and Welfare* (New York: Harper & Brothers, 1953), p. 42.
[4] *Ibid.*

fore, when we try to specify what governments have in common, we are driven back to the somewhat vague definition given above.

In spite of its vagueness, this definition implies two things about government's function in the division of labor. First, every government is the locus of ultimate power in its society; i.e., it can coerce all the other groups into obeying its decisions, whereas they cannot similarly coerce it. Therefore its social function must at least include acting as the final guarantor behind every use of coercion in the settlement of disputes.

It is conceivable that different "ultimate guarantors" of coercion might coexist in the same society, each ruling a different sphere of action (e.g., the Church in religion and the King in politics). But in our model, though power can be extremely decentralized, we assume only one organization in any area can fit the definition we have given. Consequently the government is a specialized organization distinct from all other social agents.

Thus on a purely positive basis, without ethical postulates, we can conclude that (1) the government is a particular and unique social agent and (2) it has a specialized function in the division of labor.

B. THE NATURE OF DEMOCRATIC GOVERNMENT

To avoid ethical premises, we define democratic government descriptively, i.e., by enumerating certain characteristics which in practice distinguish this form of government from others. A government is democratic if it exists in a society where the following conditions prevail:

1. A single party (or coalition of parties) is chosen by popular election to run the governing apparatus.
2. Such elections are held within periodic intervals, the duration of which cannot be altered by the party in power acting alone.
3. All adults who are permanent residents of the society, are sane, and abide by the laws of the land are eligible to vote in each such election.[5]

[5] In some democracies, women or permanent resident aliens or both are not allowed to vote.

4. Each voter may cast one and only one vote in each election.
5. Any party (or coalition) receiving the support of a majority of those voting is entitled to take over the powers of government until the next election.
6. The losing parties in an election never try by force or any illegal means to prevent the winning party (or parties) from taking office.

7. The party in power never attempts to restrict the political activities of any citizens or other parties as long as they make no attempt to overthrow the government by force.
8. There are two or more parties competing for control of the governing apparatus in every election.

Since our model society as described in Chapter 1 exhibits all these traits, the government in it is democratic.

An important conclusion can be drawn from the above definition: the central purpose of elections in a democracy is to select a government. Therefore any citizen is rational in regard to elections if his actions enable him to play his part in selecting a government efficiently. This specific definition of rationality underlies much of our later analysis.

II. THE ROLE OF POLITICAL PARTIES IN THE MODEL

The preceding discussion shows what an important role political parties play in democratic government. To demonstrate how that role is carried out in our model, we next examine the nature, motives, and operation of parties.

A. THE NATURE OF POLITICAL PARTIES

In the broadest sense, a political party is a coalition of men seeking to control the governing apparatus by legal means. By *coalition*, we mean a group of individuals who have certain ends in common and coöperate with each other to achieve them. By *governing apparatus*, we mean the physical, legal, and institutional equipment which the government uses to carry out its specialized role in the division of labor. By *legal means*, we mean either duly constituted elections or legitimate influence.

According to this definition, anyone who regularly votes for one party and occasionally contributes money or time to its campaigns is a member of that party, even if he aspires to hold no political office. The party is thus a loosely formed group of men who coöperate chiefly in an effort to get some of their number elected to office. However, they may strongly disagree with each other about the policies which those elected should put into practice.

Though this definition conforms to popular usage, it has two disadvantages as far as our model is concerned. In the first place, such a coalition does not possess a unique, consistent preference-ordering. Its members agree on some goals, but they disagree on many others. Hence the actions taken by the party as a whole are likely to form a hodgepodge of compromises—the result of an internal power struggle rather than any rational decision-making.

Second, the men who actually make specific government decisions are those who hold office, yet the broad definition of party given above implies that multitudes of other citizens also take part in this decision-making. True, their voice in the decisions need not be equal to that of office holders. But specifying just how strong it is again involves analysis of an intraparty power struggle.

Taken together, these two drawbacks offset the advantage of viewing parties as coalitions. The object of doing so is to escape the dilemma of false personification vs. over-individualism described in Chapter 1. But this broad definition of party throws us onto the over-individualistic horn, since we cannot treat the governing party as a single, rational, decision-making entity controlling government policy.

To avoid this result, we redefine party as follows: a political party is a team of men seeking to control the governing apparatus by gaining office in a duly constituted election. By *team*, we mean a coalition whose members agree on all their goals instead of on just part of them.[6] Thus every member of the team has exactly the same goals as every other. Since we also assume all the members are rational,

[6] This definition of *team* and the previous definition of *coalition* are taken from Jacob Marschak, "Towards an Economic Theory of Organization and Information," *Decision Processes*, ed. by R. M. Thrall, C. H. Coombs, and R. L. Davis (New York: John Wiley & Sons, Inc., 1954), 188–189.

their goals can be viewed as a single, consistent preference-ordering.

In effect, this definition treats each party as though it were a single person; hence it may appear to be false personification. We admit that it is an abstraction from the real world, since in reality not even the key officials of any government have exactly the same goals. Nevertheless, we are are not guilty of false personification because we do not posit the existence of any suprahuman entity. We merely assume complete agreement on goals among the members of an office-seeking coalition.

By thus narrowing our definition, we escape the dilemma posed in Chapter 1 and yet construct a model in which the government is a decision-making agent separate from its citizens. Of course, it is not separate from *all* its citizens, since some of them constitute the governing party. Yet we may reasonably assume that the vast majority of citizens belong neither to the governing team nor to the other teams competing with it for power. Therefore we can treat citizens and political parties as two mutually exclusive groups without unduly distorting reality.

There are three qualifications to this conclusion. First, in many democracies, the government's administrative apparatus is so large that it employs a significant fraction to the citizenry. But since we are not studying the impact of bureaucracy upon democracy, we assume that only a few men in each branch of administration are members of the party team. All the others are permanent employees who do not lose their jobs when a new governing party takes office. Furthermore, we assume that the team members control the policy of all the others completely. Therefore we can regard almost all employees of the government as citizens rather than party members.

Second, in some parts of our study, we treat parties as though they were imperfect coalitions instead of teams; i.e., we assume intraparty power struggles exist. We make this temporary shift of definitions because it allows us to analyze intraparty struggles, yet it leads to no conclusions incompatible with those derived from the team view of parties.

Finally, though there are other coalitions and teams in society besides political parties, we recognize only three types of political decision-makers in our model: political parties, individual citizens, and interest groups. The latter category includes both individuals and such nonparty coalitions as corporations, labor unions, and trade associations.[7]

B. THE SELF-INTEREST AXIOM

Just what goals do all the members of each party agree upon? In order to answer this question, we set forth here an axiom crucial to all the rest of our model. We assume that every individual, though rational, is also selfish. The import of this *self-interest axiom* was stated by John C. Calhoun as follows:

That constitution of our nature which makes us feel more intensely what affects us directly than what affects us indirectly through others, necessarily leads to conflict between individuals. Each, in consequence, has a greater regard for his own safety or happiness, than for the safety or happiness of others: and, where these come in opposition, is ready to sacrifice the interests of other to his own.[8]

Throughout our model, we assume that every agent acts in accordance with this view of human nature. Thus, whenever we speak of rational behavior, we always mean rational behavior directed primarily towards selfish ends.

In reality, men are not always selfish, even in politics. They frequently do what appears to be individually irrational because they believe it is socially rational—i.e., it benefits others even though it harms them personally. For example, politicians in the real world sometimes act as they think best for society as a whole even when they know their actions will lose votes. In every field, no account of human behavior is complete without mention of such altruism; its possessors are among the heroes men rightly admire.

Nevertheless, general theories of social action always rely heavily

[7] For a detailed discussion and definition of *interest groups*, see Chapter 6.
[8] John C. Calhoun, "Disquisition on Government," *Public Opinion and Propaganda*, ed. by Katz, Cartwright, Eldersveld, and Lee (New York: The Dryden Press, 1954), p. 15.

on the self-interest axiom. Practically all economic theory, for example, is based on this premise. As Adam Smith said:

Man has almost constant occasion for the help of his brethren, and it is in vain for him to expect it from their benevolence only. . . . It is not from the benevolence of the butcher, the brewer, or the baker, that we expect our dinner, but from their regard to their own interest. We address ourselves not to their humanity but to their self-love, and never talk to them of our own necessities but of their advantages.[9]

His reasoning applies equally well to politics. Therefore we accept the self-interest axiom as a cornerstone of our analysis. Precisely what self-interest means will become clear when we describe in detail how the various types of political decision-makers in the model behave.

C. THE MOTIVATION OF PARTY ACTION

From the self-interest axiom springs our view of what motivates the political actions of party members. We assume that they act solely in order to attain the income, prestige, and power which come from being in office. Thus politicians in our model never seek office as a means of carrying out particular policies; their only goal is to reap the rewards of holding office *per se*. They treat policies purely as means to the attainment of their private ends, which they can reach only by being elected.

Upon this reasoning rests the fundamental hypothesis of our model: parties formulate policies in order to win elections, rather than win elections in order to formulate policies.

At first glance, this hypothesis appears to render our model government incapable of performing its social function. In the eyes of the citizenry, the governing party's function in the division of labor is to formulate and carry out policies, not to provide its members with income, prestige, and power. Yet in our model, the governing party carries out this function only in so far as doing so furthers the private ambitions of its members. Since these ambitions are *per se* unrelated to the governing party's function, how can we expect pursuit of the

---

[9] Adam Smith, *The Wealth of Nations*, Modern Library Edition (New York: The Modern Library, 1937), p. 14.

former to accomplish the latter? Seemingly, our model contains no viable government because it confuses ends and means.

This criticism may sound plausible, but it is completely false. Even in the real world, almost nobody carries out his function in the division of labor purely for its own sake. Rather every such function is discharged by someone who is spurred to act by private motives logically irrelevant to his function. Thus social functions are usually the by-products, and private ambitions the ends, of human action. This situation follows directly from the self-interest axiom. As Joseph Schumpeter cogently stated:

It does not follow that the social meaning of a type of activity will necessarily provide the motive power, hence the explanation of the latter. If it does not, a theory that contents itself with an analysis of the social end or need to be served cannot be accepted as an adequate account of the activities that serve it. For instance, the reason why there is such a thing as economic activity is of course that people want to eat, to clothe themselves, and so on. To provide the means to satisfy those wants is the social end or meaning of production. Nevertheless, we all agree that this proposition would make a most unrealistic starting point for a theory of economic activity in commercial society and that we shall do much better if we start from propositions about profits.[10]

Applying the same reasoning to politics, he said:

Similarly, the social meaning or function of parliamentary activity is no doubt to turn out legislation and, in part, administrative measures. But in order to understand how democratic politics serve this social end, we must start from the competitive struggle for power and office and realize that the social function is fulfilled, as it were, incidentally—in the same sense as production is incidental to the making of profits.[11]

This brilliant insight summarizes our whole approach to the functioning of government. It is paralleled by the dual analysis of organizations made by sociologist Philip Selznick, who wrote:

[10] Joseph A. Schumpeter, *Capitalism, Socialism, and Democracy* (New York: Harper & Brothers, 1950), p. 282.

[11] *Ibid*. Schumpeter's profound analysis of democracy forms the inspiration and foundation for our whole thesis, and our debt and gratitude to him are great indeed.

All formal organizations are molded by forces tangential to their rationally ordered structures and stated goals. Every formal organization . . . attempts to mobilize human and technical resources as means for the achievement of its ends. However, the individuals within the system tend to resist being treated as means. They interact as wholes, bringing to bear their own special problems and purposes. . . . It follows that there will develop an informal structure within the organization which will reflect the spontaneous efforts of individuals and subgroups to control the conditions of their existence. . . . The informal structure will be at once indispensable to and consequential for the formal system of delegation and control itself.[12]

Clearly, the formal purpose of political parties—to design and carry out policies when in office—is not the only thing an analysis of government must take into account. Equally significant is the informal structure, i.e., that structure centering around the private motives of those who run each party. Our model attempts to combine both these elements into one coherent theory of government operation.

Though this theory is based on the self-interest axiom, we do not assume that the private ambitions of party members are without bounds. The self-interest of each has at least two limits: (1) he will not perform illegal acts, such as taking bribes or using his power to violate the constitution, and (2) he will not try to benefit himself at the expense of any other member of his own party team. Although both these limits are unrealistic, without them our analysis would have to be extended beyond the purview of this study.

D. THE SPECIFIC GOAL OF PARTIES

Politicians in our model are motivated by the desire for power, prestige, and income, and by the love of conflict, i.e., the "thrill of the game" common to many actions involving risk. However, they can obtain none of these *desiderata* except the last unless their party is elected to office. Therefore we do not distort the motives of party members by saying that their primary objective is to be elected. This

---

[12] Philip Selznick, "A Theory of Organizational Commitments," *Reader in Bureaucracy*, ed. by Merton, Gray, Hockey, and Selvin (Glencoe, Illinois: The Free Press, 1952), pp. 194, 195.

in turn implies that each party seeks to receive more votes than any other.

Thus our reasoning has led us from the self-interest axiom to the vote-maximizing government described in Chapter 1. The party which runs this government manipulates its policies and actions in whatever way it believes will gain it the most votes without violating constitutional rules. Clearly, such behavior implies that the governing party is aware of some definite relationship between its policies and the way people vote. In the next two chapters, we examine both these assertions in detail.

III. THE RELATION OF THE MODEL TO ETHICS AND DESCRIPTIVE SCIENCE

The model in this study occupies a twilight zone between normative and descriptive models. It is not normative, because it contains no ethical postulates and cannot be used to determine how men should behave. Nor is it purely descriptive, since it ignores all the nonrational considerations so vital to politics in the real world. Yet it is related to both these phases of political economy and has a distinct function in each.

A. NORMATIVE IMPLICATIONS

Ethical, or normative, models of democratic politics generally are constructed in the following manner:

1. The creator of the model postulates certain goals as "good."
2. He outlines the behavior necessary to achieve these goals.
3. He concludes that this behavior "should" be carried out by members of real democratic societies.

However, the creators of such models do not always consider whether the behavior they advocate as good is also rational in the economic sense. A man who is good in their eyes may be unable to perform his function in the division of labor efficiently. In fact, good behavior as they define it may be so inefficient that its prevalence would disrupt the very social state they desire. If so, their normative prescriptions are really contradictory; hence their conception of good behavior must be reëxamined.

Such contradictions cannot be discovered in a normative model unless the behavior it prescribes as good is tested for rationality. By transforming our positive model into a normative one, we can provide an excellent tool for such testing. In its positive form, our model contains a set of conditions we regard merely as descriptions of society's actual rules. But exactly the same conditions can be deduced from certain ethical precepts; hence they can be viewed either positively or normatively.

For example, consider these two parameters in the model: every citizen has one vote, and the party receiving a majority of the votes cast is elected. In our study, these rules merely describe what *is done* in society. But in the normative model constructed by Dahl and Lindblom, the identical rules denote what *ought to be done* because they are derived from the following value judgments:

Democracy is a goal, not an achievement. . . . The democratic goal is twofold. It consists of a condition to be attained and a principle guiding the procedure for attaining it. The condition is political equality, which we define as follows:

Control over governmental decisions is shared so that the preferences of no one citizen are weighted more heavily than the preferences of any other one citizen.

The principle is majority rule, which we define as follows:

Governmental decisions should be controlled by the greater number expressing their preferences in the "last say." [13]

Similarly, many other parameters which we use positively can be regarded as practical expressions of ethical axioms.

As a result, the creator or evaluator of a normative model may find that his model contains many of the same behavioral rules as ours. If so, he can use our positive description of rational behavior to check the efficiency of the behavior he considers good. Any divergence he finds casts doubt on the feasibility of his prescriptions and therefore upon just how good they really are.

[13] Dahl and Lindblom, *op. cit.*, p. 41.

Though our model can thus be used to test normative theories, we will employ it for this purpose only when there is a striking difference between rational behavior and some well-known precept for good behavior. These occasional references to an ethically ideal model must not be confused with our frequent references to an informationally ideal model. We construct the latter in Chapters 3 and 4 by assuming that perfect information is available to all decision-makers. The "certain world" which emerges serves as a positive norm for determining the impact of uncertainty and the cost of information upon democracy.[14]

B. DESCRIPTIVE IMPLICATIONS

The relevance of the model in this study to descriptive science is twofold. First, it proposes a single hypothesis to explain government decision-making and party behavior in general. Since this hypothesis leads to testable corollaries, it can be submitted to empirical proof. If verified, it may lead to nonobvious conclusions about the actions and development of parties, thus adding to our knowledge of reality.[15]

Second, the model tells us what behavior we can expect if men act rationally in politics. Therefore it can perhaps be used to discover (1) in what phases of politics in the real world men are rational, (2) in what phases they are irrational, and (3) how they deviate from rationality in the latter.

In all these ways, we hope the model will help guide empirical research to investigate important issues rather than trivial ones.

---

[14] However, the world of perfect information is so radically different from any "uncertain world" that we cannot carry our informationally ideal model too far. If we did, most of the institutions in it would become useless as bases for comparison with our actual model. Therefore we will sketch only a few qualities of the informationally ideal model and ignore many of the problems which would arise if we tried to describe it in detail.

[15] The reasoning in the model also embodies a second hypothesis: that citizens and other political decision-makers behave rationally. Furthermore, the analysis is so constructed that the first hypothesis is usually developed by means of the second. As a result, most of the ramifications of rationality are independent of vote-maximizing, but not vice versa. Therefore the description of behavior which emerges from the model cannot always be used to test the vote-maximizing hypothesis, though it can be used to test the rationality hypothesis.

Nevertheless, the model is not an attempt to describe reality accurately. Like all theoretical constructs in the social sciences, it treats a few variables as crucial and ignores others which actually have some influence. Our model in particular ignores all forms of irrationality and subconscious behavior even though they play a vital role in real-world politics.

The fact that our study is positive but not descriptive gives rise to an ineradicable difficulty of exposition. The statements in our analysis are true of the model world, not the real world, unless they obviously refer to the latter. Thus when we make unqualified remarks about how men think, or what the government does, or what strategies are open to opposition parties, we are not referring to *real* men, governments, or parties, but to their model counterparts in the rational world of our study.

This distinction must be kept constantly in mind; otherwise the reader may condemn many of our statements as factually erroneous when they are really not factual assertions at all. If confusion arises in spite of our precautions, we ask the reader this indulgence: whenever he is tempted to think an assertion empirically false, let him provisionally assume it refers solely to the model. If it then falls into place logically, this assumption is correct; if not, our analysis stands in need of improvement.

IV. SUMMARY

In this study, *government* is defined as that specialized agency in the division of labor which is able to enforce its decisions upon all other agencies or individuals in the area. A *democratic* government is one chosen periodically by means of popular elections in which two or more parties compete for the votes of all adults.

A *party* is a team of individuals seeking to control the governing apparatus by gaining office in an election. Its function in the division of labor is to formulate and carry out government policies whenever it succeeds in getting into power. However, its members are motivated by their personal desire for the income, prestige, and power which come from holding office. Thus, carrying out their social function is to them a means of achieving their private ambitions. Though this arrangement may seem odd, it is found throughout the division of labor because of the prevalence of self-interest in human action.

Since none of the appurtenances of office can be obtained without being elected, the main goal of every party is the winning of elections. Thus all its actions are aimed at maximizing votes, and it treats policies merely as means towards this end.

Though our model is a purely positive one, it can be used to test the rationality of behavior prescribed in normative political models. In descriptive science, it (1) advances the vote-maximizing hypothesis as an explanation of democratic political behavior and (2) constructs a positive norm by which to distinguish between rational and irrational behavior in politics.

3

The Basic Logic
of Voting

Introduction

IN ORDER to plan its policies so as to gain votes, the government must discover some relationship between what it does and how citizens vote. In our model, the relationship is derived from the axiom that citizens act rationally in politics. This axiom implies that each citizen casts his vote for the party he believes will provide him with more benefits than any other.

Though this definition seems obvious, it is actually based upon concepts which are both complex and ambiguous. In this chapter we examine them carefully in order to show what "rational voting" really implies.

I. UTILITY INCOME FROM GOVERNMENT ACTIVITIES

The *benefits* voters consider in making their decisions are streams of utility derived from government activity. Actually, this definition is circular, because we define *utility* as a measure of benefits in a citizen's mind which he uses to decide among alternative courses of action. Given several mutually exclusive alternatives, a rational man always takes the one which yields him the highest utility, *ceteris paribus*; i.e., he acts to his own greatest benefit. This follows directly from the definition of rationality which is given in Chapter 1.

All citizens are constantly receiving streams of benefits from government activities. Their streets are policed, water purified, roads repaired, shores defended, garbage removed, weather forecast, etc. These benefits are exactly like the benefits they receive from private economic activity and are identified as government-caused only by their source. Of course, there are enormous qualitative differences between the benefits received, say, from national defense and from eating mince pie for dessert. But no matter how diverse, all benefits must be reduced to some common denominator for purposes of allocating scarce resources. This is equally true of benefits within the private sector. The common denominator used in this process we call *utility*.

It is possible for a citizen to receive utility from events that are only remotely connected to his own material income. For example, some citizens would regard their utility incomes as raised if the government increased taxes upon them in order to distribute free food to starving Chinese. There can be no simple identification of "acting for one's own greatest benefit" with selfishness in the narrow sense because self-denying charity is often a great source of benefits to oneself. Thus our model leaves room for altruism in spite of its basic reliance upon the self-interest axiom.

Using this broad concept of utility, we can speak of a *utility income* from government activity. This income includes benefits which the recipient does not realize he is receiving. It also includes benefits he knows he is receiving but the exact source of which he does not know. For example, many citizens are probably not aware that the water they drink is inspected by a government agency. If inspection were discontinued, they might not realize their utility incomes had fallen until they received polluted water. Even then, not all of them would know that a cessation of government activity had caused this drop in income.

The fact that men can receive utility income from government actions without being aware of receiving it may seem to violate the usual definition of *income*. Nevertheless, we must insist upon it, because an important political strategy of governments is making voters aware of benefits they are already receiving. However, only benefits which voters become conscious of by election day can influence their voting decisions; otherwise their behavior would be irrational.

II. THE LOGICAL STRUCTURE OF THE VOTING ACT

A. TERMINOLOGY OF THE ANALYSIS

By defining income as a flow of benefits, we have involved ourselves in time, since flows can only be measured as rates per unit of time. The unit of time we use is the *election period*. It is defined as the time elapsing between elections, and it forms the principal unit of judgment in a voter's mind.

At least two election periods enter into a rational voter's calculations: the one following the coming election, and the one ending on election day. We will refer to these periods $t + 1$ and t respectively.

To illustrate the verbal analysis, we also employ several other symbols as follows:

U stands for an individual voter's real or hypothetical utility income from government activity during one election period.

A is the incumbent party, i.e., the governing party in period t.

B is the opposition party, i.e., the party out of power in period t. (In the first part of the analysis, we assume a two-party system.)

U^a stands for utility income actually received during a period. It is the utility income provided by the party in power during that period.

U^i stands for the utility income which a voter believes is the highest he could possibly have received during some period. It is the utility income which the ideal government would have provided him if it had been in power during that period.

E stands for expected value.

B. THE TWO PARTY DIFFERENTIALS

Each citizen in our model votes for the party he believes will provide him with a higher utility income than any other party during the coming election period.[1] To discover which party this is, he compares the utility incomes he believes he would receive were each party in office. In a two-party system, this comparison can be set up as a simple subtraction:

$$E(U^A_{t+1}) - E(U^B_{t+1})$$

The difference between these two expected utility incomes is the citizen's *expected party differential*. If it is positive, he votes for the incumbents; if it is negative, he votes for the opposition; if it is zero, he abstains.[2]

At first glance, rational voting thus appears to be a very simple matter. But its apparent ease is deceiving, for a crucial question remains: how should a rational voter calculate the expected utility incomes from which he derives his expected party differential? It is in answering this question that we encounter difficulties.

When a man votes, he is helping to select the government which will govern him during the coming election period (i.e., period $t+1$). Therefore as we have just shown, he makes his decision by comparing future performances he expects from the competing parties. But if he is rational, he knows that no party will be able to do everything that it says it will do. Hence he cannot merely compare platforms; instead he must estimate in his own mind what the parties would actually do were they in power.[3]

Since one of the competing parties is already in power, its performance in period t gives him the best possible idea of what it will do in the future, assuming its policies have some continuity.[4] But

---

[1] From now on, the term *utility income* refers specifically to utility income from government activity unless otherwise noted.

[2] We discuss the decision rule for multiparty systems later in this chapter.

[3] The governing party in our model has such broad powers that perhaps it could carry out all its promises. Nevertheless, we assume here that it cannot for two reasons: (1) in the real world and in our own uncertainty model, government cannot foresee all the obstacles it will encounter; clearly this fact has repercussions upon the structure of voters' thinking; and (2) in a two-party system, each party deliberately makes ambiguous promises; hence platforms are poor harbingers of actions even in our model. The second point is discussed in detail in Chapter 8.

[4] The tendency of every rational party to maintain continuity in its policies is discussed in Chapter 7.

it would be irrational to compare the current performance of one party with the expected future performance of another. For a valid comparison, both performances must take place under the same conditions, i.e., in the same time period. Therefore the voter must weigh the performance that the opposition party would have produced in period t if it had been in power.

True, this performance is purely hypothetical; so he can only imagine what utility income he would have derived from it. But party B's future is hypothetical, too—as is that of party A. Thus he must either compare (1) two hypothetical future utility incomes or (2) one actual present utility income and one hypothetical present one. Without question, the latter comparison allows him to make more direct use of concrete facts than the former. Not only is one of its terms a real entity, but the other can be calculated in full view of the situation from which it springs. If he compares future utility incomes, he enjoys neither of these advantages. Therefore, we believe it is more rational for him to ground his voting decision on current events than purely on future ones.

As a result, the most important part of a voter's decision is the size of his *current party differential*, i.e., the difference between the utility income he actually received in period t and the one he would have received if the opposition had been in power.[5] Algebraically, this entity is calculated as follows:

$$(U_t^A) - E(U_t^B)$$

It is the major determinant of his expected party differential.

However, this conclusion does not mean that citizens in our model ignore the future when deciding how to vote. Obviously, such an attitude would be irrational, since the purpose of voting is to select a future government. Therefore the rational man in our model applies two future-orienting modifiers to his current party differential in order to calculate his expected party differential.

---

[5] To avoid confusion, we adopt the following rule: whenever the term *party differential* appears without the adjective *current* immediately preceding it, it always denotes the *expected* party differential.

C. THE TREND FACTOR AND PERFORMANCE RATINGS

The first of these modifiers we call simply the *trend factor*. It is the adjustment each citizen makes in his current party differential to account for any relevant trend in events that occurs within the current election period. For example, let us assume that a voter believes the present government made many mistakes upon first taking office but has steadily improved and is now governing expertly. He may feel that this expertness will prevail throughout the next election period if the incumbents are reëlected. Therefore he adjusts his current party differential to eliminate the impact of their initial blunders. Conversely, if he feels the government started out superbly but has continuously degenerated, he may project only its bad performance into his expected party differential.

The second modifier comes into play only when the citizen cannot see any difference between the two parties running; i.e., when he thinks they have identical platforms and current policies.[6] To escape from this deadlock, he alters the basis of his decision to whether or not the incumbents have done as good a job of governing as did their predecessors in office.

Our use of this particular tie-breaking device may seem rather arbitrary. Why should a rational man pay attention to the past in selecting a future government? Why should the present similarity of parties cause him to drag past governments into his decisions?

The answer to these questions is derived from the impact of elections *per se* upon party behavior. In effect, every election is a judgment passed upon the record of the incumbent party. But the standards used to judge its record are of two types. When the opposition's policies in period t have differed from those of the incumbents, the judgment expresses the voters' choice between the future projections of these two policy sets. But if the opposition's policies

[6] When perfect information exists, citizens think parties' policies are identical only when they really are identical. But in a world where men are not fully informed, some actual differences between parties may escape notice because they are not significant enough to exceed voters' perception thresholds. For a further explanation of this possibility, see Section III of this chapter.

have been identical with those of the incumbents, mere projection provides the voters with no real choice. In this case, their judgment expresses whether they rate the incumbents' record as good or bad according to some abstract standard.

Thus every election is a signaling device as well as a government selector. However, in a two-party system, it is limited to giving one of two signals. The incumbents always regard reëlection as a mandate to continue their former policies. Conversely, the opposition party regards its triumph as a command to alter at least some of the incumbents' policies; otherwise, why would people have voted for it? In short, the outcome calls for either "no change" or "change." Hence it always makes a difference which party is elected, no matter how similar their records in period t. If the opposition wins, it is sure to carry out policies different from those the incumbents would have carried out had they been reëlected.

However, no one knows in advance just what policy changes the opposition will make if it is elected. Nor can they be discovered by looking at the opposition's hypothetical record in period t, since (we are here assuming) it is identical with that of the incumbents. But if men do not know what change signifies, how can they rationally vote for or against it?

Rational men are not interested in policies per se but in their own utility incomes. If their present utility incomes are very low in their own eyes, they may believe that almost any change likely to be made will raise their incomes. In this case, it is rational for them to vote against the incumbents, i.e., for change in general.

On the other hand, men who are benefiting from the incumbents' policies may feel that change is likely to harm rather than help them. True, the opposition might introduce new policies which would raise their utility incomes. But their incomes are so high already that they fear any break in the continuity of present policies. Hence they rationally vote for the incumbents, i.e., against change in general.

Clearly, both actions are rational responses to the fact that elections inevitably signal change or no change. They show that even when the parties running have identical records in period t, many citizens may reasonably expect different utility incomes from each party in period $t + 1$. Therefore abstention is rational only if a citizen believes that either (1) the policy changes that will be made if the opposition is elected will have no net effect upon his utility income or (2) these changes may affect his income, but the probability that they will raise it is exactly equal to the probability that they will lower it; i.e., the expected change is zero.

Two things are to be noted about this reasoning. First, we have admitted a degree of uncertainty into our certainty model. However, the purpose of this model is to prepare for analysis of the uncertainty model; hence we feel justified in taking uncertainty into account whenever it affects the basic structure of rational behavior.

Second, we have argued that the incumbents' record can be judged as good or bad even when it is identical with the record of the opposition. But what standard for judgment exists in this case? With what can the incumbents' record be compared?

In the real world, men often compare what government is doing with what it should be doing without referring to any other party. Instead they are implicitly comparing the utility incomes they are actually receiving with those they would be receiving if the ideal government were in power. Of course, every man does not have the same ideals as every other. Yet each man can use his private conception of the ideal government to assign a *performance rating* to the incumbent party or any other party.[7] Algebraically, it is computed as follows:

$$\left[\frac{U_t^i}{U_t^a} \right]$$

Performance ratings are extremely useful for comparing governments operating in different time periods or even in different areas.[8] They are necessary for such comparisons because absolute levels of utility income from different time periods cannot be compared di-

[7] To compute the ratings of parties not now in office, it is necessary (1) to substitute the real (or hypothetical) incomes they did (or would) provide for the actual income being received and (2) to select the appropriate ideal income so that both terms of the fraction concern the same time period.

[8] Our use of ratios to denote performance ratings is purely arbitrary; any other mathematical measure which allows relative comparisons can be substituted without changing the argument.

rectly, as we saw earlier. The performance rating of a government may change for the following reasons: (1) it changes its actions while other conditions remain the same; (2) it keeps the same actions, and they give rise to the same utility as before, but other circumstances change so that the ideal utility-income level alters; or (3) it keeps the same actions, but other circumstances change so that these actions no longer produce the same utility incomes.

In our model, performance ratings enter a voter's decision-making whenever he thinks both parties have the same platforms and current policies. At first glance, this rule seems to imply discontinuity in the voter's thinking, but in fact it does not. Every rational voter knows that if the opposition party is elected, it will alter some of the policies now being followed by the incumbents. But whenever the two parties have different platforms or current policies, he also knows just what changes will be made. Therefore he can choose between parties by deciding how he likes these specific changes.

However, when he believes the two parties have identical platforms and current policies, he no longer knows what specific changes will occur if the opposition wins. Therefore he is forced to base his decision upon his attitude towards change in general. There is no shift in his method of deciding how to vote; rather a shift in the evidence available causes him to discard one tool and use another. The object of both tools is the same—to estimate the gain he will get from voting for one party instead of the other.

Thus voters use performance ratings only when their current party differentials are zero and not always then. A man's current party differential may be zero for two reasons: (1) both parties have identical policies and platforms; or (2) though their policies and platforms are different, they produce identical utility incomes for him. In the latter case, performance ratings are useless to him because he already knows what changes will take place if the opposition wins. Since these changes do not alter his utility income, he abstains. But in the former case he does not know what changes the opposition will make; hence he needs some way to determine his attitude toward change in general. We have already shown that (1) this attitude depends upon how good a job he thinks the incumbents are doing in providing him with utility income and (2) he can rate the incumbents' performance against an ideal performance. But by what standard does he evaluate, say, a rating of 40 percent as good or bad?

Formulating such a standard is what requires the voter to consider the performances of past governments. In our model, each voter develops his own standard out of his experiences with other governments. By computing their performance ratings, he creates a measuring rod with which he can discover whether the incumbents have been doing a good, bad, or indifferent job of governing. He votes for them if their rating is good, against them if it is bad, and not at all if it is indifferent.[9] Thus he may rationally assign a non-zero value to his expected party differential even when both parties have identical records in period t.

III. PRELIMINARY DIFFICULTIES CAUSED BY UNCERTAINTY

So far we have glibly spoken of voters computing their party differentials and performance ratings without pointing out how difficult such computation is. In order to find his current party differential, a voter in a two-party system must do the following: (1) examine all phases of government action to find out where the two parties would behave differently, (2) discover how each difference would affect his utility income, and (3) aggregate the differences in utility and arrive at a net figure which shows by how much one party would be better than the other. This is how a rational voter would behave in a world of complete and costless information—the same world in which dwell the rational consumer and the rational producer of traditional economic theory.

In the real world, uncertainty and lack of information prevent even

[9] When voting is costless, a voter using preference ratings always votes if the incumbents have done a good (or bad) job, but this is not true when voting is costly. In the latter case, the losses (or benefits) he expects from change in general must be large enough to outweigh the cost of voting; otherwise he will abstain even though the incumbents do not have an indifferent rating. For a more detailed discussion of abstention when voting is costly, see Chapter 14.

the most intelligent and well-informed voter from behaving in precisely the fashion we have described. Since he cannot be certain what his present utility income from government is, or what it would be if an opposition party were in power, he can only make estimates of both. He will base them upon those few areas of government activity where the difference between parties is great enough to impress him. When the total difference in utility flows is large enough so that he is no longer indifferent about which party is in office, his *party differential threshold* has been crossed. Until then, he remains indifferent about which party is in power, even if one would give him a higher utility income than the other. The existence of thresholds raises the probability that the expected party differential will be zero, i.e., that abstention will occur. It also makes it possible to change a voter's mind by providing him with better information about what is already happening to him.

At this point, we encounter two major problems. First, when we open the door of our model to uncertainty, we must also admit such undesirables as errors, false information, and ignorance. Because in this chapter we deal only with the basic logic of voting, we will postpone consideration of these factors until later except for one proviso. Throughout this thesis, we assume that no false (i.e., factually incorrect) information exists, though incomplete information can exist. Thus we exclude deliberate lies from our model, though errors and misleading data may remain.

The second problem is rooted in the very concept of a voter's changing his mind about how to vote. As we have shown, every voter makes his voting decisions by comparing various real and hypothetical streams of utility income. To decide what impact each government act has upon his income, he appraises it as good or bad in the light of his own view of "the good society." This procedure is rational because every citizen in our model views government as a means to the achievement of the good society as he sees it.

Thus a man's evaluation of each party depends ultimately upon (1) the information he has about its policies and (2) the relation between those of its policies he knows about and his conception of the good society. Once a voter has even provisionally decided how to vote, he can be persuaded to change his mind only if one of these two factors is altered. To simplify the analysis, we assume that every citizen has a fixed conception of the good society and has already related it to his knowledge of party policies in a consistent manner. Therefore only new information can persuade him to change his mind.

In essence, we are assuming that citizens' political tastes are fixed. Even though these tastes often change radically in the long run, we believe our assumption is plausible in the short run, barring wars or other social upheavals. In fact, fixed political tastes seem far more plausible to us than fixed consumption tastes, which are usually assumed in demand studies.

IV. VARIATIONS IN MULTIPARTY SYSTEMS

Our analysis has so far been in terms of a two-party system, but its conclusions can easily be extended to a multiparty system. In the latter, a voter follows the same rules as in the former, but compares the incumbent party with whichever of the opposition parties has the highest present performance rating, i.e., would yield him the largest utility income if it were now in office.

However, there is one eventuality in a multiparty system that does not arise in a two-party system: a rational voter may at times vote for a party other than the one he most prefers. For example, when the Progressive Party ran a candidate in the American Presidential election of 1948, some voters who preferred the Progressive candidate to all others nevertheless voted for the Democratic candidate. They did so because they felt their favorite candidate had no chance at all, and the more people voted for him, the fewer would vote Democratic. If the Democratic vote fell low enough, then the Republicans—the least desirable group from the Progressive point of view—would win. Thus a vote for their favorite candidate ironically increased the probability that the one they favored least would win. To avoid the latter outcome, they voted for the candidate ranking in the middle of their preference ordering.

Clearly, this is rational behavior, but it contradicts our simple rule for how voters should act. This discrepancy demands an explanation. First we must point out that in our model, elections are devices for the selection of governments, though they actually serve many purposes besides this one. They can also be (1) means of creating social solidarity, as they are in modern communist countries, (2) expressions of political preference, (3) devices for releasing personal aggression in legitimate channels (e.g., in political campaigns), and (4) incentives for citizens to inform themselves about current events. Nevertheless, we are interested in elections solely as means of selecting governments, and we define rational behavior with that end in mind.

A rational voter first decides what party he believes will benefit him most; then he tries to estimate whether this party has any chance of winning. He does this because his vote should be expended as part of a selection process, not as an expression of preference. Hence even if he prefers party A, he is "wasting" his vote on A if it has no chance of winning because very few other voters prefer it to B or C. The relevant choice in this case is between B and C. Since a vote for A is not useful in the actual process of selection, casting it is irrational.

Thus an important part of the voting decision is predicting how other citizens will vote by estimating their preferences. Each citizen uses his forecast to determine whether the party he most prefers is really a part of the relevant range of choice. If he believes it is not, then rationality commands him to vote for some other party.

In the absence of any information whatever about what other voters are likely to do, the rational voter always votes for the party he prefers. He also does so whenever the information he has leads him to believe his favorite party has a reasonable chance of winning. The precise stochastic meaning of "reasonable" cannot be defined *a priori*; it depends upon the temperament of each voter. However, the less chance of winning he feels his favorite party has, the more likely he is to switch his vote to a party that has a good chance.

The exact probability level at which he switches will partly depend upon how important he thinks it is to keep the worst party from winning. For example, let us assume that there are three parties: Right, Center, and Left. Voter X prefers Right to Center and Center to Left, but he believes that Right has the least chance of winning. If he greatly prefers Right to Center and is almost indifferent between Center and Left, he is less likely to switch his vote from Right to Center than if he slightly prefers Right to Center but abhors Left.

This situation becomes even more complex when we consider *future-oriented* voting. A voter may support a party that today is hopeless in the belief that his support will enable it to grow and someday become a likely winner—thus giving him a wider range of selection in the future. Also, he may temporarily support a hopeless party as a warning to some other party to change its platform if it wants his support. Both actions are rational for people who prefer better choice-alternatives in the future to present participation in the selection of a government.[10]

V. SUMMARY

In a world where he is furnished with complete, costless information, the rational citizen makes his voting decision in the following way:

1. By comparing the stream of utility income from government activity he has received under the present government (adjusted for trends) with those streams he believes he would have received if the various opposition parties had been in office, the voter finds his current party differentials. They establish his preference among the competing parties.

2. In a two-party system, the voter then votes for the party he prefers. In a multiparty system, he estimates what he believes are the preferences of other voters; then he acts as follows:

   a. If his favorite party seems to have a reasonable chance of winning, he votes for it.

   b. If his favorite party seems to have almost no chance of win-

---

[10] For a more detailed discussion of voting in multiparty systems, see Chapters 8 and 9.

ning, he votes for some other party that has a reasonable chance in order to keep the party he least favors from winning.

c. If he is a future-oriented voter, he may vote for his favorite party even if it seems to have almost no chance of winning in order to improve the alternatives open to him in future elections.

3. If the voter cannot establish a preference among parties because at least one opposition party is tied with the incumbents for first place in his preference ordering, he then acts as follows:[11]

a. If the parties are deadlocked even though they have differing platforms or current policies or both, he abstains.

b. If the parties are deadlocked because they have identical platforms and current policies, he compares the performance rating of the incumbent party with those of its predecessors in office. If the incumbents have done a good job, he votes for them; if they have done a bad job, he votes against them; and if their performance is neither good nor bad, he abstains.

---

[11] The case in which two or more opposition parties are tied for first place is not covered by our decision rules. However, it seems rational for a citizen to vote for whichever of these top-ranking parties he thinks has the best chance of winning. For other considerations which might have a bearing upon his decision, see Chapter 9.

4

The Basic Logic
of Government
Decision-Making

***

Introduction

TRADITIONALLY economic theory assumes that the social function and private motive of government both consist of maximization of social utility or social welfare. Our hypothesis differs from this view in three ways: (1) in our model, government's social function is not identical with its private motive; (2) we specify only the latter, which is the maximization of votes instead of utility or welfare; and (3) the government is a party competing with other parties for control of the governing apparatus. In this chapter we use the last two of these axioms to describe the basic principles of government decision-making in our model democracy.

I. FUNDAMENTAL PRINCIPLES OF GOVERNMENT DECISION-MAKING

A. THE CONCEPT OF MARGINAL OPERATIONS

Because the government in our model wishes to maximize political support, it carries out those acts of spending which gain the most votes by means of those acts of financing which lose the fewest votes. In other words, expenditures are increased until the vote-gain of the marginal dollar spent equals the vote-loss of the marginal dollar financed.

At first glance, this procedural role for government action looks very similar to the traditional rule based on social utility. The latter states that government should continue spending until marginal social return falls to a level equal to marginal social cost, i.e., the marginal return obtainable in the private sector. Although it appears that our hypothesis merely substitutes a vote function for the social-utility function, in fact the two rules are radically different. The government in our model is competing for votes with other political parties now out of office; hence its planning must take into account not only the voters' utility functions, but also the proposals made by its opponents.

Furthermore, opposition parties usually do not have to commit themselves on any issue until after the incumbent party's behavior as the government has revealed its policy. Therefore when the incumbents initiate a program, they can only guess how their opponents will react. But the opposition knows what policy the incumbents have on any given issue and can select the optimum strategy to counteract it. Thus government decision-making occurs in a tangled context of economic optimums and political warfare.

In our model, at the beginning of each election period the newly elected government draws up a master plan to guide its actions throughout the period. We could assume that every such plan is worked out from the basic acts of government down to the last detail as though there had been no government before. However, this would both describe the actual procedure inaccurately and change its logical structure.

Therefore we assume that the new government makes only partial alterations in the scheme of government activities inherited from the preceding administration; it does not recreate the whole scheme.[1] This postulate is both realistic and useful in formulating relatively simple rules for government behavior. In addition, it allows us to correlate government's plans with the utility functions of individual voters because citizens decide how to vote by means of the marginal impact of government activity upon their utility functions rather than its total impact.

Government activity includes providing such basic social conditions as police protection, enforcement of contracts, maintenance of national defense, etc. Thus the total utility a man derives from government action includes his gains from law and order in society and security in world politics. Even if this total utility income exceeds his total loss of utility in taxes and to government acts he dislikes, he may still strongly disapprove of some marginal government activity. A vote against any party is therefore not a vote against government *per se* but net disapproval of the particular marginal actions that party has taken.

Thus both the government and the voters are interested in marginal alterations in the structure of government activity. By *marginal alterations* we mean partial changes in the structure of government behavior patterns which each administration inherits from its predecessor. These changes may be of great significance absolutely (e.g., the alteration of defense spending by several billion dollars may have striking repercussions upon the economy). Furthermore, a series of marginal changes may alter the whole structure of government acts; so the meaning of marginality is related to the time units chosen.[2] Nevertheless, it is legitimate to focus attention upon marginal government acts in the short run, which is what concerns us in this chapter.

[1] The preceding administration is the same as the present one in cases of reëlection.

[2] In this respect, our concept resembles that of marginal cost in economics.

B. THE MAJORITY PRINCIPLE

Though such focusing drastically narrows the range of choice open to a government's consideration, it still faces a staggering choice problem, for there are numerous margins and multitudes of alternatives at each. In order to present our model of how government behaves under these circumstances, we make six simplifying assumptions:

1. All decisions are made by a central unit in the government which can look at all margins of possible action.
2. At each margin, there are only two alternatives of action, M and N.
3. All government choices are independent of each other; i.e., the outcome of each decision has no bearing on the possible choices or outcomes of any other decision.
4. There are only two parties competing for control of the government, one of which is now in office.
5. Each party knows the nature of all the utility functions of individual voters, so that it can tell whether and by how much each voter prefers M or N for every choice it is considering. By this we assume intrapersonal cardinality of utility, but we say nothing about interpersonal comparisons.
6. Voters are informed without cost of all possible government decisions and their consequences, and they make voting decisions rationally, as described in Chapter 3.

Under these radically oversimplified conditions, the government subjects each decision to a hypothetical poll and always chooses the alternative which the majority of voters prefer. It must do so because if it adopts any other course, the opposition party can defeat it. For example, if the government acts as the majority prefers in everything except issue x, the opposition can propose a platform identical to the government's except for issue x, where it stands with the majority. Since the voters are indifferent between parties on all other issues, the whole contest narrows down to issue x, and the opposition, having supported the majority position, gains more votes than the incumbents. Thus to avoid defeat, the government must support the majority on every issue.

II. OPPOSITION STRATEGIES AGAINST THE MAJORITY PRINCIPLE

Following the *majority principle* is the incumbents' best policy, but it does not guarantee victory in every election. The opposition party can sometimes defeat a majority-pleasing government by using one of three possible strategies.

A. COMPLETE MATCHING OF POLICIES

The simplest opposition strategy is adoption of a program which is identical with that of the incumbents' in every particular. This maneuver forces citizens to decide how to vote by comparing the incumbent's performance rating with those of previous governments. But in a certain world, the incumbents can easily discover and adopt the majority position on every issue; hence their performance rating is likely to be high enough to insure reëlection. In addition, the only circumstances which cause a majority-pleasing government to have a low performance rating also cause other strategies to work even better than the 100 percent matching maneuver. Therefore the latter would rarely be used in our hypothetical world.

B. A COALITION OF MINORITIES

Under certain conditions, the opposition can defeat a government which uses the majority principle by taking contrary stands on key issues, i.e., by supporting the minority. To explain these conditions, we make use of the following symbols:

U   stands for the utility income a voter would get from a possible government policy on some issue.

M   is the policy alternative on any issue which is favored by a majority of those citizens who are not indifferent about that issue.

N   is the policy alternative on any issue which is favored by a minority of those citizens who are not indifferent about that issue.

P   is the total set of issues which arise during an election period.
S   is a subset in P containing issues 1 through s, the first of which to arise (issue 1) need not be the first issue to arise in P but is the earliest issue in P on which the opposition party takes a minority stand.
i   stands for any individual issue.
X   is the incumbent party.
Y   is the opposition party.

The opposition party can always defeat the incumbents if there is some S in P which has the following characteristics:

1. More than half the citizens who vote are in the minority on some issues in S; i.e., they prefer N_i to M_i at least once.
2. Each citizen who holds the minority view on some but not all issues in S has a stronger preference for those policies he favors when in the minority than for those he favors when in the majority.
3. The opposition party need not commit itself on any issue in S until the incumbents have revealed their position on all issues therein, nor does it have to reveal its position on any other issue in P until after the incumbents have committed themselves on that issue.

Throughout this chapter, we refer to these characteristics as condition one, condition two, and condition three respectively.

Conditions one and two can be expressed more precisely in symbols as follows: there are more voters for whom $\sum_{i=1}^{s} (U_N - U_M)_i > 0$ than for whom $\sum_{i=1}^{s} (U_N - U_M)_i < 0$. In other words, more voters are minority oriented toward S than are majority oriented toward it.

Those for whom $\sum_{i=1}^{s} (U_N - U_M)_i = 0$ are ambivalent.[3]

---

[3] This notation assumes intrapersonal cardinality of utility, as stated earlier in the chapter. However, the verbal argument preceding it does not depend upon this assumption; it is equally valid under purely ordinal assumptions. For proof of this assertion, see footnote 14 of this chapter.

Condition one implies that the government does not always please the same set of men when it takes the majority position; i.e., the composition of the majority differs from decision to decision. This outcome could never occur if a particular set of citizens, comprising more than 50 percent of the electorate, agreed upon all issues government faced. Therefore the coalition-of-minorities strategy works only when no majority of voters exhibits perfect consensus on all issues.

Furthermore, condition two means that once the government has been elected, most citizens would rather have it follow the minority's views on every issue in S than the majority's views on every issue therein. This does not mean they are antidemocratic, for a democracy requires majority rule only in choosing its government. However, it implies that consensus is weak, since men are more vehement about their minority views than about the views they share with a majority of others.

How these conditions favor the coalition-of-minorities strategy can be shown by an example. Assume that A, B, and C are the whole electorate, and government makes decisions on two issues. On the first issue, government takes a position which A and B favor slightly and C opposes strongly. The government's decision on the second issue is strongly opposed by A, but slightly favored by B and C. Thus government action pleases the majority in each case. Nevertheless, both A and C incur net losses from government activity, since the pleasure each receives on one issue is outweighed by the unhappiness he gets on the other. Consequently, each will vote for a party which espouses the minority view on both issues.

In such a situation, it might seem wiser for the incumbents to adopt a minority-pleasing strategy themselves. However, condition three prevents them from gaining by doing so. When the opposition can refrain from committing itself until after the incumbents have acted, it can counteract whatever strategy they adopt. If the government employs the majority principle consistently, the opposition defeats it by supporting the minority on every issue. Conversely, if the government takes a minority position on even one issue, the opposition can triumph by matching it on every other issue and supporting the majority on that one. In short, the incumbents cannot win when all three conditions hold.

If we retain the first two conditions but weaken condition three, the opposition still has an advantage, though it can conceivably lose.[4] For instance, assume the same situation exists as in our previous example except for the following change: the opposition must commit itself on each issue in P after the incumbents reveal their stand on that issue but before they do so on the next one (we assume issues arise one at a time). In this case, it is possible for the incumbents to defeat the opposition whenever voter B's preference for the majority view is stronger on the first issue than on the second. The government chooses the majority view on the first issue in S (as it always must), and the opposition counters with the minority view. But on the second issue, the government picks the minority view, forcing the opposition to support the majority.[5] Since B gains more from the incumbents' position on the first issue compared to that of the opposition than he loses from their position on the second, he prefers the incumbents to the opposition. C supports the opposition and A the government; hence the incumbents win even though conditions one and two hold.

Thus when the weakened version of condition three is in effect, the opposition can be certain of victory only if a fourth condition also holds:

4. No matter what stands the incumbents take on all issues in S after issue 1, the opposition party can always match these stands

[4] Its advantage is the ability to decide which issue in P will be issue 1 in S; i.e., to decide when S starts. The incumbents must adopt the majority position on the first issue in S because the opposition has supported the majority (i.e., matched the incumbents) on all previous issues. The incumbents can never support a minority until after the opposition has done so. If they did, the opposition would support the majority on that issue, match the incumbents on all subsequent issues, and win the election. The set S begins when the opposition first decides not to match the incumbents and instead supports the minority on some issue. That issue is always issue 1 in S; hence the opposition has the initiative and can strike where it wishes. The other issues in S need not follow issue 1 immediately in P, but they must be subsequent to it.

[5] If the opposition also supports the minority on issue 2 it loses the election in our example, because the contest is narrowed to issue 1, on which the majority support the incumbents, as explained in the preceding footnote.

or adopt opposite ones in such a way that more voters will prefer the opposition's policy set than prefer the incumbents' policy set. We refer to this characteristic of S as condition four.

Condition four can be expressed more exactly in symbols as follows: there are more voters for whom $\sum_{i=1}^{s} (U_Y)_i > \sum_{i=1}^{s} (U_X)_i$ for at least one possible opposition strategy than for whom $\sum_{i=1}^{s} (U_Y)_i < \sum_{i=1}^{s} (U_X)_i$ for that strategy. Admittedly, this is a very general statement, but we cannot make it more specific because of the enormous number of strategies possible when conditions one and two hold and there are many issues or many voters or both.

If S conforms to condition four, the incumbents cannot gain victory by forcing the opposition to adopt a heterogeneous strategy instead of a straight coalition of minorities. A *heterogeneous* strategy is one in which each party supports some minorities and some majorities in S, as in the example given above. Though the incumbents can force the opposition to adopt such a strategy even when condition four holds, they cannot win by doing so. No maneuvering on their part can overcome the advantage seized by the opposition when it supported the minority on issue 1 in S. Thus when conditions one, two, and four hold, the incumbents are always defeated unless uncertainty is introduced into the model.

Of course, once the opposition party gets into office, it faces the same dilemma that its predecessor could not solve. Furthermore, if the same issues arise again, it must handle them in the manner indicated by its campaign promises; i.e., if it had upheld minority views on every issue, it will enact those views when it becomes the government.[6] In this case it is vulnerable to the strategy whereby its rival matches it on every issue but one, on which the rival supports the majority. Thus unless conditions one, two, or four change, the

---

[6] For proof of a party's need to carry out its promises, see Chapter 7.

opposition can count on being defeated itself at the end of one term in office.

In short, the two parties regularly alternate in power, each lasting only one election period at a time. This conclusion may seem to undermine our hypothesis: if the government knows it will inevitably be defeated in the next election, why should it bother to maximize votes? The answer is twofold: (1) if it fails to do so, the voters may not reëlect it when it is next due to take office, and (2) in reality, uncertainty prevents the opposition from defeating the incumbents with the regularity possible in a certain world even when conditions one, two, and four hold.[7]

In the real world, an opposition party is most likely to try a minority-coalition strategy after the incumbents have been in office a long time. Otherwise this maneuver is risky because no one knows with certainty whether conditions one, two, and four actually prevail. But when the "ins" have been governing for several terms consecutively, they have had to make so many decisions that (1) they have probably made many enemies and (2) the likelihood of a varying majority composition on several issues is high. Therefore the opposition may be willing to abandon the majority position on some issues in hopes of creating a successful alliance among the dissenters to government action.

C. THE ARROW PROBLEM

The opposition's third possible strategy against the government, like the second, works only when there is a lack of consensus in the electorate. If voters disagree in certain particular ways about what goals are desirable, the government may be defeated because it cannot follow the majority principle even if it wants to do so. To study this situation, we drop the simplifying assumption that there are only two alternatives for each decision. Instead we assume that some issues can be resolved by any one of the three mutually exclusive policies f, g, and h.[8] Let us further assume that on at least

[7] See Chapter 7 for a discussion of the first point and Section III of this chapter in regard to the second point.

[8] This three-choice case covers all cases involving more than two alternatives.

one issue our three voters, A, B, and C, rank the three alternatives as follows:

| | Voter | | |
Choice	A	B	C
First	f	g	h
Second	g	h	f
Third	h	f	g

No alternative has majority support for first choice; in fact, any alternative that the government chooses can be defeated in a paired election by some other alternative. If the government picks f, both B and C prefer h. If the government chooses h, both A and B would vote for an opposition which picked g. Finally if the government selects g, the opposition can choose f, which both A and C prefer to g. As long as the government must commit itself first, the opposition can choose some other alternative, match the government's program on all other issues so as to narrow the election to this one, and defeat the incumbents—no matter what alternative the incumbents choose!

Perhaps it seems that the voters will see through the strategy of the opposition, because they realize that once the opposition gets into power, it must face the same dilemma. However, the crux of the problem is not the voters' action in the election, but the structure of their preferences. As Professor Arrow has shown, the government in such a situation cannot adopt any rational policy.[9] No matter what it does, it is wrong because a majority would have preferred some other action. It surely is not rational for voters to refuse to vote for the alternative they prefer when offered a choice —yet only thus can the strategy of the opposition be defeated. The fact is that nothing the voters can do is rational, in the sense of selecting a stable, preferred alternative, as long as their preferences are so disparate.

Since government faces more than two alternative policies in al-

[9] Kenneth J. Arrow, *Social Choice and Individual Values* (New York: John Wiley & Sons, Inc., 1951). Much of the contents of this section is taken directly from Arrow's work.

most every decision, we may assume *a priori* that it encounters this dilemma at least once during every election period.[10] Any other conclusion requires an extreme degree of consensus among voters on every detail of every issue—a condition we believe unlikely. Therefore, as long as we hold to the other assumptions we made at the start of this analysis, the incumbents will always be defeated by the opposition. The opposition need only follow the policy-matching strategy, thus narrowing the election down to some Arrow-problem issue, and wait for the government to commit itself on that issue. Then it merely selects the policy that defeats whatever the government has chosen, and—presto!—it is elected!

III. THE ROLE OF CERTAINTY IN THE MODEL

At this point, our model begins to disintegrate because of the assumption of certainty; i.e., parties know what voters prefer, and voters know the consequences of government acts. This perfect knowledge allows Arrow problems to dominate attention and force the social system into a breakdown, particularly if they involve important issues. For if no government can possibly be reëlected, then party motivation for action cannot long remain the desire to be reëlected. Experience will soon convince each party that this desire is futile.

Therefore, once elected, a government has no reason to follow the majority principle on any issue. It knows that if a single instance of the Arrow problem is encountered, no matter how trivial, it will lose to the opposition. Since this is overwhelmingly likely, the government will act according to some rule other than the majority principle, such as immediate material gain for its members. Our hypothesis that governments act so as to maximize votes seems to lead to its own abandonment.[11]

[10] From now on, we refer to any such dilemma as an "Arrow problem."

[11] Perhaps we can conclude from this that democracy cannot function in a certain world unless consensus among voters is almost complete on all issues. In the real world, uncertainty masks the dilemmas which society would face if it had to confront its diversity squarely; hence democracy is possible. This reasoning demonstrates how fundamental uncertainty is to political life in all large societies.

This pessimistic conclusion depends upon the feasibility of an issue-matching strategy, i.e., the ability of the opposition to narrow the contest to a few issues by agreeing with the incumbents on all others. Such a strategy is possible only if the opposition is sure (1) which issues involve Arrow problems and (2) which alternative in each issue will defeat the one the government chooses. Without certainty on these matters, the opposition runs an enormous risk when it matches the incumbents everywhere else, since this removes any possibility of winning on any other issue.

On the other hand, the whole idea of the majority principle rests on the opposition's ability to adopt an issue-matching strategy if the incumbents even once fail to support the majority's views. Again, the opposition must be certain that on some particular issue the incumbents have adopted a minority position. Without such certainty, no party would dare reduce the whole election to one issue. Therefore both the derivation of the majority principle and its undermining by the Arrow problem depend on the assumption of certainty.

Precisely the same argument applies to the minority-coalition strategy. If the opposition knows that conditions one, two, and four hold, it can always defeat the incumbents by taking minority positions on at least some issues. Therefore the incumbents have no incentive to please the majority at all, since their cause is hopeless. The certainty which allows the majority principle to function simultaneously undermines it whenever these three conditions hold.

If we try to escape these two dilemmas by introducing uncertainty, we save the incumbents from inevitable defeat, but at the same time we allow them to abandon the majority principle. However, we shall deal with these developments later.[12] For the moment, we retain certainty but at the same time ignore its effect upon the motivation of party behavior; i.e., we assume that parties are never discouraged from their desire to be reëlected by their continual defeat after one term in office. Hence maximization of votes remains the central goal of their behavior. This admitted dodge allows us to keep hold of the majority principle long enough to make some useful deductions from it.

[12] See Chapters 5, 6, 7, and 9.

IV. THE PREVALENCE OF THE "WILL OF THE MAJORITY"

A. THE RULE OF THE PASSIONATE MAJORITY

From the preceding analysis, it is clear that government does not always follow the majority principle even in a certain world. When the opposition adopts a coalition-of-minorities strategy, government may support the minority occasionally so as to maximize chance of a tie outcome. Or if an opposition party gains office by following a minority-coalition strategy, it will carry out minority-pleasing policies whenever similar issues arise again. Finally, when Arrow problems arise, there is no majority position to support. Hence at first glance the majority principle seems to be a useless concept altogether.

However, if we exclude Arrow problems, it leads directly to the following conclusion: in a two-party system, both parties nearly always adopt any policy that a majority of voters strongly prefer, no matter what strategies the parties are following. Neither party can gain from holding the minority view unless the majority hold their opinions lukewarmly; hence a passionate majority always determines policy.

To show just what a passionate majority is, let us assume that voters attach utility to various policy outcomes as depicted in Table 1.

	TABLE 1 Voters			TABLE 2 Voters		
	A	B	C	A	B	C
Issue 1						
Alternative M	1	10	8	1	10	8
Alternative N	100	9	5	100	9	5
Issue 2						
Alternative M'	10	10	16	10	10	16
Alternative N'	9	9	17	9	9	20

Note: Numbers stand for units of utility.

If so, the opposition party cannot adopt a minority-coalition strategy (policies N and N') to counteract the incumbents' majority strategy (M and M') even though voter A tremendously prefers receiving N to receiving M'. This possibility is ruled out because C would be willing to trade the minority outcome on issue 2 for the majority outcome on issue 1; i.e., he is more passionate about his majority view than he is about his minority view. If we alter his passion so that he would be willing to reverse the trade mentioned (as in Table 2), then the coalition-of-minorities strategy works.[13]

This example illustrates several characteristics of the *rule of the passionate majority*. First, interpersonal cardinality is irrelevant. This is true because we can multiply any or all citizens' utility figures by any positive numbers without changing the results, as long as all the figures for any one man are multiplied by the same number. Thus the fact that A's utility income goes up 99 units if M' is substituted for M does not necessarily overcompensate for B's loss of one unit from the same change, since there is no way to compare units interpersonally.

Second, the factor which determines whether a man takes a passionate-majority stand is not his relative gain from each issue but his total gain from the whole combination of issues. For example, in Table 1, C gets 37.5 percent more utility from M than from N but only 6.25 percent more utility from N' than from M'; hence we might suspect that relative gain explains C's willingness to trade N for M. But this is false, as Table 2 shows. C is now willing to trade M for N' even though he gets only 25 percent more utility from N' than from M' and still gets 37.5 percent more from M than from N. Clearly his total gain on all issues taken together determines how he votes rather than the rate of gain on any particular issue.[14]

[13] It is clear from this reasoning that the conditions underlying a passionate majority are the exact opposite of conditions one and two.

[14] Even intrapersonal cardinality can be eliminated without altering the rule of the passionate majority. We retain it here because (1) it makes exposition easier and (2) it fits into our use of utility in the rest of the study. However, we could use a strictly ordinal approach by comparing bundles of policies rather than utilities. For example, in Table 1, voter C prefers bundle MM' to bundle NN', but in Table 2 his preference is reversed. If we merely state that his taste for policies has changed, we can derive the same conclusions as before without men-

Finally, the example shows that a passionate majority is not necessarily more passionate about its views than the minority it overrules. In other words, parties do not compare the intensity of the majority's feelings with those of the minority; they appraise the willingness of each citizen to trade the outcomes he prefers when in a majority for those he prefers when in a minority. Citizen A clearly has a more intense desire to get N instead of M than anyone else has about any issue; yet in Table 1 his passion is outweighed by the weaker passion of citizens B and C.[15]

Thus we cannot judge how passionate a majority is by its feelings about any one issue. The members of a passionate majority may only care slightly whether alternative M is chosen rather than alternative N; while the minority may frantically desire N. The crucial point is whether the citizens in the majority have a greater preference for their position on this issue than they do for minority positions they hold on other issues. Thus parties do not judge passion by comparing voters with each other; instead they compare the intensity of each voter's feelings on certain issues with the intensity of his feelings on others.

This fact raises two questions: (1) are there any interpersonal comparisons in politics? (2) what does the rule of the passionate majority really signify?

B. THE POLITICAL SIGNIFICANCE OF PASSIONATE MAJORITIES

Interpersonal comparisons are in fact the essence of politics, because its function is the settlement of conflicts between men. Furthermore, since we have defined utility as a measure of benefit, and since

---

tioning utility at all. Every other part of our study involving utility can be similarly transposed into ordinal or indifference analysis; hence none of our conclusions depend upon cardinality of utility, whether inter- or intrapersonal. The only reason we do not use a strictly ordinal approach throughout is that it renders exposition more difficult.

[15] This outcome is even more striking if we assume that the utilities of all three voters are measured in the same units, i.e., that interpersonal cardinality is possible. Clearly, A could then bribe B and C to prefer N and everyone would gain—perhaps substantially. Yet when vote-selling is prohibited, A's relatively enormous desire for N is inevitably frustrated. For a detailed discussion of vote-selling in such situations, see Chapter 10.

all conflicts concern benefits, these comparisons are at root utility comparisons. However, they are ordinal, not cardinal; cardinality is supplied by the assumption that each citizen can cast one and only one vote. This axiom implies that each man's political views are just as important as any other man's, even if one holds his views with intense fervor and the other is nearly indifferent. The fact that each is a citizen is what makes his views significant, not the fact that he is (or is not) fervent about them. Hence neither passion nor its absence adds to the political weight of his opinions in a certain world.

But if this is true, what can the rule of the passionate majority signify? Its real meaning is that majority rule prevails in government policy formation only when there is a consensus of intensities as well as a consensus of views. By *consensus of intensities* we mean that most citizens agree on which issues are most important even if they disagree about what policy to follow on each issue; i.e., they care most about having the right policy followed on the same issues, though they may have different ideas about what the right policies are. By *consensus of views* we mean that on any issue a majority of citizens favor one alternative over the others—they have the same opinion about which policy is right.

These two types of consensus are independent of each other, since each may exist alone. Even when they both exist at once, the majority supporting a given policy may not be the same majority which supports some other policy. However, there will be a single set of citizens, comprising a majority of voters, who have very similar importance rankings of all issues. This similarity need not eliminate the possibility of minority-favoring actions, because there may be a small subset of policies within which conditions one, two, and four hold. By matching the incumbents on all other policies, the opposition can narrow the election to this subset and apply the coalition-of-minorities strategy. Nevertheless, the fact that it matches the incumbents on all other policies shows that the majority position usually prevails even in this case.

Furthermore, even when Arrow problems are encountered, the rule of the passionate majority has significant repercussions. Beneath a complex of alternatives that causes Arrow problems, there usually rests some more fundamental policy decision. For example, there are myriad ways to set up a social security program; hence adoption of any one may involve the government in an Arrow problem. But the question of whether or not aged people should somehow receive more than token public assistance can be reduced to a yes or no basis, and a majority opinion found. If the majority appears strongly to favor this principle, both parties will adopt it. The range of alternatives on the social security issue is thus narrowed to different definitions of "more-than-token" and different methods of administration. Though this still leaves a large area of choice, it does provide a standpoint on the basic issue which both parties adopt and around which the actual alternatives cluster. We conclude that in a two-party democracy, government policies at root follow whatever a majority strongly desires, and the range of deviation from its aspirations is relatively small.

Thus democracy leads to the prevalence of the majority's views whenever most citizens agree with each other more emphatically than they disagree with each other. One extremely important social force causing both agreement and disagreement is the division of labor. Because it increases men's dependence on one another, it creates a need for agreement. However, it also increases specialization; therefore it breeds disparate points of view about what policies are best for society.

Furthermore, because each man earns most of his income in his area of specialization, and because the benefits of social coöperation are largely indivisible, every citizen is likely to have more intense feelings about his specialty—which is relatively unique—than about his general interests—which he shares with most others. Thus specialization is a politically divisive force in a democracy which encourages men to ally as minorities to thwart the will of the majority.[16] We shall see later how this fact leads to logrolling and

---

[16] This conclusion is similar to the one reached by David Riesman in his analysis of "veto groups." See David Riesman, *The Lonely Crowd* (New Haven: Yale University Press, 1950), pp. 244–255. For a further discussion of how such disunity may paralyze democracy, see Chapters 8 and 9 of the present study.

other tactics by which a group of minorities agree to exploit the majority.[17]

V. THE BUDGET PROCESS

A. BUDGET DECISIONS UNDER THE MAJORITY PRINCIPLE

At the beginning of this chapter we stated that the government increases its spending until the vote gain of the marginal dollar spent equals the vote loss of the marginal dollar of financing. In other words, when a newly elected (or reëlected) government sets up its plan of action, it asks about each expenditure, "Is it worth its cost in votes in terms of votes gained?" just as a profit-making firm asks about each of its expenditures, "Is it worth its cost in dollars in terms of added revenue?"

But the government takes over many of the activities of its predecessor without really considering doing away with them, though it may consider marginal alteration of their quantity or reorganization of their administration. Hence it starts out with a mass of essential activities which it knows by experience are worth their cost in votes. Also, there will probably exist a set of basic revenue-raising devices which the government knows cost less in votes than would cessation of those activities they support. Thus the crucial weighing of votes occurs at the margins of both expenditure and revenue patterns.

Most governments separate the early stages of expenditure-planning from the early stages of revenue-planning as a part of their internal division of labor. Two sets of plans are drawn up and submitted to some central balancing agency, which must delimit the expenditure pattern and find some kind of financing, whether taxed, printed, or borrowed, for all of it. If a government is acting so as to maximize votes, these plans are rated by their additions to or subtractions from the individual utility incomes of every voter. The balancing agency weighs each additional act of spending against the additional financing needed for it and decides whether it will gain

[17] See Chapters 12 and 13.

or lose votes, in light of the utility functions of all voters and the possible strategy of the opposition.

The government is likely to adopt any act of spending which, coupled with its financing, is a net addition of utility to more voters than it is a subtraction, i.e., it pleases more than it irritates. Otherwise the opposition may approve it and make an issue of it in the forthcoming campaign. Conversely, whenever a proposed expenditure irritates more voters than it pleases, the party in power will most likely refuse to carry it out. The government continues to weigh proposals in this manner long after its first plan is formulated, since conditions change and new possibilities must be considered.

Thus the pressure of competition motivates the government in the same way that it motivates private firms, though the number of competitors is much smaller, and the competition is for votes instead of dollars. This pressure even causes parties to innovate so as to meet new social needs and keep technically in step with their competition.

B. BUDGET DECISIONS UNDER OTHER CONDITIONS

The preceding description of government budgeting applies when the government follows the majority principle, but it need not employ that principle under all conditions. As we have seen, whenever the opposition uses a coalition-of-minorities strategy or is kept from adopting an issue-matching strategy by uncertainty, the government is freed from the necessity of agreeing with the majority on every issue.

As a result, it is not interested in the net impact upon a voter's utility income of each action but of all its actions taken together. Upon occasion, it is willing to irritate more voters than it pleases, if subsequent actions will placate those irritated and yet not completely cancel the satisfaction of those pleased. This means the government can no longer weigh acts individually, but must look at the effect of all of them as a unit. Consequently its decisions become much more complex.

As an example, let us say that the government is pondering some problem that has just arisen at T_n, which is any moment between T_b, the beginning of the election period, and T_e, the date of the election. All of its actions from T_b to T_n must be considered as given, since they are already affecting individual utility incomes. Also, a blueprint has previously been drawn up for the future acts from T_n to T_e, which were originally coördinated with the now-given acts into a single master plan covering the whole period. Unforeseen events cause constant deviations from this master plan, each of which is actually a reformulation of the whole plan from T_n to T_e, in the light of the acts already taken from T_b to T_n. Thus every single unforeseen decision involves a new prediction of every voter's net utility income position on election day.

In practice, no government actually carries out such elaborate calculations. Not only does it lack information about the shapes of individual utility functions, but also it cannot possibly make such staggering calculations for each decision. Nevertheless, the rudiments of this kind of thinking appear in the government's keeping an eye on various groups in society to see how they are doing and to discover what actions should be taken to appease them or ensnare their votes. By simplifying the millions of voters into a small number of blocs, and merging the thousands of acts into a few major policy groups, the government can actually make the kind of recalculations discussed. It can take into account how a given policy will affect farmers, labor, businessmen, etc., and how this policy will fit into the net effect that its whole program will have had on each of these homogeneous groups by election day, given the actions already taken.

We conclude that governments in our model world either (1) make each spending decision separately by means of the majority principle, or (2) fit each decision into the entire pattern and re-calculate the whole impact of their spending program upon all voters. Which of the two methods they follow depends upon the degree of uncertainty in their knowledge of voters' utility functions, and the strategies adopted by opposition parties.

VI. HOW GOVERNMENT ACTS ARE RELATED TO VOTERS' UTILITY FUNCTIONS

In Chapter 3, we stated that how a voter casts his ballot depends upon what actions the government takes and what actions the opposition says it would take were it in office. In this chapter, we have shown that the actions a government takes depend upon how the government thinks voters will cast their ballots. These statements delineate a relationship of mutual interdependence, which can be transposed into a set of equations as follows:

t stands for the whole election period.
V stands for actual votes cast for the incumbents.
V' stands for expected votes the government feels will be cast for it.
A stands for government actions.
U stands for voters' utility incomes from government action.
e stands for the date of the election at the end of period t.
P stands for the strategies of the opposition parties.
f_1 stands for a functional relationship.

1. The actions of the government are a function of the way it expects voters to vote and the strategies of its opposition:

$$A_t = f_1(V'_e, P_t)$$

2. The government expects voters to vote according to changes in their utility incomes and the strategies of opposition parties:

$$V'_e = f_2(U_t, P_t)$$

3. Voters actually vote according to changes in their utility incomes and alternatives offered by the opposition:

$$V_e = f_3(U_t, P_t)$$

4. Voters' utility incomes from government activity depend upon the actions taken by government during the election period:

$$U_t = f_4(A_t)$$

5. The strategies of opposition parties depend upon their views of the voters' utility incomes and the actions taken by the government in power:

$$P_t = f_5(U_t, A_t)$$

This set of five equations has five unknowns: expected votes, actual votes, opposition strategies, government actions, and individual utility incomes.

We have rearranged our ideas in equation form to show the circularity of our analytical structure: votes depend upon actions, and actions depend upon votes. The media through which the dependence operates are, in each case, the utility incomes of individuals and the strategies adopted by opposition parties. Other variables must be added later when we introduce the cost of information, but the basic relationship remains the same.

VII. SUMMARY

According to our hypothesis, governments continue spending until the marginal vote gain from expenditure equals the marginal vote loss from financing. The determinants of vote loss and vote gain are the utility incomes of all voters and the strategies of opposition parties. Thus governments are engaged in political warfare as well as maximization problems.

Under conditions of certainty, a government's best strategy is to adopt choices which are favored by a majority of voters. Before making any expenditure, it takes a hypothetical poll to see how voters' utility incomes are affected by the expenditure and the necessary financing. If it fails to adopt the majority's views, its opponents will do so and will fight the election on this issue only, thereby insuring defeat for the incumbents.

However, conforming to the will of the majority does not guarantee reëlection for the incumbents. Sometimes the opposition can form a coalition of dissenters and win by upholding the minority view on key issues, and at other times no clear majority position exists. In both cases, the incumbents' downfall is caused by lack of strong concensus in the electorate combined with the opposition's ability to refrain from committing itself until after the government acts.

Thus majority rule does not always prevail on specific issues, but it usually does in a two-party system whenever the majority strongly favors a certain policy. Such passionate majorities exist when citizens feel more strongly about the policy views most others share with them than about those regarding which they are in the minority. By encouraging specialization of viewpoint, the division of labor tends to break up passionate majorities and foster minority-coalition governments.

When government is following the majority principle, it plans its budget by taking a hypothetical poll on each decision. When it is using some other strategy, it judges every action as a part of its whole spending plan for the election period. Unforeseen events force it to recalculate the whole plan in the light of what it has already done.

Since governments plan their actions to please voters and voters decide how to vote on the basis of government actions, a circular relation of mutual interdependence underlies the functioning of government in a democracy.

Part II

The General Effects of Uncertainty

5

The Meaning of Uncertainty

I. THE NATURE OF UNCERTAINTY

UNCERTAINTY is any lack of sure knowledge about the course of past, present, future, or hypothetical events. In terms of any particular decision, it may vary in removability, intensity, and relevance.

Most uncertainty is removable through the acquisition of information, if a sufficient quantity of data is available. However, some uncertainty is intrinsic to particular situations. For example, the outcome of a free election is uncertain before the election occurs because voters can change their minds at the last minute. Determinists might disagree by claiming that sufficient information about each voter would enable a superintelligent mind to predict the outcome infallibly. However, we do not wish to engage in the perennial free will vs. determinism controversy. The agents in our model rarely have enough data to eliminate all uncertainty even when it is theoretically removable. Therefore we merely assume that the intensity of uncertainty can be reduced by information, which can be obtained only by the expenditure of scarce resources.

The intensity of uncertainty in a given situation is expressed by the degree of confidence with which a decision-maker makes his decision. If added knowledge clarifies the situation in his mind and points more strongly to one alternative as being the most rational, his confidence varies directly with the amount of data he has. Conversely, additional information may contradict what he knows already, so that his confidence falls as he learns more. However, as a general rule, the more information a decision-maker acquires, the more confident of making the right decision he becomes. And the more confident he is, the less he must discount the gains from being right in planning his overall allocation of resources. Therefore, information is valuable if it increases confidence in a correct decision, even if it does not change the decision tentatively arrived at. However, marginal returns from this use of data rapidly diminish towards zero; i.e., the more confident a man is about his decision, the less he believes he can gain from further information.

Uncertainty is irrelevant to a given decision if the decision is trivial, or if the uncertainty concerns knowledge not germane to it. Thus a man may have an extremely high degree of confidence about some of his decisions even if he lives in a world of tremendous uncertainty. Uncertainty must refer to particular events; it is not a general condition.

All three of these dimensions of uncertainty can be merged into the *level of confidence* with which a decision-maker makes each decision.[1] Absolute confidence means uncertainty has been removed; though this is rare. And since the level of confidence refers to a particular decision, only revelant uncertainty will influence it.

We will not often make explicit reference to the level of confidence in our discussions of the cost of information and its impact upon political rationality.[2] However, we have set it forth here in order to clarify those parts of our analysis where its use is implicit.

[1] The term *level of confidence* as used herein does not have exactly the same meaning as the statistical term *confidence level*. The latter is a technical term with a precise definition, whereas the former is more generalized in nature.

[2] Nor will we attempt to analyze the various methods of making decisions under conditions of uncertainty. For a thorough discussion of this topic, see Kenneth J. Arrow, "Alternative Theories of Decision-Making in Risk-Taking Situations," *Econometrica*, XIX (1951), 404–437.

II. REASON, KNOWLEDGE, AND INFORMATION

A distinction of which we will make more explicit use is that between reason, contextual knowledge, and information. *Reason* is facility with the processes of logical thought and the principles of causal analysis; we assume that all men possess it. *Contextual knowledge* we define as cognizance of the basic forces relevant to some given field of operations. It is a grasp of relations among the fundamental variables in some area, such as mathematics, economics, or the agriculture of ancient China. Thus contextual knowledge (1) is more specific than reason, (2) is not common to all men but is acquired to a greater or less degree through education, and (3) can be an object of specialization. *Information* is data about the current developments in and status of those variables which are the objects of contextual knowledge.

Thus a man may know the monetary structure of a country without being informed on the present level of the interest rate, the outstanding money supply, etc. Lack of contextual knowledge is ignorance, which is to be distinguished from lack of information. To combat ignorance, a man needs education; whereas to combat lack of information (if he already has knowledge) he needs only information, which is less expensive than education but still costly.

From these definitions, we can see that a man can be knowledgeable without being informed, or informed without being knowledgeable, but he cannot interpret information without contextual knowledge. Therefore, when we speak of an informed citizen, we will be referring to a man who has both contextual knowledge and information about those areas relevant to his decision-making.

III. THE FORMS OF UNCERTAINTY IN OUR MODEL

Let us turn from semantics to specifying the types of uncertainty which we will encounter. Voters and political parties are the two major classes of actors in our model, and each class has several forms of uncertainty associated with it.

Voters may be uncertain in the following ways:

1. They may be aware that their total utility incomes have altered, but be uncertain about what caused them to do so, particularly about whether government or private action was responsible.
2. They may not know the repercussions upon their own utility incomes of some proposed (or undertaken) government action, mainly because they do not know what changes in objective conditions it would cause.
3. They may be completely unaware of certain actions being carried out by the government, or of alternatives the government could have undertaken, or of both.
4. They may be uncertain how much influence their own views have on the formation of government policy.
5. They may be uncertain about how other citizens plan to vote.

In short, voters are not always aware of what the government is or could be doing, and often they do not know the relationship between government actions and their own utility incomes.

Political parties (including the one in office) may be uncertain in the following ways:

1. They may not know what decisions the nonpolitical elements of the economy are going to make; i.e., they may be unable to predict the economic conditions with which they must deal in running the government.
2. They may not know how a given government act will affect the utility incomes of voters, even if they know what objective conditions it will produce.
3. They may not know what objective consequences a given government act will have, even if they know how voters' utility incomes will be affected by every possible set of consequences.
4. They may not know how much influence any one voter has over other voters.
5. They may not know whether voters are aware of what the government is doing and how it affects them, or how much additional information is necessary to make voters thus aware.
6. They may not know what policies opposition parties will adopt on any given issue. If this type of uncertainty exists, a party will

be unable to forecast how voters will react to its own policy, even if it knows the way voters will be affected by that policy and the nature of their utility functions.

IV. SUMMARY

Uncertainty is any lack of sure knowledge about the course of events. It may be present in any part of the political decision-making process, and usually affects both political parties and voters by controlling the level of confidence with which they make decisions.

In discussing uncertainty, we can usefully distinguish between types of knowledge. Contextual knowledge illuminates the basic causal structure of some field of operations; while information provides current data on the variables significant in that field.

6

How Uncertainty Affects
Government Decision-
Making

Introduction

UNCERTAINTY divides voters into several classes because it affects some people more than others. Furthermore, it gives rise to persuasion, since some of the voters who are most certain try to influence those who are least certain. Thus two criteria for differentiating among voters are created by uncertainty: the confidence with which a voter holds his party preference, and the intensity with which he advocates whatever views he has.

Objectives

In this chapter we attempt to prove the following propositions:

1. Some rational men are politically active, others are passive or confused, and still others react to politics with habitual behavior patterns.

2. Political leadership is possible only in an uncertain world, and leaders gain rational followers in rough proportion to the followers' lack of information.
3. Every democratic government decentralizes its own power if discovering the opinions of its constituents is difficult, no matter how centralized its constitutional organization is.
4. In an uncertain world, it is irrational for a democratic government to treat all men as though they were politically equal.

I. HOW UNCERTAINTY GIVES RISE TO PERSUASION

As long as we retain our original assumption of certainty, no citizen can possibly influence another's vote. Each knows what would benefit him most, what the government is doing, and what other parties would do if they were in power. Therefore his political taste structure, which we assume fixed, leads directly to an unambiguous decision about how he should vote. If he remains rational, no persuasion can change his mind. In such a world, even if a voter passionately wants his party to win, it is futile for him to try to influence anyone else to vote for it.

But as soon as uncertainty appears, the clear path from taste structure to voting decision becomes obscured by lack of knowledge. For some voters, the decision remains obvious; they want a specific party to win because its policies are clearly the most beneficial to them. But others are highly uncertain about which party they prefer. They are not sure just what is happening to them, or what would happen to them if another party were in power. They need more facts to establish a clear preference. By providing these facts, persuaders find an opportunity to become effective.

Persuaders are not interested *per se* in helping people who are uncertain become less so; they want certainty to produce a decision which aids their cause. Therefore they provide only those facts which are favorable to whatever group they are supporting. We have assumed that these "facts" will never be false, but they need not tell the whole truth. And they probably will not, because persuaders are, by definition, propagandists in the original sense of the word—they present correct information organized so as to lead to a specific conclusion.

As long as we assume rationality, only people who have already made up their own minds can persuade others.[1] Therefore persuaders are at one extreme of the uncertainty scale—they are certain what voting decision is best for them.[2] They are also extremists on the intensity scale, since they are interested enough in one party's victory to proselyte for it.

Not all would-be persuaders are voters; parties are obviously persuaders too. Those who are voters we call *agitators*, i.e., voters who use scarce resources to influence other voters. Having informed themselves well enough to be certain of their own decisions, agitators are practically immune to the persuasion of their opponents, since we assumed persuasion can be done only by providing information, not by changing tastes. Agitators are usually motivated by a desire to see the policies of a specific party enacted, or by gratitude to a party for having carried out some policy they favor. But whether their motive is simple repayment for a political favor, or the most idealistic altruism, they are willing to invest scarce resources—at least time, and perhaps more—in agitating.

II. TYPES OF VOTERS OTHER THAN AGITATORS

Some voters are well-informed enough to have made definite and certain voting decisions, but they are not interested in persuading others to agree with them. We call these voters *passives* if they have arrived at a party preference, and *neutrals* if they are indifferent among parties. Being certain, neither passives nor neutrals are open to influence. However their behavior on election day differs—passives vote, neutrals abstain.[3]

So far we have dealt only with voters who are certain about how

[1] It is true that in the real world, persuading others is often a means of confirming one's own insecurely held beliefs, but we ignore that possibility in our model.

[2] This does not mean that it is impossible for further information to change a persuader's mind. For an exact definition of *certain*, see Section II of this chapter.

[3] Throughout this chapter we assume that the cost of voting is zero. When it is not zero, some passives will also abstain. For a detailed discussion of how voting costs affect participation, see Chapter 14.

they want to vote. This does not mean that they know every fact relevant to their voting decision, nor that they are absolutely sure it is the best one they can make. It means they know enough to have reached a definite decision, and they regard as negligible the probability that any further information would cause them to change it. Hence they do not deliberately seek further information.[4]

Many citizens, however, are uncertain about how to vote. Either they have not made up their minds at all, or they have reached some decision but feel that further information might alter it. Here we can distinguish three categories: *baffleds* are those who have not made up their minds; *quasi-informed passives* are those who have reached tentative decisions favorable to some party; and *quasi-informed neutrals* are those who have reached the tentative conclusion that there is no significant difference between present parties or between this government and preceding ones. If these voters are still uncertain on election day, the quasi-informed passives vote, but the baffleds and quasi-informed neutrals abstain.

Finally, some rational men habitually vote for the same party in every election. In several preceding elections, they carefully informed themselves about all the competing parties, and all the issues of the moment; yet they always came to the same decision about how to vote. Therefore they have resolved to repeat this decision automatically without becoming well-informed, unless some catastrophe makes them realize it no longer expresses their best interests. Like all habits, this one saves resources, since it keeps voters from investing in information which would not alter their behavior. Thus it is a rational habit. Habitual voters are either *loyalists*, who always vote for the same party, or *apathetics*, who always abstain because they believe their party differentials are forever zero.

In summary, here are the types of voters who have decided to vote, listed in order of the confidence with which they hold their decisions: agitators, passives, loyalists, and quasi-informed passives. Here are those who have decided to abstain, ranked in the same way:

---

[4] There are two qualifications to this assertion: (1) men who are certain may accidentally encounter information which upsets their certainty even though the probability of their doing so is low, and (2) agitators may seek more information for use in persuading others rather than for making their own voting decisions.

neutrals, apathetics, quasi-informed neutrals, and baffleds. Only five of the eight types are normally open to persuasion. In order of their susceptibility, they are baffleds, quasi-informed neutrals, quasi-informed passives, apathetics, and loyalists.

III. THE ROLE OF THRESHOLDS

In Chapter 3, we introduced the notion of political thresholds, a concept which has considerable bearing on the nature of persuasion. For example, a loyalist may know that conditions today differ somewhat from those extant when he chose a party to vote for habitually, but unless conditions are remarkably different, he will not reëxamine this habit. The change must be large enough to cross some *perception threshold* before he is moved to reconsider his behavior pattern. Another example is a baffled who has information leading to a preference for one party, but is so unsure that this information is complete that he discounts it to below his *action threshold*. Of if a passive discovers that his party differential has become very large, he may start trying to persuade others to vote as he does. Thus he crosses his *agitation threshold*, and becomes an agitator instead of a passive.

These thresholds are crucial to the process of influencing voters. If an agitator wants to know just how much information to give a baffled (or a group of baffleds) so as to get his vote but not waste resources overconvincing him, the agitator must know where the baffled's action threshold is, and how close he is to it. Similarly, a party seeking to convert passives into agitators needs to know how much policy-alteration pay-off is required to push the passives across their agitation thresholds. Thus the judgments of agitators, parties, and other persuaders about how many resources they should invest in persuasion depend upon their estimations of how close key blocs of voters are to various thresholds.

It is also a threshold that keeps baffleds from wavering back and forth between parties with every additional bit of information they get. Under conditions of perfect certainty, the slightest iota of difference between parties would be enough to determine a man's vote. But in the real world, and in the world of our uncertainty model, he knows that minute differences he sees are likely to be either illusory or counterbalanced by others he does not see. Therefore he will wait for a significant degree of difference between parties before relinquishing his neutrality.

IV. THE NATURE AND FORMS OF LEADERSHIP IN THE MODEL

Wherever men can be influenced, other men appear whose specialty is influencing them; so it is in our model. Uncertainty renders many voters willing to heed leaders who seem to know the way toward those social goals the voters hold. Thus they follow the leaders' counsel about which government policies to approve of and which to oppose. Subtler forms of leadership insinuate themselves into the reporting of news, the setting of political fashions, and the shaping of cultural images of good and evil.

We assumed in Chapter 3 that voters' tastes in government were fixed, because they were simply rational deductions from the voters' views of the good society. However, in an uncertain world, roads leading toward the good society are hard to distinguish from those leading away from it. Thus, even though voters have fixed goals, their views on how to approach those goals are malleable and can be altered by persuasion. Consequently, leadership can be exercised on most policy questions, because nearly all policies are means to broader social goals rather than ends in themselves.

Leadership we define as the ability to influence voters to adopt certain views as expressing their own will. Leaders are men with influence over voters—usually not full control of their votes, but at least some impact on their views about the best policies for parties to espouse. Leadership in this sense can exist only under conditions of uncertainty, because whenever men know the repercussions of every conceivable act, they need no advice to discover what is best for them. True, even under certainty men need leaders to decide what to do in the absence of universal consensus, and to coördinate the division of labor. But this is different from deciding what *should* be done, i.e., what policies are most beneficial to the individual voters.

Why do leaders lead? In our model, all leaders are motivated by the desire to improve their own positions in society. By thus attributing all human action to selfishness, we are not limiting it to the narrow sense of that word. We also include a broad sense which may call for great self-sacrifice. Nevertheless, most leaders will be at least partially motivated by the possibility of acquiring some direct benefit for themselves—economic, political, or social.

There are three types of leaders in our model: political parties, interest groups, and favor-buyers.[5] *Political parties* are followers as well as leaders, for they mold their policies to suit voters so as to gain as many votes as possible. Having done this, they attempt to lead all voters to believe these policies are best for them. *Interest groups* are leaders who try to get government to adopt some particular policy beneficial to themselves by claiming to represent voters. They seek to implant their own views in voters' minds so that they do represent voters; then the government may be impressed enough to aid them. *Favor-buyers* are men who wish a party to act in some way which benefits them, and will in return influence voters to support that party. Favor-buyers claim to represent no one except themselves; they are merely engaged in trading their influence over voters for specific acts they want done. Their influence often consists of money they can devote to campaigns on behalf of the party they are dealing with. Any one leader may practice all three kinds of leadership simultaneously, but we will keep them separate for analytical purposes.

V. THE FUNCTIONING OF INTERMEDIARIES

A. GOVERNMENT'S NEED FOR REPRESENTATIVES

Uncertainty is so basic to human life that it influences the structure of almost every social institution. The government in a democracy is no exception to this rule. To cope with uncertainty, it is

---

[5] Though all leaders are really individual men, we here speak of groups as leaders because the men in each group try to persuade nonmembers to act in ways favorable to the group as a whole.

forced to employ intermediaries between itself and its constituents.

These intermediaries have two functions, both derived from the relationship between government acts and individual utility functions described in Chapter 4. As we saw there, government plans its acts by looking at individual utility functions and discovering what voters want. For this purpose it needs representatives *of* the people who can simplify the otherwise impossible task of exploring every individual's utility function. Also, individuals decide how to vote by comparing the acts of government and the proposals of opposition parties. Therefore government sends its own representatives *to* the people to convince them that its acts are worthy of their approval. Other parties, of course, employ representatives to convince the people that the incumbents should be replaced.

Uncertainty thus helps convert democracy into representative government. Another powerful force which has the same effect is the division of labor. To be efficient, a nation must develop specialists in discovering, transmitting, and analyzing popular opinion, just as it develops specialists in everything else. These specialists are the representatives. Their existence makes it rational for the government to be influenced by a small proportion of its citizenry rather than to act on behalf of all citizens seen in the abstract.

The government in our model world wants to enact policies which fit the desires of its constituents, but it does not know what these desires are. Therefore it employs, as a part of its own institutional structure, a group of men whose function is to scatter into the corners of the nation and discover the will of the people. They keep the government's central planning agency informed about what people want so that it can make decisions that will maximize the government's chance for reëlection.

Since the information and opinions these liaison agents supply have a strong influence upon government decisions, in effect some of the power of the central planning agency is shifted onto the agents. Government's power therefore becomes spread out among many representatives instead of being concentrated entirely in one agency. Theoretically, the government will continue to decentralize its power until the marginal gain in votes from greater conformity to popular desires is outweighed by the marginal cost in votes of lesser ability to coördinate its actions.

The qualitative nature of this power decentralization depends upon the way in which the citizenry is divided into heterogeneous groups. If the major variations are geographical, then the government will become spatially decentralized; i.e., representatives from each relatively homogeneous area will hold power, even though they may ostensibly live and act in some central location. If society's main divisions are along social, racial, or economic lines, then power will filter out to representatives of groups rather than areas. The quantity of decentralization depends upon the technical development of communications. As communication facilities improve, less decentralization is necessary to keep in contact with the popular will.

This kind of government decentralization is necessary regardless of whether the formal structure of the government calls for decentralized elections. The government must have agents "taking the pulse of the people" in each area (or group) even if all votes are pooled nationally and no local (or group) representatives are elected. Where citizens do elect nonnational representatives, decentralization has a constitutional as well as a functional basis. Consequently it is likely to be less flexible than in purely national systems like our model.

B. NONGOVERNMENT INTERMEDIARIES

In representing the people to the government, official agents of both the people and the government must be as accurate as possible. Their job is to tell the government what people actually want it to do. But in many cases, most citizens do not know what they want government to do. As we shall see later, they do not keep themselves informed about most of the problems government faces; so they have no opinions about how it should solve these problems. As a result, there is nothing for representatives to represent on many issues, in so far as most of their constituents are concerned.[6]

[6] If government knew the exact shape of everyone's utility function, it could discover what was best for each person even if the person himself did not know

However, every government decision concerns a few men directly and immediately. These men are often well-informed about it and have definite ideas about what government should do. In order to get the government to adopt their views, they claim that these views represent what the people want. Furthermore, their claims are not limited by any need for accuracy; in fact, they have every reason to exaggerate (though our assumption of no false information prevents outright lying). Thus they masquerade as representatives of a majority of citizens, even though they are actually lobbyists for some particular group or organization.

Since most people do not express any views directly to the government, it must listen to the lobbyists and try to guess just how representative their proposals really are. The government in our model does not care whether these proposals are good for its citizens. All it wants to know is whether a majority of voters already approve of them or would do so if informed about them. For this reason, self-styled representatives try to persuade the government not only that their proposals are beneficial to the electorate—in which case the electorate will appreciate them *post facto*—but also that the electorate already desires them.

But since everyone can make such a claim, the government will not be impressed unless some proof is adduced to support it. Therefore these representatives try to create a following which in fact does desire their proposals. By moulding public opinion in their favor, they hope to force the government to support their views, since government adapts itself to public opinion whenever it discovers consensus therein.

In guessing how representative lobbyists really are, each political party usually discounts their claims of support. Congressional hearings are replete with individuals who claim to speak for thousands of citizens, but who admit under cross-examination that their organizations have a dozen or so members and no further influence. It is not even clear that a *bona fides* association like the United

_____

this because he lacked information possessed by the government. In this sense, perfect representation could operate even when voters had no opinions. But government is motivated by voters' opinions, not their welfare, since their opinions about welfare are what influence voting.

Auto Workers always represents all its members. On any particular issue, large groups of members may disagree with the official position of the organization.

But even though the government discounts the claims made by private intermediaries, it cannot avoid being influenced by them. The government must try to discover what people want. Unless it can ask them directly by means of polls—which are expensive and difficult to interpret—it must rely either on guesses or on those representatives who come forth and state their views. Furthermore, the government is interested in the intensity with which each voter holds his opinions, since it must weigh the net effect of a great many actions upon him. It will therefore risk imparting a slight injury to one voter if, by doing so, it gives a great boon to another one. With some exceptions, those who come forth to press their views upon government are likely to be more intensely interested than those who keep silent. A rational government cannot ignore this fact in its policy-making.

In addition, the government needs resources to convince people that its policies are good ones. It also has to defend itself from the attacks of opposition parties and of interest groups who disagree with its decisions. To acquire the money for these tasks, it can sell favors to men who need government action and are willing to pay for it. Opposition parties do the same thing, but they are limited to sales with promises of delivery when elected.

Favor-buying is usually nothing so crude as bribery; it is the subtler device of making campaign contributions in return for a favorable disposition of attitudes by a party: pro-free-enterprise, pro-labor, anti-free-trade, etc. The payments received by the party may not even be in money. Instead they may be editorial policies, weight thrown in a crucial electoral district, or willingness to refrain from opposing certain policies.

Thus political favors are often paid for by some form of agitation; in fact, most agitators are recruited from the ranks of favor-buyers. Naturally, the man with the greatest potential influence as an agitator gets the most favors in return for his services. Therefore, in deciding just how much it will set policy to suit various favor-seekers, political parties must estimate their *influence coefficients*, i.e., the numbers by which the favor-seekers' own votes must be multiplied in calculating their political weight.

C. THE NET POLITICAL EFFECTS OF UNCERTAINTY

Since both buyers and sellers in favor-buying transactions stand to gain, we must admit that their actions are rational. Conversely, pursuit of rationality will lead them to take such actions. Hence rationality under conditions of uncertainty leads government to construct policies often aimed more at the good of a few voters than at the good of all, or even of a majority.[7] To act otherwise would be irrational.

As a result, voters in a democracy do not have equal influence on policy formation even though each has only one vote. Possession of resources other than a ballot definitely increases a citizen's potential influence upon government policy. Active membership in an organization claiming to represent many voters may even further augment this influence. These are not new conclusions; the only novelty is that we have shown them to be the necessary outcome of rational action on the part of the government and its citizens. In spite of the universal, equal franchise, government cannot rationally regard every voter as being of the same importance as every other. Because some citizens have influence coefficients much higher than unity, a rational government must give them more weight in forming policy than it gives most of their fellow citizens.

Even in the world of perfect certainty, voters have different degrees of influence over each particular government decision. The division of labor and the diversity of tastes create countless relatively homogeneous groups of voters, each with interests different from the others. Because any specific government decision is of different significance to each group, the groups are not equally desirous of influencing the decision. Therefore a rational government

[7] This conclusion presupposes that only a few voters attempt to influence any specific government policy directly even when many or all are affected by it. In Chapter 13, we prove that this presupposition is valid in our model.

is swayed more by some voters at one time and others at another time, and disparity of influence marks any particular decision. But there is no inequality of total importance among voters. The government is never willing to incur the loss of A's vote to gain the favor of B, *ceteris paribus*, because it has no reason to regard B as more important than A.

Uncertainty destroys this net equality of influence. The government may know that it will lose A's vote if it favors B, but perhaps it also knows that B's aid will maximize its chance of persuading baffleds C and D to support it. Consequently, it is willing to cast A overboard in order to get B to help it. Uncertainty allows the unequal distributions of income, position, and influence—all of which are inevitable in any economy marked by an extensive division of labor—to share sovereignty in a realm where only the equal distribution of votes is supposed to reign.[8]

VI. SUMMARY

Uncertainty divides voters into groups with varying degrees of confidence in their voting decisions. Since those who are least sure can be influenced by further information, uncertainty leads to attempts at persuasion by men who provide correct but biased information.

The possibility of persuasion gives rise to competition for leadership among political parties, interest groups, and favor-buyers. In forming policy, parties try to follow the wishes of voters, but once their policy is formed, they endeavor to lead all voters to accept it as desirable. Interest groups want government to adopt policies favorable to them, so they pose as representatives of popular will. They try simultaneously to create real public opinion supporting their views and to convince government that such public opinion exists. Favor-buyers represent only themselves, but are willing to support political parties in return for specific favors.

Because the government's central planning agency is uncertain

[8] It is conceivable that the distribution of income in such a society could be equalized, though the distributions of position and influence could not. However, no large, complex economy has ever embodied equal income distribution, so we may regard achieving it as a practical impossibility.

about what people want, it must rely on intermediaries between it and the citizenry to find out. The interest groups described above are one type of intermediary; government's own decentralized agents are another. Favor-buyers function as intermediaries in an opposite fashion by helping government create opinion sympathetic to policies it has already decided upon. But all these intermediaries exact a price—they get an influence over policy formation greater than their numerical proportion in the population.

Thus uncertainty forces rational governments to regard some voters as more important than others. By doing so it modifies the equality of influence which universal suffrage was designed to insure.

7

The Development of
Political Ideologies as
Means of Getting Votes

Introduction

OUR basic hypothesis states that political parties are interested in gaining office *per se*, not in promoting a better or an ideal society. But if this is true, how can we explain the appearance of political ideologies? Why does nearly every democratic party ostensibly derive its policies from some specific philosophy of governing?

Our answer is that uncertainty allows parties to develop ideologies as weapons in the struggle for office. In this role, ideologies are assigned specific functions that shape their nature and development.

We define an *ideology* as a verbal image of the good society and of the chief means of constructing such a society. In modern political science, ideologies are nearly always viewed partly as means to political power employed by social classes or other groups, rather than as mere representations of actual goals. No *Weltanschauung* is accepted at face value, because it is seen as tainted with its es-pousers' desire to gain power.[1]

In keeping with this view, we also treat ideologies as means to power. However, in our model, political parties are not agents of specific social groups or classes; rather, they are autonomous teams seeking office *per se* and using group support to attain that end.

Objectives

In this chapter we attempt to prove the following propositions:

1. Because of uncertainty, widely varying ideologies may be em-ployed by political parties even if all are motivated solely by the desire to maximize votes.
2. Some rational voters decide how to vote ideologically instead of by comparing policies.
3. The competitive struggle for office compels parties in our model to be both honest and consistent in formulating policies and ideologies and developing them over time.
4. Rational and institutional immobilities sometimes cause ideolo-gies and policies to lag behind the real conditions relevant to party behavior.

I. THE ROLE OF UNCERTAINTY

A. IDEOLOGIES IN A CERTAIN WORLD

Even in a certain world, political parties are caught in the classic dilemma of all competitive advertisers. Each must differentiate its product from all near substitutes, yet it must also prove this product has every virtue that any of the substitutes possesses. Since no party can gain by opposing a passionate majority, all parties espouse whatever policies an overwhelming portion of the electorate agree

[1] For a brilliant exposition of this view, see Karl Mannheim, *Ideology and Utopia*, Harvest Book Series (New York: Harcourt, Brace and Company, 1955), pp. 96–97.

upon and strongly desire. But citizens will see little point in voting if all choices are identical, so differences between platforms must be created to entice voters to the polls.[2]

But in a certain world, these differences are strictly on the policy level, because party platforms contain no ideological elements whatever. When voters can expertly judge every detail of every stand taken and relate it directly to their own views of the good society, they are interested only in issues, not in philosophies. Hence parties never need to form *Weltanschauungen* at all, but can merely take *ad hoc* stands on practical problems as they arise.

B. HOW UNCERTAINTY MAKES IDEOLOGIES USEFUL TO VOTERS

Uncertainty alters this whole situation by removing the voters' perfect competence at relating every party decision to their own ideologies. Voters do not know in great detail what the decisions of the government are, and they cannot find out except at a significant cost. Even if they did know, they could not always predict where a given decision would lead. Therefore, they would be unable to trace the consequences of each decision accurately and relate them to their own ideologies. Nor do they know in advance what problems the government is likely to face in the coming election period.

Under these conditions, many a voter finds party ideologies useful because they remove the necessity of his relating every issue to his own philosophy. Ideologies help him focus attention on the differences between parties; therefore they can be used as samples of all the differentiating stands. With this short cut a voter can save himself the cost of being informed upon a wider range of issues.

Furthermore, a citizen may decide for whom to vote by means of

---

[2] This statement may seem inconsistent with our argument in Chapter 3 that it always makes a difference which party is elected, even when all have identical platforms. Nevertheless, such identity reduces the incentive to vote because it makes the party differential smaller than it would be if parties had different platforms. As a result, the probability that the party differential will be outweighed by the cost of voting is increased, thus raising the likelihood of abstention. For a more detailed discussion of participation in democratic elections, see Chapter 14.

ideologies rather than past records. Instead of comparing government behavior with opposition proposals, he compares party ideologies and supports the one most like his own. Thus he votes on ideological competency, not on specific issues. Such behavior is rational in two situations (1) having informed himself reasonably well, the voter cannot distinguish between parties on an issue basis, but can on an ideology basis; or (2) he votes by means of ideologies in order to save himself the cost of becoming informed about specific issues. In both cases, his behavior differs from that described in Chapter 3 because he uses an *ideology differential* to make his decision, since he is without sufficient data to formulate a nonzero party differential.

Use of the ideology differential is rational only in the short run. All rational voters cast ballots in order to influence the actions of political parties, not their statements. But ideologies *per se* are only statements. Therefore if a voter can distinguish between parties only by their ideologies, the parties are in fact identical in so far as the voter's welfare is concerned. They behave the same way, even though they talk differently; so it matters not which he supports.

Thus well-informed voters who use ideologies as a last resort in decision-making will quit voting, no matter what their ideology differentials are, if their party differentials remain zero in election after election. Ideological differences between parties will have ceased to be meaningful in their eyes.

But a citizen who regards ideologies as cost-saving devices is not employing them as a last resort. They are to him a first resort, used to save the cost of calculating his party differential. This procedure is rational as long as there is an actual behavioral difference between parties which has a known correlation with their ideologies. For example, assume a citizen paid the cost of informing himself about the issues and discovered that party A's policies were much more beneficial to him than those of parties B and C. However, he had already guessed this because party A's ideology appealed to him more than any other. Therefore, since it is much cheaper to keep informed about ideologies than about issues, from then on he does the former as a rational short cut to the latter.

This behavior is a compromise between being a loyalist and being fully informed about politics. Unlike the loyalist, the man who uses his ideology differential as a cost-saver knows something about current affairs. But he does not know as much as a citizen using issues to make his decisions, because there are many more issues than philosophic axioms in politics. We call such compromisers *dogmatists* because they look at doctrines rather than behavior when choosing a party to support.

C. HOW UNCERTAINTY MAKES IDEOLOGIES USEFUL TO POLITICAL PARTIES

In a world beclouded by uncertainty, ideologies are useful to parties as well as to voters. Each party realizes that some citizens vote by means of ideologies rather than policies; hence it fashions an ideology which it believes will attract the greatest number of votes. For reasons we discuss later, this ideology must be both internally consistent and consistent with the party's concrete policies. But these provisos still leave a wide range of possible ideologies open to each party.

Even so, it might at first seem that all the parties in our model will have very similar ideologies. True, they wish to differentiate their products slightly so as to claim uniqueness. But since each party seeks to appeal to as many citizens as possible, and since all parties are faced by the same citizenry, why would they espouse strikingly different ideologies, as do parties in the real world?

Three factors in our model explain how wide ideological variance can develop out of our vote-maximizing hypothesis. They are the heterogeneity of society, the inevitability of social conflict, and uncertainty. The fact that the world's resources are limited creates in every society an inherent tension among social groups. When these groups are well-defined, this tension prevents any one political ideology from strongly appealing to all groups simultaneously as long as voters are rational. For example, an ideology which specifically plays up to managers of industry will always be less than optimum for workers in industry, even if the industry is state owned.

Thus each party can ideologically woo only a limited number of social groups, since its appeal to one implicitly antagonizes others. But because of uncertainty, it is not obvious which combination of groups yields the largest number of votes. Furthermore, society is dynamic; hence the right combination in one election may turn out to be the wrong one in the next. Therefore it is quite possible for parties to disagree about what social groups to appeal to. This fact, combined with their inherent desire to differentiate their products, means that parties in our model may design widely varying ideologies in spite of their identical objectives.

Party ideologies can remain different only in so far as none is demonstrably more effective than the rest. For example, let us assume that three parties form and appeal to three different social groups, and one of these parties consistently wins by overwhelming votes. In order to "get back in the swim," the other two parties must revise their ideologies to attract votes from the same group as the perennial winner. Then each party will be trying to combine a specific segment of the predominant group with parts of minority groups for electoral victory. As a result, their ideologies will resemble each other much more closely than before.

Democrat / Clinton

Uncertainty about effectiveness is thus necessary if ideological diversity is to persist. Clearly, if everyone knew which type of ideology would win, all parties would adopt it. Differentiation would then be made on a more subtle level. Here again we encounter the passionate majority. Where it exists, party platforms can diverge only if parties are uncertain about just what the majority is for, or on levels of subtlety beyond that of passionate consensus.

Another way ideologies help parties cope with uncertainty is by short cutting the process of calculating what policies will gain the most votes. In our model, each party designs its ideology to appeal to that combination of social groups which it feels will produce the most support. If its design is accurate, policies chosen for their consistency with the ideology will automatically please the citizens being courted by the party.

This short cut removes the necessity of relating each policy decision directly to voter reaction; therefore it reduces the cost of decision-making. However, its application is limited in two ways. First, the ideology may not be specific enough to lead unambiguously to action—more than one alternative may be ideologically acceptable. Second, voters are ultimately interested in actions, not ideologies, so each party must frequently check its actions directly against the voters' preferences. It cannot always rely on being ideologically correct any more than a rational voter can always rely solely on his ideology differential in deciding for whom to vote.

D. HOW COMPETITION AMONG PARTIES AFFECTS IDEOLOGIES

Though uncertainty brings ideologies to life in our model, another factor determines what happens to them after they are born. This dual causality results from their use by voters as short cuts to the consideration of policies. Because uncertainty exists, voters need such short cuts; so parties create them. But their subsequent development depends upon their relation to the policies they stand for, not upon uncertainty.

In order to be rational short cuts, ideologies must be integrated with policies closely enough to form accurate indicators of what each party is likely to do in the future. When policies change significantly, ideologies must also change; otherwise they are not effective signals and the citizens in our model will not use them. Thus whatever factors influence the development of policies also influence the development of ideologies.

The major force shaping a party's policies is competition with other parties for votes. Not only does competition determine the content of party policies, as we saw in Chapter 4, but also it controls (1) their stability and (2) their relation to the party's public statements. Thus competition determines whether parties will be responsible and honest.

An ideology is a public statement about party policy, since it either contains or implies specific proposals for action. Therefore by analyzing the general relation between a party's actual policies and its policy statements, we can discover some of the qualities its ideology will exhibit. This relation is relatively independent of uncertainty, though it does presuppose voters possess less than perfect knowledge of the future.

In the next section of this chapter, we shift our focus from ideologies in particular to the broader concepts of reliability, integrity, and responsibility as applied to political parties. Though we believe our examination of these concepts is interesting *per se*, its main purpose is to establish certain traits of party behavior relevant to our later analysis of ideologies.

II. RELIABILITY, INTEGRITY, AND RESPONSIBILITY

So far we have shown that parties may develop ideologies because they are useful to themselves and to voters, and that ideological diversity may persist through time. Now we try to prove that a party's ideology must be consistent with either (1) its actions in prior election periods, or (2) its statements in the preceding campaign (including its ideology), or (3) both.

A. THE ROLE OF RELIABILITY AND RESPONSIBILITY IN THE MODEL

In order to analyze the concepts of reliability, integrity, and responsibility it is necessary to label the time periods, party actions, and party statements relevant to the next election. Let us assume there are two parties, X and Y, and that subscripts denote time periods. Let X_1 stand for the *statements* of party X during period T_1, and let (X_1) denote its *actions* during that period. Finally, let the time periods be as follows:

T_1 The campaign prior to the present election period (in which statements about the present period were made).

T_2 The present election period, except the campaign at its end.

T_3 The campaign at the end of the present election period (in which statements about the next election period are made).

T_e Election day, the day separating T_3 and T_4.

T_4 The next election period.

Thus Y_3 denotes the statements made by party Y while campaigning for the right to hold office during T_4. We assume also that X was in power during T_2 and (X_2) represents its actions as the government. These are to be compared with Y_2, since an opposition party can make statements but cannot take action.[3]

What voters must make judgments about in the election are (X_4) and (Y_4), but these potential future actions can be predicted only through knowledge of events in periods T_1, T_2, and T_3.[4] One method is to compare X_3 and Y_3; this would be rational because these statements are about the same situation, i.e., T_4. However, this procedure ignores the record of the incumbent party which in our model is the outstanding item in voters' thinking.

Therefore, in our previous analysis of how rational citizens vote, we stated that they compare (X_2) and Y_2, even though they are selecting a government to govern in T_4. True, they would rather compare the record of the incumbent party with the promises of the opposition, i.e., (X_2) and Y_3. But these are not logically comparable, because they refer to different situations $(T_2$ and $T_4)$. Since actions already taken are better evidence than those merely promised, we shifted each voter's comparison to (X_2) and Y_2, also allowing him to employ a trend factor if he desired.

If voters follow this course, there must be some relation between the behavior—real or hypothetical—of each party in T_2 and the behavior it will produce in T_4 if elected on T_e. This relation is compounded of reliability and responsibility.

A party is *reliable* if its policy statements at the beginning of an

---

[3] This limitation on opposition parties results from the peculiarities of our model, which has no legislature. However, we can easily revise our axioms to include a "showcase" legislature in which the leaders of opposition parties can express their opinions, debate with the incumbents, make investigations, and even take votes. As long as none of its activities has any coercive power over the governing party, such a legislature is perfectly consistent with the rest of our model. But the very impotence of these activities leads us to consider them as statements rather than actions.

[4] Period T_1 can here be construed as including some statements and actions which preceded the campaign just before period T_2. Even in our model, voters consider events from many previous election periods in judging the integrity and responsibility of each party. But because conditions change, parties change their policies, and rational citizens realize that not all such changes are irresponsible. Therefore citizens take account of some but not all past actions and weight them differently. To avoid a lengthy formalization of this process, we have arbitrarily cut off the past at the campaign preceding T_2 in our formal analysis. However, it should be remembered that this truncation is only for the sake of simplicity.

election period—including those in its preëlection campaign—can be used to make accurate predictions of its behavior (or its statements if it is not elected) during the period. Thus a party which always does the exact opposite of what it says it will do is reliable even though it is not honest.

A party is *responsible* if its policies in one period are consistent with its actions (or statements) in the preceding period, i.e., if it does not repudiate its former views in formulating its new program. Therefore, if a party has both responsibility and reliability, its actions in T_2 are linked with its probable behavior in T_4. Responsibility implies that the platform statements in T_3 are related to and develop from its actions (or statements) in T_2. Reliability implies that its behavior during T_4 can be predicted from its platform statements at T_3. This linkage makes it rational for voters to choose a party to govern them during T_4 by comparing (X_2) and Y_2.

B. THE NECESSITY FOR RELIABILITY AND RESPONSIBILITY IN POLITICS

Though reliability and responsibility are useful in our model, perhaps either or both can be eliminated without destroying political rationality. To examine this possibility, let us briefly consider how democracy would work if parties exhibited (1) neither reliability nor responsibility, (2) responsibility without reliability, and (3) reliability without responsibility.

The absence of reliability means that voters cannot predict the behavior of parties from what the parties say they will do. The absence of responsibility means party behavior cannot be predicted by consistently projecting what parties have done previously. When both are absent, the only possible basis for prediction is an inconsistent relation between the past and future actions of each party. But unless circumstances are changing with extreme rapidity, almost every feasible relation between a party's past and future actions exhibits consistency. If each party caters to a particular social group, its future services to the group will not conflict with its past ones as long as the group's interests are stable. Similarly, parties pursuing purely ideological goals act consistently over time. In short, it is irrational for an unreliable party to adopt behavior which is systematically inconsistent.

Therefore when neither reliability nor responsibility exists, no political predictions can be made. But rational behavior is impossible without at least some way of forecasting future events. *Ipso facto*, a democracy in which parties lack both reliability and responsibility cannot be rational. But does this mean both must be present?

Where parties are responsible but lack reliability, voters looking at past party records in order to deduce what the parties will do in the future ignore all party statements. However, the only recent record of action is that of the incumbents. During the current election period, the opposition has done nothing but make statements, and because it lacks reliability, these statements are meaningless as guides to its future behavior. But if the opposition has been out of office long, conditions may have changed so much that its actions when last in office are useless as a guide to what it would do if elected now. Hence some systematic relationship between a party's statements and its subsequent actions is necessary for rational voting.

The converse case occurs when parties are reliable but not responsible. Then voters depend solely on what parties say they are going to do, not on what they have done, to predict what they will do. Nevertheless, the past record of each party is necessary for judging just how reliable it is, since its record must be compared with its preceding promises. However, a persistent relation need exist only between promises and behavior, not between the actions of one period and those of the next. This kind of election system is both rational and feasible; in it voters compare X_3 and Y_3 instead of (X_2) and Y_2. However, as we pointed out before, they are ignoring the record of the incumbent party, which we believe to be a central item in any rational consideration of how to vote.

We conclude that reliability is a logical necessity in any rational election system, and that responsibility—though not logically necessary—is strongly implied by rationality as we define it. Of course, this conclusion does not prove that reliability and responsibility actually exist in our model. We can demonstrate that they do—and therefore that our model is rational—only by showing that political parties are inexorably driven by their own motives to be both reliable and responsible.

C. HOW EACH PARTY'S MOTIVES CAUSE IT TO BE HONEST AND RESPONSIBLE

Citizens in our model cast their ballots only to influence government policies. They are interested in each party's statements only insofar as those statements serve as guides to the policies the party will carry out when in office. When the party is already in office, its current actions provide a better guide to what it will do than do its current statements. Therefore the incumbent party need not be reliable as long as it is responsible.

But opposition parties cannot be judged by their current actions in office because there are none. Their last governing acts occurred at least a full election period before the one for which they are now being considered for office. Since conditions change over time, these acts are not very useful as sole indicators of what the party is going to do in the future, especially if election periods are long. Therefore opposition parties must be reliable; i.e., voters must be able to predict their actions reasonably well from what they say.

If an opposition party is not reliable, it will be unable to gain the confidence—and hence the votes—of rational citizens. They would rather vote for a party that can be relied upon to carry out its imperfect proposals than one whose behavior cannot be predicted at all. In fact, rational men will vote for an unreliable opposition party only if the incumbents and all reliable parties have such abysmal proposals that random policy selection is preferable to them. And if many men feel this way, they will probably found a new party rather than vote for one whose future actions are unpredictable. Thus, because voters regard reliability as an asset for any party out of office, all opposition parties are driven by competition to acquire it.

In addition, the incumbent party is never certain that it will be reëlected; hence it must be prepared to become an opposition party if necessary. But if it is unreliable when in office, rational citizens will regard it as equally unreliable when it is in opposition. Parties are thus forced to be reliable when in office so as to avoid creating reputations that will keep them out of office for a long time once they are defeated. In short, the struggle for votes compels all parties to be reliable.

Furthermore, the form their reliability takes is quite likely to be integrity. A party has *integrity* if its policy statements at the beginning of an election period are reasonably borne out by its actions during the period (or by its statements if it is not elected). We must use the qualifying adverb *reasonably* because no party fully controls all the factors relevant to the carying out of its policies. As a result, every party runs into more or less severe obstacles; so whether it in fact has integrity must be decided subjectively by the voters themselves.

In politics, as in all human activity, integrity is by far the most efficient form of reliability. If A can always be sure that B will try to do whatever B says he is going to do, A can pass judgment on B's future action much more easily than if B always does the opposite of what he says he will, or tries to do only half of it, or never tries to do any of it. In other words, integrity is the simplest relation between statements and true intentions. Hence when it exists, fewer resources are required to predict an agent's future behavior than are required by any other form of reliability. Where analysis is complex and costly anyway, as it is in politics, this saving can be crucial.

Because integrity is thus essential to efficient interpersonal relations, rational men come to value it *per se*. A perfect liar and a perfectly honest man are equally reliable, but almost all ethical systems honor the latter and chastise the former. This valuation occurs in part because communication in a society of honest men is cheaper than in a society of liars. Similarly, in politics men rationally prefer parties which are honest to those which are not, *ceteris paribus*. As a result, competition tends to force all the parties in our model to be relatively honest.[5]

The same force also causes parties to exhibit responsibility. Once a party is elected, it must decide what policies to enact. Even if it is not honest, it will probably try to carry out the promises it made in

[5] This conclusion is somewhat modified later in Chapters 8 and 9.

its campaign. Its objective is to maximize votes, and these promises were effective in doing just that. Therefore the party is likely to embody them in its next campaign platform too, making adjustments to fit any changed circumstances. Its desire to hang onto a good thing causes it to be responsible.

Conversely, desire to get rid of a loser puts opposition parties under pressure to alter their promises. If they lost by an overwhelming vote, this pressure may cause drastic irresponsibility. But if the vote was close, the pressure to hold their previous supporters by maintaining most of their platform may prevail. Eventually the first pressure will move them into an equilibrium in which the second pressure is dominant; i.e., each election will be so close that the losers will refrain from seriously revising their policies.

At this point, opposition parties will be kept responsible by the penalties of irresponsibility. If a party frequently adopts new policies inconsistent with its old ones, voters will suspect that it cannot be trusted to carry out any long-range policies at all. Like integrity, responsibility is a trait which makes rational planning easier; hence men value it and honor its possessors. To take advantage of this fact, every part will be as responsible as changing circumstances permit, unless its policies are forcefully rejected by nearly all voters.

III. IDEOLOGICAL COHERENCE AND STABILITY

Any party which is both responsible and reliable will probably have an ideology which is relatively coherent and immobile. In other words, its ideology will not be internally contradictory but will be at least loosely integrated around some social *Weltanschauung*. And the party will not radically shift its policies and doctrines overnight, but will only slowly change their nature.

We have already seen how uncertainty leads parties to form ideologies. Simple logic dictates that these ideologies exhibit at least some *coherence* because no party can rationally espouse a policy set containing mutually exclusive proposals (unless no one can predict they are mutually exclusive before they are carried out). Furthermore, if a party uses its ideology to attract the support of specific social groups, it will attempt to organize its policies in some relation to the ideology. Since the ideology itself consists partly of action proposals, this organization will effect an integration of theory and policy.

The more closely these two facets are molded into a single *Weltanschauung*, the more attractive the party becomes to those voters whose views closely approximate this *Weltanschauung*—and the less attractive it becomes to all other voters. Each party wants to appeal to as many voters as possible, or at least as many as possible within some range of the social spectrum. Hence no party makes its ideology adhere too rigidly to any one philosophic outlook. On the other hand, it does not merely put forth an unorganized jumble of policies, since it wishes to appear ideologically competent so as to attract dogmatic voters.

We can therefore expect ideologies to be coherent but not integrated; e.g., a party may be basically pro-A in outlook, but with something for B, C, and D added in the quasi-coördinated fashion. Exactly how well integrated ideologies are depends upon the number of major parties competing for office, as we shall see in the next two chapters.

Ideological *immobility* is characteristic of every responsible party, because it cannot repudiate its past actions unless some radical change in conditions justifies this. Therefore its doctrinaire policies alter slowly to meet the needs of the moment. Once more uncertainty is the decisive factor, because it may prevent the party from knowing what policies are actually most appropriate. In the absence of this knowledge, responsibility makes it ideologically immobile, i.e., tends to encourage slow rather than rapid changes in doctrine. Such immobility often causes party behavior to lag behind what it would be if the party were perfectly informed. Yet this is a rational lag, because it is rational for a party to be responsible in the absence of information to the contrary.

Rational immobility is strongly reinforced by the institutional immobilities associated with every social organization. Because individual men become identified with certain policies, it is often necessary for a party to shift its leadership before it can shift its platform. This means that intraparty power conflicts influence just how rapidly its policies change. Different groups within the party use varying shades of the dominant party ideology as weapons against each other. In their struggle for power, each tries to convince influential party members that it is the bearer of the ideas most likely to win votes in the general elections.

This struggle for power within each party is somewhat similar to the conflict between parties. Uncertainty about what ideas are most efficacious as vote-getters permits a diversity of views to exist within a party, just as it permits different party ideologies to exist in society. However, party members select an ideology to represent the party on a basis different from that with which voters select an ideology. Party members choose an ideology which will win votes, not one they believe in, since their objective is the acquisition of office, not the creation of a better society.

Such continual readjustment of ideologies within each party means that no party can be perfectly responsible because its institutional structure is too dynamic. Its leadership alters; consequently its policy emphasis may shift from one election period to the next. Even on a purely rational basis, changing conditions would call for an abrogation of perfect responsibility. It is irrational to hold rigidly to the same policies when new situations arise. Nevertheless, parties are rarely able to adjust their ideologies at exactly the speed which conditions warrant. Thus rational responsibility and institutional immobility give rise to lags and discontinuities.

IV. CONFLICTS BETWEEN IDEOLOGIES AND VOTE-GETTING

According to our basic hypothesis, parties seek as their final ends the power, income, and prestige that go with office. Ideologies develop out of this desire as means to gaining office. But the maintenance of ideologies may become a subsidiary end with direct rewards in terms of prestige, especially if a change in ideology is regarded by the public as loss of integrity or responsibility. Thus the means to a larger end becomes an end in itself, and its attainment may sometimes conflict with attainment of the larger end.

In the real world, this irrational development is a common phenomenon in social organizations. Even when an organization is created to serve one specific purpose, it develops other purposes connected with its survival *per se* and with the prestige to be gained from operating it. The conditions for conflict between major and minor goals are thereby created.

Of course, where two policy alternatives are identical from the point of view of winning votes, the one most acceptable ideologically will be chosen and vice versa; there is no conflict here. But conflicts do arise, and occasionally maintenance of an ideological stand takes precedence over the all-out drive for office. At such times, an observer might be tempted to conclude that our hypothesis cannot explain the real world. It appears that the hypothesis which makes ideologies the end and office the means is being upheld instead.[6]

This conclusion is equivocal, however. No matter which end—espousing ideologies or holding office—is viewed as the final one, the other will be a subsidiary end necessary to the attainment of the first. It will even take rational precedence over the main goal in some situations where short-run setbacks lead to greater long-run progress towards the final end. Therefore the test of occasional precedence cannot decide between these hypotheses. The real issue is which end takes precedence more often—often enough to be called prevalent. We contend that the desire to obtain and keep power *per se* plays a larger role in the practical operation of democratic politics than the desire to implement ideological doctrines or serve particular social groups. Naturally our contention is merely an opinion.

[6] There are two interpretations of the hypothesis that makes ideologies the end and office the means. The first claims that those who seek to implement a certain ideology do so purely for the good of society, i.e., to bring about the social state it depicts. This view has generally been abandoned in favor of the second view. According to the latter, social groups use ideologies as smoke screens or tools; their real end is whatever benefits them most. We accept the second, or *group-serving*, interpretation in the above analysis. Ideologies are not really the final end in either this hypothesis or our own; in both they are really the means to some other end.

V. SUMMARY

Uncertainty restricts each voter's ability to relate every government act to his own view of the good society. Therefore acquaintance with each party's view of the good society—its ideology—helps him make his voting decision without knowing about every policy specifically. Voters thus use ideologies to cut their information costs.

Parties also find ideologies useful in gaining the support of various social groups and in short cutting decisions about which policy will gain the most votes. A diversity of party ideologies can exist only because uncertainty prevents any one from being proven superior. If a superior one does emerge, other parties imitate it and subtler differentiation takes place.

In our model, it is necessary for each party's ideology to bear a consistent relation to its actions and to develop without repudiating the party's former acts. Any other procedure makes rational voting nearly impossible; hence voters impute value to parties with these traits. To win votes, all parties are forced by competition to be relatively honest and responsible in regard to both policies and ideologies.

Though ideologies are never internally contradictory, they may be only loosely integrated, since they are designed to attract many social groups. Their stability over time has both logical and institutional roots which prevent policies from being altered smoothly to fit changing conditions. Thus ideologies cause lags and discontinuities that may cost a party votes.

In this way conflicts arise between the maintenance of ideological purity and the winning of elections. The former may occasionally take precedence over the latter, but our hypothesis is upheld as long as parties behave most of the time as though election is their primary objective.

8

The Statics and
Dynamics of Party
Ideologies

Introduction

IF POLITICAL ideologies are truly means to the end of obtaining votes, and if we know something about the distribution of voters' preferences, we can make specific predictions about how ideologies change in content as parties maneuver to gain power. Or, conversely, we can state the conditions under which ideologies come to resemble each other, diverge from each other, or remain in some fixed relationship.

Objectives

In this chapter we attempt to prove the following propositions:

1. A two-party democracy cannot provide stable and effective government unless there is a large measure of ideological consensus among its citizens.

114

2. Parties in a two-party system deliberately change their platforms so that they resemble one another; whereas parties in a multiparty system try to remain as ideologically distinct from each other as possible.

3. If the distribution of ideologies in a society's citizenry remains constant, its political system will move toward a position of equilibrium in which the number of parties and their ideological positions are stable over time.

4. New parties can be most successfully launched immediately after some significant change in the distribution of ideological views among eligible voters.

5. In a two-party system, it is rational for each party to encourage voters to be irrational by making its platform vague and ambiguous.

I. THE SPATIAL ANALOGY AND ITS EARLY USE

To carry out this analysis, we borrow and elaborate upon an apparatus invented by Harold Hotelling. It first appeared in a famous article on spatial competition published in 1929, and was later refined by Arthur Smithies.[1] Our version of Hotelling's spatial market consists of a linear scale running from zero to 100 in the usual left-to-right fashion. To make this politically meaningful, we assume that political preferences can be ordered from left to right in a manner agreed upon by all voters. They need not agree on which point they personally prefer, only on the ordering of parties from one extreme to the other.

In addition, we assume that every voter's preferences are single-peaked and slope downward monotonically on either side of the peak

[1] Harold Hotelling, "Stability in Competition," *The Economic Journal*, XXXIX (1929), 41–57, and Arthur Smithies, "Optimum Location in Spatial Competition," *The Journal of Political Economy*, XLIX (1941), 423–439. For other aspects of the spatial-competition problem, see F. Zeuthen, "Theoretical Remarks on Price Policy: Hotelling's Case with Variations," *Quarterly Journal of Economics*, XLVII (1933), 231–253; Erich Schneider, "Bemerkungen zu Einer Theorie der Raumwirtschaft," *Econometrica*, III (1935), 79–105; A. P. Lerner and H. W. Singer, "Some Notes on Duopoly and Spatial Competition," *Journal of Political Economy*, XLV (1937), 145–186; and August Lösch, *The Economics of Location* (New Haven: Yale University Press, 1954).

(unless his peak lies at one extreme on the scale). For example, if a voter likes position 35 best, we can immediately deduce that he prefers 30 to 25 and 40 to 45. He always prefers some point X to another point Y if X is closer to 35 than Y and both are on the same side of 35. The slope downward from the apex need not be identical on both sides, but we do presume no sharp asymmetry exists.

These assumptions can perhaps be made more plausible if we reduce all political questions to their bearing upon one crucial issue: how much government intervention in the economy should there be? If we assume that the left end of the scale represents full government control, and the right end means a completely free market, we can rank parties by their views on this issue in a way that might be nearly universally recognized as accurate. In order to coördinate this left-right orientation with our numerical scale, we will arbitrarily assume that the number denoting any party's position indicates the percentage of the economy it wants left in private hands (excluding those minimal state operations which even the most Hayekian economists favor). Thus the extreme left position is zero, and the extreme right is 100. Admittedly, this apparatus is unrealistic for the following two reasons: (1) actually each party is leftish on some issues and rightish on others, and (2) the parties designated as right wing extremists in the real world are for fascist control of the economy rather than free markets. However, we will ignore these limitations temporarily and see what conclusions of interest we can draw from this spatial analogy.

Both Hotelling and Smithies have already applied their versions of this model to politics. Hotelling assumed that people were evenly spaced along the straight-line scale, and reasoned that competition in a two-party system would cause each party to move towards its opponent ideologically. Such convergence would occur because each party knows that extremists at its end of the scale prefer it to the opposition, since it is necessarily closer to them than the opposition party is. Therefore the best way for it to gain more support is to move toward the other extreme, so as to get more voters outside of it—i.e., to come between them and its opponent. As the two parties move closer together, they become more moderate and less extreme in policy in an effort to win the crucial middle-of-the-road voters, i.e., those whose views place them between the two parties. This center area becomes smaller and smaller as both parties strive to capture moderate votes; finally the two parties become nearly identical in platforms and actions. For example, if there is one voter at every point on the scale, and parties A and B start at points 25 and 75 respectively, they will move towards each other and meet at 50, assuming they move at the same speed (Fig. 1). Like the two grocery

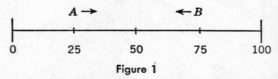

Figure 1

Note for Figures 1–10: Horizontal scale represents political orientation (see pp. 115–116). Vertical scale represents number of citizens.

stores in Hotelling's famous example, they will converge on the same location until practically all voters are indifferent between them.

Smithies improved this model by introducing elastic demand at each point on the scale. Thus as the grocery stores moved away from the extremes, they lost customers there because of the increased cost of transportation; this checked them from coming together at the center. In our model, this is analogous to political extremists becoming disgusted at the identity of the parties, and refusing to vote for either if they become too much alike. At exactly what point this leakage checks the convergence of A and B depends upon how many extremists each loses by moving towards the center compared with how many moderates it gains thereby.

II. THE EFFECTS OF VARIOUS DISTRIBUTIONS OF VOTERS

A. IN TWO-PARTY SYSTEMS

An important addition we can make to this model is a variable distribution of voters along the scale. Instead of assuming there is one voter at each point on the scale, let us assume there are 100,000 voters whose preferences cause them to be normally distributed with a mean of 50 (Fig. 2). Again, if we place parties A and B initially at 25 and 75, they will converge rapidly upon the center. The possible loss of extremists will not deter their movement toward each other, because there are so few voters to be lost at the margins

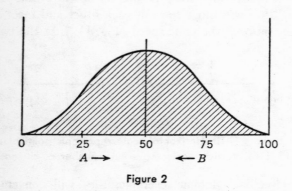

Figure 2

compared with the number to be gained in the middle. However, if we alter the distribution to that shown in Figure 3, the two parties will not move away from their initial positions at 25 and 75 at all; if they did, they would lose far more voters at the extremes than they could possibly gain in the center. Therefore a two-party system need not lead to the convergence on moderation that Hotelling and Smithies predicted. If voters' preferences are distributed so that voters are massed bimodally near the extremes, the parties will remain poles apart in ideology.

The possibility that parties will be kept from converging ideologically in a two-party system depends upon the refusal of extremist voters to support either party if both become alike—not identical, but merely similar. In a certain world—where information is complete and costless, there is no future-oriented voting, and the act of voting uses up no scarce resources—such abstention by extremists would be irrational. As long as there is even the most infinitesimal difference between A and B, extremist voters would be forced to vote for the one closest to them, no matter how distasteful its policies seemed in comparison with those of their ideal government. It is always rational *ex definitione* to select a greater good before a lesser, or a lesser evil before a greater; consequently abstention would be irrational because it increases the chances of the worse party for victory.

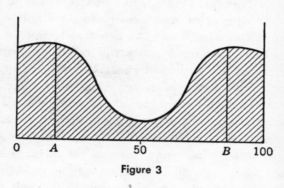

Figure 3

Even in a certain world, however, abstention is rational for extremist voters who are future oriented. They are willing to let the worse party win today in order to keep the better party from moving towards the center, so that in future elections it will be closer to them. Then when it does win, its victory is more valuable in their eyes. Abstention thus becomes a threat to use against the party nearest one's own extreme position so as to keep it away from the center.[2]

Uncertainty increases the possibility that rational extremist voters will abstain if the party nearest them moves toward its opponent, even if it does not become ideologically identical with the latter. When information is limited and costly, it is difficult to detect infinitesimal differences between parties. Perhaps even relatively significant differences will pass unnoticed by the radical whose own

[2] In reality, since so many ballots are cast, each individual voter has so little influence upon the election that his acts cannot be realistically appraised as a threat to any party, assuming the actions of all other citizens are given. Since we deal with this atomistic problem fully in Chapter 13, we evade it here by assuming each man behaves as though his vote has a high probability of being decisive.

views are so immoderate that all moderates look alike. This means that the differential threshold of such extremists is likely to be very high—they will regard all small differences between moderate parties as irrelevant to their voting decision, i.e., as unreal distinctions.

Having established the rationality of abstention by extremist voters, let us again consider a bimodal distribution of voters with modes near each extreme (Fig. 3). In a two-party system, whichever party wins will attempt to implement policies radically opposed to the other party's ideology, since the two are at opposite extremes. This means that government policy will be highly unstable, and that democracy is likely to produce chaos. Unfortunately, the growth of balancing center parties is unlikely. Any party which forms in the center will eventually move toward one extreme or the other to increase its votes, since there are so few moderate voters. Furthermore, any center party could govern only in coalition with one of the extremist parties, which would alienate the other, and thus not eliminate the basic problem. In such a situation, unless voters can somehow be moved to the center of the scale to eliminate their polar split, democratic government is not going to function at all well. In fact, no government can operate so as to please most of the people; hence this situation may lead to revolution.

The political cycle typical of revolutions can be viewed as a series of movements of men along the political scale.[3] Preliminary to the upheaval, the once centralized distribution begins to polarize into two extremes as the incumbents increasingly antagonize those who feel themselves oppressed. When the distribution has become so split that one extreme is imposing by force policies abhorred by the other extreme, open warfare breaks out, and a clique of underdogs seizes power. This radical switch from one extreme to the other is partly responsible for the reign of terror which marks most revolutions; the new governors want to eliminate their predecessors, who have

---

[3] The following description should not be construed as a causal explanation of revolutions; it is rather a translation of the events that occur in them into movements along the scale we have developed. Hence we make no attempt to discuss why revolutions follow the cycle portrayed. For an analysis of this problem, see Lyford P. Edwards, *The Natural History of Revolution* (Chicago: University of Chicago Press, 1927).

bitterly opposed them. Finally violence exhausts itself, a new concensus is reached on the principles of the revolution, and the distribution becomes centralized again—often under a new dictatorship
as rigid as the old, but not faced with a polarized distribution of
opinions.[4]

Under more normal circumstances, in countries where there are
two opposite social classes and no sizeable middle class, the numerical distribution is more likely to be skewed to the left, with a small
mode at the right extreme (Fig. 4). The large mode at the left rep-

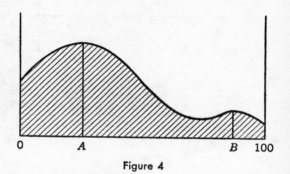

Figure 4

resents the lower or working class; on the right is the upper class.
Here democracy, if effective, will bring about the installation of a
leftish government because of the numerical preponderance of the
lower classes. Fear of this result is precisely what caused many
European aristocrats to fight the introduction of universal suffrage.
Of course, our schema oversimplifies the situation considerably. On
our political scale, every voter has equal weight with every other,
whereas in fact the unequal distribution of income allows a nu-
merically small group to control political power quite disproportionate to its size, as we saw in Chapter 6.

In spite of this oversimplification, it is clear that the numerical
distribution of voters along the political scale determines to a great
extent what kind of democracy will develop. For example, a distribu-

[4] The application of this model to revolutions was suggested by Robert A.
Dahl and Kenneth Arrow. Professor Dahl develops a similar model in *A Preface
to Democratic Theory* (Chicago: University of Chicago Press, 1956), pp. 90–102.

tion like that of Figure 2 encourages a two-party system with both parties located near the center in relatively moderate positions. This type of government is likely to have stable policies, and whichever party is in power, its policies will not be far from the views of the vast majority of people. On the other hand, if a nation's voters are distributed as shown in Figure 5, a multiparty system will almost inevitably result.

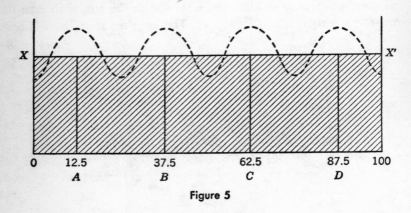

Figure 5

B. THE NUMBER OF PARTIES IN EQUILIBRIUM

Before examining the dynamics of multiparty systems, we should point out that our political version of Hotelling's model does not suffer from the outstanding limitation of the economic version he used. In Hotelling's spatial market, it was impossible to reach stable equilibrium with more than two grocery stores. The ones in the middle would always become the target of convergence from either side; consequently they would leap to the outside to keep from being squeezed. There was no device to restrict the perfect mobility that caused this disequilibrium.

But political parties cannot move ideologically past each other. As we saw in the last chapter, integrity and responsibility create relative immobility, which prevents a party from making ideological leaps over the heads of its neighbors. Thus ideological movement is restricted to horizontal progress at most up to—and never beyond—

the nearest party on either side. Coupled with our device of variable distribution, this attribute of the model nearly always insures stable equilibrium.

It is true that new parties can be introduced between two formerly adjacent ones or outside one of them. Nevertheless, this possibility cannot upset stable equilibrium in the long run for two reasons. First, once a party has come into being, it cannot leap over the heads of its neighbors, as explained. Second, there is a limit to the number of parties which can be supported by any one distribution. When that limit is reached, no more new parties can be successfully introduced. The parties extant at that point arrange themselves through competition so that no party can gain more votes by moving to the right than it loses on the left by doing so, and vice versa. The political system thus reaches a state of long-run equilibrium in so far as the number and positions of its parties are concerned, assuming no change in the distribution of voters along the scale.

Whether the political system contains two or many parties in this state of equilibrium depends upon (1) the nature of the limit upon the introduction of new parties and (2) the shape of the distribution of voters. We will examine these factors in order.

In our model, every party is a team of men who seek to attain office—a party cannot survive in the long run if none of its members get elected.[5] But in order to get at least some of its members elected, the party must gain the support of a certain minimum number of voters. The size of this minimum depends upon the type of electoral system in operation.

To get any of its members in office at all, a party in our model must win more votes than any other party running. This arrangement encourages parties which repeatedly lose to merge with each other so as to capture a combined total of votes larger than the total

[5] This definition of party does not cover many actual parties that continue to exist even though their chances for election are practically zero; e.g., the Vegetarians and Socialists in the United States. These parties are politically irrational from the point of view of our hypothesis; i.e., the motives we posit as politically rational are not the ones impelling their members. Even future-oriented rationality does not cover them, since past experience demonstrates that their future chances of election are also nearly nonexistent unless some highly unlikely catastrophe occurs.

received by the party which repeatedly wins. Such amalgamation continues until each of the survivors has a reasonable chance of winning a majority of the votes cast, which is the only way it can be sure of gaining office. Thus the winner-take-all outcome of a plurality electoral structure tends to narrow the field to two competing parties.[6]

Where proportional representation exists, a party which wins only a small percentage of the total vote may place some of its members in the government, since coalition governments often rule.[7] Thus the minimum amount of support necessary to keep a party going is much smaller than in a plurality system; so a multiparty system is encouraged. Nevertheless, each party must still obtain a certain minimum number of votes in order to elect members of the legislature who might possibly enter a coalition. For this reason, a given distribution of voters can support only a limited number of parties even under proportional representation.[8] Therefore the conditions for equilibrium exist in both two- and multiparty systems.

The type of electoral structure extant in a political system may be either a cause or a result of the original distribution of voters along the scale. Thus if the distribution has a single mode around which nearly all voters are clustered, the framers of the electoral structure may believe that plurality rule will not cause any large group to be ignored politically. Or if the distribution has many small modes, the law-makers may choose proportional representation in order to allow sizeable extremist groups to have a voice in government.

Causality can also be reversed because the number of parties in

[6] For a more extensive discussion of this assertion, see V. O. Key Jr., *Politics, Parties, and Pressure Groups* (New York: Thomas Y. Crowell Company, 1953), pp. 224–231.

[7] A detailed analysis of the problems raised by coalition governments is presented in the next chapter.

[8] Another reason why new parties cannot form *ad infinitum* is that political parties are specialized agencies in the division of labor, as explained in Chapter 2. Therefore not everyone can be in a political party; in fact, in a given society, there is probably a definite limit imposed by efficiency on the number of persons who can specialize in being party members. The size of this limit depends upon such factors as the importance of government action in that society, the need for differing representation (i.e., the scattering of voters on the scale), the social prestige and economic income attached to being in politics, and the general standard of living produced by the division of labor.

existence molds the political views of rising generations, thereby influencing their positions on the scale. In a plurality structure, since a two-party system is encouraged and the two parties usually converge, voters' tastes may become relatively homogeneous in the long run; whereas the opposite effect may occur in a proportional representation structure.

From this analysis it is clear that both the electoral structure and the distribution of voters are important in determining how many parties a given democracy will contain when it reaches equilibrium. Each factor influences the other indirectly, but it also has some impact independent of the other. For example, if a proportional representation system is established in a society where the distribution of voters has a single mode and a small variance, it is possible that only two parties will exist in equilibrium because there is not enough political room on the scale for more than two significantly different positions to gain measurable support.[9]

Having explored the impact of the two major types of electoral structure upon the number of parties in a political system, we will concentrate our attention from now on upon the impact of the distribution of voters along the scale. In order to do so, we assume that this distribution is the only factor in determining how many parties there are.[10]

C. IN MULTIPARTY SYSTEMS

Multiparty systems—those with three or more major parties—are likely to occur whenever the distribution of voters is polymodal. The

[9] This example ignores the possibility of a tiny third party occupying a crucial balancing position between two other large parties. Actually such an outcome is also possible in a plurality system if the government is chosen by a series of district elections rather than a single national election. As in Great Britain, a small party may gain only a few seats in the legislature, but if the two large parties are equally powerful, its decisive role in the balance of power may keep it alive even though it never gains office in the government directly. Our plurality model precludes this outcome because we posit election on a strictly national basis. In the next chapter we present a proportional representation model in which such small but powerful parties can exist.

[10] Of course there are many factors influencing the number of parties in a given system, but most of them can be subsumed under the electoral structure (which we just discussed) or the distribution of voters (which we are about to discuss).

existence of two or more outstanding modes creates conditions favorable to one party at each mode, and perhaps balancing parties between them. Figure 5 represents an extreme example of this structure, since voters are equally distributed along the scale (on XX'); i.e., each point on the scale is a mode (or the distribution can be seen as having no modes). However, not every point can support a party if we assume that the electoral structure allows only a certain number of parties to compete for power with reasonable chances of success. Therefore a definite number of parties will spring up along the scale and maneuver until the distance between each party and its immediately adjacent neighbors is the same for all parties. In Figure 5 we have assumed that the total number of parties is limited to four; hence in equilibrium they will space themselves as shown (assuming extremists abstain if parties A and D move toward the center).[11]

An important difference between a distribution like that in Figure 5 and one like that in Figure 2 is that the former provides no incentive for parties to move toward each other ideologically. Party B in Figure 5, for example, cannot gain more votes by moving toward A or towards C. If it started toward C, it would win votes away from C, but it would lose just as many to A; the reverse happens if it moves toward A. Therefore it will stay at 37.5 and maintain its ideological purity—unlike party B in Figure 2.[12] The latter party is pulled toward the center because, by moving toward A, it wins more votes among the moderates than it loses among the extremists, as mentioned before.

Thus it is likely that in multiparty systems, parties will strive to distinguish themselves ideologically from each other and maintain

[11] As new voters appear on the scene, they may cluster around the four locations where parties exist and thus form a tetramodal distribution like that shown by the dotted line in Figure 5. In other words, a perfectly even distribution is probably not stable over time but tends to become a distribution with definite modes and less populated areas between them. Such a development further restricts the manner in which new parties may enter the system, since it makes some locations much more desirable than others but also concentrates extant parties at the most favorable spots.

[12] At this point we are ignoring the possibility of B's gaining power by forming a coalition with either A or C or both. The forces influencing B's movement when it is in such a coalition are described in Section III of the next chapter.

the purity of their positions; whereas in two-party systems, each party will try to resemble its opponent as closely as possible.[13]

This phenomenon helps to explain certain peculiarities of the two political systems. If our reasoning is correct, voters in multiparty systems are much more likely to be swayed by doctrinal considerations —matters of ideology and policy—than are voters in two-party systems. The latter voters are massed in the moderate range where both ideologies lie; hence they are likely to view personality, or technical competence, or some other nonideological factor as decisive. Because they are not really offered much choice between policies, they may need other factors to discriminate between parties.

Voters in multiparty systems, however, are given a wide range of ideological choice, with parties emphasizing rather than soft-pedalling their doctrinal differences. Hence regarding ideologies as a decisive factor in one's voting decision is usually more rational in a multiparty system than in a two-party system. In spite of this fact, the ideology of the government in a multiparty system (as opposed to the parties) is often less cohesive than its counterpart in a two-party system, as we shall see in the next chapter.

III. THE ORIGIN OF NEW PARTIES

In analyzing the birth of new parties, we must distinguish between two types of new parties. The first is designed *to win elections*. Its originators feel that it can locate itself so as to represent a large number of voters whose views are not being expressed by any extant party. The second type is designed *to influence already existent parties* to change their policies, or not to change them; it is not primarily aimed at winning elections.

Of course, no party is ever begun by people who think it will never get any votes, or win any offices, especially if our hypothesis about party motivation is true. Nevertheless, some parties—founded by perfectly rational men—are meant to be threats to other parties and

[13] A two-party system like that shown in Figure 3 will not exhibit ideological convergence. However, as we have pointed out, it is doubtful whether such a distribution can function as a democracy, since internal conflict will be intense no matter which party wins.

not means of gaining immediate power or prestige. An example is the States' Rights Party of 1948, intended to threaten the Democrats because of their policy on civil rights. Such blackmail parties are future oriented, since their purpose is to alter the choices offered to voters by the extant parties at some future date.

To distinguish between these two kinds of parties is often difficult, because many parties founded primarily to gain office actually perform the function of influencing the policies of previously existing parties. This impact has been typical of third parties in United States history, none of which ever won a national election, though many had great influence upon the platforms of parties that did win. Thus if we classify new parties by intention, nearly all of them are of the "real" type; whereas if we classify them by results, most of them, at least in American history, are of the "influence" type. However, we will assume that the new parties we discuss are designed to win elections, unless otherwise specified.

No party, new or old, can survive without gaining the support of a sizeable fraction of the electorate—a support active enough to be expressed by votes in elections. This does not mean that a party must locate right in the midst of a big lump of voters on our political scale; rather it must be nearer a large number of voters than any other parties are. Its location is as dependent upon where other parties are as it is upon where voters are.

New parties are most likely to appear and survive when there is an opportunity for them to cut off a large part of the support of an older party by sprouting up between it and its former voters. An outstanding case in point is the birth of the Labour Party in England, which can be illustrated very roughly by Figure 6. Before 1900, there were two major British parties, the Liberals (A) and the Tories (B). They were under the usual two-party pressure to converge. However, the enfranchisement of the working class in the late nineteenth century had shifted the center of voter distribution far to the left of its old position. And the Liberal Party, even after it moved to the left, was to the right of the new center of gravity, although it was the more left of the two parties. The founders of the Labour Party correctly guessed that they could out-flank the Liberals by forming a new party (C) to the left of the latter, which they did. This trapped the Liberals between the two modes of the electorate, and their support rapidly diminished to insignificant size.[14]

The crucial factor in this case was the shift of the electorate's distribution along the political scale as a result of the extension of suf-

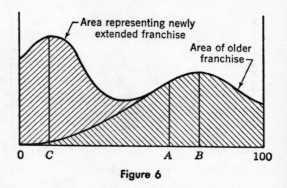

Figure 6

frage to a vast number of new voters, many of whom were near the extreme left. Whenever such a radical change in the distribution of voters occurs, existent parties will probably be unable to adjust rapidly because they are ideologically immobile. New parties, however, are not weighed down by this impediment. Unencumbered by ideological commitments, they can select the most opportune point on the scale at which to locate, and structure their ideologies accordingly. Opportunities to do so will be especially tempting if the old parties have converged toward the previous center of gravity as a result of the normal two-party process, and the new distribution is heavily skewed to one or both extremes. This is roughly what happened in the case of the Labour Party.

Another situation which may be productive of new parties is a social stalemate caused by a voter distribution like that in Figure 3. Where voters are massed bimodally at opposite ends of the scale,

[14] Interestingly enough, now that the Liberal Party has dwindled in support, the British electoral system has reverted to its former two-party pattern. Since the new center of gravity is far left of the old, the Conservative Party has moved farther leftward than the Labour Party has moved rightward. Nevertheless, a tendency toward convergence clearly exists.

peaceful democratic government is difficult, as mentioned previously. A faction desirous of compromise may grow up, thus altering the distribution so it resembles the one shown in Figure 7. Here an opportunity exists for a new party to be formed at C. If this party grows as a result of continuous shifts of voters to the center, eventually a

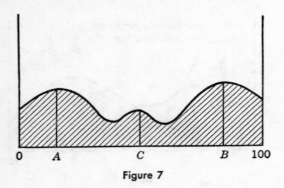

Figure 7

new situation like that in Figure 8 may appear. The center has become preponderant, but has split into three parts because new parties have arisen to exploit the large moderate voting mass.

It is clear that a major prerequisite for the appearance of new parties is a change in the distribution of voters along the political scale. A shift in the universality of franchise, a weakening of traditional views by some cataclysmic event like World War II, a social

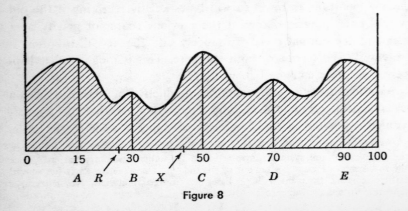

Figure 8

revolution like that following upon industrialization—any such disturbing occurrence may move the modes on the political scale. A change in the number of voters *per se* is irrelevant; it is the distribution which counts. Hence women's suffrage does not create any new parties, although it raises the total vote enormously.

There is one situation in which a new party is likely to appear without any change in voter distribution, but this will be the influence type of party, not the kind that aims at getting itself elected. When one of the parties in a two-party system has drifted away from the extreme nearest it toward the moderate center, its extremist supporters may form a new party to pull the policies of the old one back toward them. In Figure 9, party B has moved away to the left of its

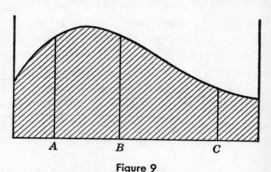

Figure 9

right-wing members because it wants to gain votes from the large mass of voters near the leftish mode. In order to threaten party *B* with defeat unless it moves back toward the right, the right-wing extremists found party C. This party cannot possibly win itself, but it can throw the election to A by diverting extremist votes from *B*.

To get rid of this menace, party B must adopt some of C's policies, thus moving back to the right and taking the wind out of C's sails. This will cause party C to collapse, but it will have accomplished its purpose of improving the platform of one of the real contenders, *B*, in the eyes of its extremist supporters. As mentioned previously, the States' Rights Party formed in 1948 had just such an aim.

In situations like this, it is a movement of party ideology, not of voter distribution, which gives rise to a new party. Party ideologies are relatively immobile in multiparty systems; so this type of new party will appear almost exclusively in two-party systems. Fear of these blackmail parties may strongly counteract the centripetal pull normal to such systems.

IV. IDEOLOGICAL COHERENCE AND INTEGRATION

A. ALTERATION OF OUR MODEL TO INCLUDE MULTIPOLICY PARTIES

In Chapter 7 we showed that each party's ideology will be coherent but not integrated. That is, it will not contain internal contradictions, but neither will it be too closely tied to any one philosophic *Weltanschauung*. This outcome results from the conflicting desires each party feels when forming its ideology. On the one hand, it wishes to appeal to as many voters as possible; on the other hand, it wishes to have a strong appeal for each individual voter. The first desire implies a platform containing a wide range of policies representing many different ideological outlooks. The second desire implies a close integration of policies around the philosophic viewpoint of whichever voter is being wooed. Obviously, the more either desire is achieved, the less will the other be satisfied.

This dualism can be depicted on our graph of political space. First we must remove the assumption that each party's platform contains only its stand on the proper degree of government intervention in the economy. Let us assume instead that each party takes stands on many issues, and that each stand can be assigned a position on our left-right scale.[15] Then the party's net position on this scale is a weighted average of the positions of all the particular policies it upholds.

[15] We can state this assumption formally as follows: all citizens agree on a left-right ordering of the stands taken by the various parties on any given issue. Thus it is not necessary for every citizen to have the same cardinal ordering of stands on the left-right scale as every other; i.e., citizen A may feel that party X's stand on some issue is at point 35, while citizen B may believe the same stand is at point 30, but both must agree it is on the same side of party Y's stand on that issue and bears the same ordinal relation to the stands of parties W, Y and Z. Although in the text we implicitly assume agreement on the exact location of each party stand in order to simplify the argument, our conclusions also follow from purely ordinal premises.

Furthermore, each citizen may apply different weights to the individual policies, since each policy affects some citizens more than others. Therefore the party has no unique, universally recognized net position. Some voters may feel it is more right-wing than others, and no one view can be proved correct. However, there will be some consensus as to the range in which the party's net position lies; so we can still distinguish right-wing parties from center and left-wing ones.

Under these conditions, the rational party strategy is to adopt a spread of policies which covers a whole range of the left-right scale. The wider this spread is, the more viewpoints the party's ideology and platform will appeal to. But a wider spread also weakens the strength of the appeal to any one viewpoint, because each citizen sees the party upholding policies he does not approve of.

Thus a voter's judgment of each party becomes two-dimensional: he must balance its net position (the mean of its policies) against its spread (their variance) in deciding whether he wants to support it. If some party has a mean identical with his own position (which we assume single-valued) but an enormous variance, he may reject it in favor of another party with a mean not as close to him but with a much smaller variance. In short, voters choose policy vectors rather than policy scalars, and each vector is really a weighted frequency distribution of policies on the left-right scale.

B. INTEGRATION STRATEGIES IN TWO-PARTY AND MULTIPARTY SYSTEMS

If we assume that each point on the political scale represents a definite Weltanschauung, the width of the spread formed by a party's policies varies inversely with their integration around a single such Weltanschauung. Therefore, the degree of integration in a party's ideology depends upon what fraction of the scale it is trying to cover with its policy spread. We have already seen that this fraction will be smaller in a multiparty system than in a two-party system, simply because dividing a constant in half yields larger parts than dividing it into any greater number of equal pieces. If we rule out any overlapping of policy spreads, we may conclude that ideologies will be more integrated in multiparty systems than in two-party systems. Each party's platform will more clearly reflect some one philosophic viewpoint, around which its policies will be more closely grouped. This accords with our previous conclusion that each party in a multiparty system will try to differentiate its product sharply from the products of all other parties, whereas each party in a two-party system will try to resemble its rival.

To illustrate this conclusion, let us compare Figure 2 with Figure 5. In Figure 2, after parties A and B have approached each other near the center of the scale, each is drawing votes from half the scale. Its supporters range in viewpoint from those at one extreme to those at dead center; hence it must design a policy spread which includes all of them. But there are more voters in the middle than at the extremes. Therefore each party structures its policies so that its net position is moderate, even though it makes a few concessions to the extremists. In this way, it hopes to keep the extremists from abstaining and yet woo the middle-of-the-roaders massed around 50.

In contrast to the parties in Figure 2, those in Figure 5 do not have to appeal to a wide range of viewpoints. The policy span of each is much narrower, and any attempt to widen it soon causes a collision with another party. This restricts each party's spread even if we allow overlapping to occur.

For example, party B in Figure 5 cannot gain by trying to spread its policies so as to please voters at positions 10 and 60. If it wishes to retain its net position at 35, it can only cast a few policies out as far as 10 and 60. But parties A and C are massing most of their policies so as to please voters at 10 and 60 respectively; hence B cannot hope to compete with A and C in these locations. In fact, B is much better off concentrating its policies around 35, since this keeps it from spreading itself too thin and losing votes to A and C from its own bailiwick. Thus no party in a multiparty system has much incentive to spread out or to overlap another ideologically, and each will closely integrate its policies around some definite philosophic outlook.

C. OVERLAPPING AND AMBIGUITY IN TWO-PARTY SYSTEMS

If we allow overlapping in a two-party system, the results are radically different from those just described. Each party casts some policies into the other's territory in order to convince voters there that its net position is near them. In such maneuvering, there is much room for skill because different voters assign different weights to the same policies. For example, assume that there are two social groups, farmers and workers, whose positions are respectively right and left of 50. They have exactly opposite views on two laws, one on farm price supports and the other on labor practices. However, the farmers weigh the farm law heavily in their voting decisions and consider the labor law much less significant; whereas the workers' emphasis is just the reverse. Each group thus views any party's net position differently from the way the other views it. Realizing this, a clever party will take a stand favoring farmers on the farm law and workers on the labor law. By doing so, it can establish a net position simultaneously close to both groups, even though they are far apart from each other!

This possibility of having a net position in many different places at once makes overlapping policies a rational strategy in a two-party system. Therefore, in the middle of the scale where most voters are massed, each party scatters its policies on both sides of the mid point. It attempts to make each voter in this area feel that it is centered right at his position. Naturally, this causes an enormous overlapping of moderate policies.

However, each party will sprinkle these moderate policies with a few extreme stands in order to please its far-out voters. Obviously, each party is trying to please an extreme opposite to that being pleased by the other party. Therefore it is possible to detect on which side of the mid point each party is actually located by looking at the extremist policies it espouses. In fact, this may be the only way to tell the two parties apart ideologically, since most of their policies are conglomerated in an overlapping mass in the middle of the scale.

Clearly, both parties are trying to be as ambiguous as possible about their actual net position. Therefore why should they not accomplish the same end by being equally ambiguous about each policy? Then every policy stand can cover a spread of voters, too. Not only can voters differently weight individual policies, they can also interpret the meaning of each policy differently—each seeing it in a light which brings it as close as possible to his own position. This vastly widens the band on the political scale into which various interpretations of a party's net position may fall.

Ambiguity thus increases the number of voters to whom a party may appeal. This fact encourages parties in a two-party system to be as equivocal as possible about their stands on each controversial issue. And since both parties find it rational to be ambiguous, neither is forced by the other's clarity to take a more precise stand.

Thus political rationality leads parties in a two-party system to becloud their policies in a fog of ambiguity. True, their tendency towards obscurity is limited by their desire to attract voters to the polls, since citizens abstain if all parties seem identical or no party makes testable promises. Nevertheless, competition forces both parties to be much less than perfectly clear about what they stand for. Naturally, this makes it more difficult for each citizen to vote rationally; he has a hard time finding out what his ballot supports when cast for either party. As a result, voters are encouraged to make decisions on some basis other than the issues, i.e., on the personalities of candidates, traditional family voting patterns, loyalty to past party heroes, etc. But only the parties' decisions on issues are relevant to voters' utility incomes from government, so making decisions on any other basis is irrational. We are forced to conclude that rational behavior by political parties tends to discourage rational behavior by voters.

This conclusion may seem startling, since it implies that there is a conflict between party rationality and voter rationality in a two-party system. But in fact this conflict has also been observed by students of political behavior, as the following quotation shows:

The tendency toward agreement between parties under a bipartisan system flows from the fact that party leaders must seek to build a majority of the electorate. In the nation as a whole a majority cannot be built upon the support of organized labor alone; the farmers cannot muster enough votes to form a majority; businessmen are decidedly in a minority. Given the traditional attachment to one party or another of large blocs of voters in all these classes, about the only way in which a party can form a majority is to draw further support from voters of all classes and interests. To succeed in this endeavor party leaders cannot afford to antagonize any major segment of the population. A convenient way to antagonize an element in the population is to take at an inopportune moment an unequivocal stand on an issue of importance. Similarities of composition, hence, contribute to two features of American parties: their similarity of view and their addiction to equivocation and ambiguity.[16]

Our model of "political space" has led us to exactly the same conclusion: parties will try to be similar and to equivocate. And the more they succeed, the more difficult it is for voters to behave rationally.

Does this mean that our assumption of rationality leads to a contradiction in a two-party system? Apparently the more rational political parties are, the less rational voters must be, and vice versa. How does this affect our model?

D. A FUNDAMENTAL TENSION IN OUR MODEL

To answer these questions, we must review briefly the basic structure of our mythical political system. In it are two sets of agents: voters and parties. Each set uses the other to achieve its own goal. Voters have as their goal the attainment of a government responsive to their wants; they make use of parties to run this government. Parties have as their goal the rewards of being in office; they make use of voters to get elected. Thus the interlocking of two different goal-pursuing processes forms the political system.

The only end common to both sets of agents is the continuance of the system. Otherwise, neither set cares whether the other's goals are achieved unless that achievement is beneficial to itself. Therefore if a member of one set can gain by impairing the ability of all the members of the other set to attain their goals, he will do so. This

[16] V. O. Key Jr., *op. cit.*, pp. 231–232.

follows from our axiom that each man seeks his own good and to get it will sacrifice the good of others, if necessary.

To put it more concretely, if any party believes it can increase its chances of gaining office by discouraging voters from being rational, its own rational course is to do so. The only exception to this rule occurs when voter irrationality is likely to destroy the political system. Since parties have a stake in this system, they are irrational if they encourage anything which might wreck it.

However, it is not obvious that ambiguous policies and similar ideologies are likely to destroy democracy. What they might do is make voting less than perfectly rational as a mechanism for selecting governments. But rationality as we define it is not a dichotomous concept; i.e., the possible states of rationality are not limited to 100 percent and 0 percent. Therefore making voting less than perfectly rational does not render it absolutely useless but merely reduces its efficiency as a government-selection process. Knowing this, parties will not be deterred by fear of the end of democracy when they increase ambiguity and match each other's platforms.

Voters have two defenses against being forced into irrationality. The first is to limit the operations of parties by law. In the United States, parties have been forced to make financial reports, refrain from fraudulent statements, submit their primaries to public control, accept only limited contributions from any one source, and otherwise act in ways not likely to exploit the citizenry. Since it would be irrational for citizens to allow parties to exploit them, these laws indirectly protect voters from being forced into irrationality. But voters can hardly expect to induce government to pass laws against platform ambiguity and similarity, so this defense is not much help.

The second defense is to change the political system from a two-party one to a multiparty one. This will cause parties to narrow the spread of their policies, differentiate their platforms more sharply, and reduce ambiguity. However, such a conversion will also give rise to tremendous problems not present in two-party systems, as we shall see in the next chapter. Therefore it is doubtful whether the change would improve prospects for rational voting; they might get worse.

After weighing all these considerations, we may conclude that our model is not necessarily contradictory. However, it does contain two sets of agents in tension with each other. If either of these is allowed to dominate the other fully, the model may become contradictory; i.e., one of the two sets of agents may cease to behave rationally. Thus if parties succeed in obscuring their policy decisions in a mist of generalities, and voters are unable to discover what their votes really mean, a *rationality crisis* develops. Since such a crisis is even more likely to occur in a multiparty system, we will defer our analysis of it until the next chapter.

V. A BASIC DETERMINANT OF A NATION'S POLITICS

From everything we have said, it is clear that a basic determinant of how a nation's political life develops is the distribution of voters along the political scale, assuming our oversimplified model has some application in the real world. In the first place, the number of modes in the distribution helps determine whether the political system will be two-party or multiparty in character. This in turn determines whether party ideologies will be similar and ambiguous or different and definite; hence it influences the difficulties voters face in behaving rationally. Second, whether democracy can lead to stable government depends upon whether the mass of voters is centrally conglomerated, or lumped at the extremes with low density in the center; only in the former case will democracy really work. Third, the distribution's stability determines whether new parties will constantly be replacing the old, or the old will dominate and new ones merely influence their policy.

Of course, the distribution of voters is not the only factor basic to a nation's policies. For example, some theorists argue that the use of single-member districts instead of proportional representation is the main cause of a two-party political system.[17] Nevertheless,

[17] We have already discussed this point in Section II of this chapter.

whether it is seen as a cause in itself or as a result of more fundamental factors, the distribution is a crucial political parameter.

What forces shape this important parameter? At the beginning of
our study, we assumed that voters' tastes were fixed, which means
that the voter distribution is given. Thus we dodged the question
just posed, and have been evading it ever since. Even now we cannot
answer, because the determinants are historic, cultural, and psychological, as well as economic; to attempt to analyze them would be
to undertake a study vast beyond our scope.

All we can say is the following: (1) the distribution of voters is a
crucial determinant molding a nation's political life, (2) major
changes in it are among the most important political events possible,
and (3) though parties will move ideologically to adjust to the distribution under some circumstances, they will also attempt to move
voters toward their own locations, thus altering it.

VI. SUMMARY

We can turn Harold Hotelling's famous spatial market into a
useful device for analyzing political ideologies by adding to it (1)
variable distribution of population, (2) an unequivocal left-to-right
ordering of parties, (3) relative ideological immobility, and (4)
peaked political preferences for all voters.

This model confirms Hotelling's conclusion that the parties in a
two-party system converge ideologically upon the center, and
Smithies' addendum that fear of losing extremist voters keeps them
from becoming identical. But we discover that such convergence depends upon a unimodal distribution of voters which has a low
variance and most of its mass clustered around the mode.

If the distribution of voters along the scale remains constant in a
society, its political system tends to move towards an equilibrium in
which the number of parties and their ideological positions are fixed.
Whether it will then have two or many parties depends upon (1) the
shape of the distribution and (2) whether the electoral structure is
based upon plurality or proportional representation.

No tendency toward imitation exists in a multiparty system; in fact, parties strive to accentuate ideological "product differentiation" by maintaining purity of doctrine. This difference between the two systems helps explain why certain practices are peculiar to each.

New parties are usually intended to win elections, but they are often more important as means of influencing the policies of previously existent parties. Since old parties are ideologically immobile, they cannot adjust rapidly to changes in voter distribution, but new parties can enter wherever it is most advantageous. Influence parties may crop up in two-party systems whenever convergence has pulled one of the major parties away from the extreme, and its extremist supporters want to move it back towards them.

If we assume a party's position on the scale is a weighted average of the positions occupied by each of its policy decisions, we can account for the tendency of parties to spread their policies: they wish to appeal to many different viewpoints at once. Parties in a two-party system have a much wider spread of policies—hence a looser integration of them—than those in a multiparty system. In fact, in two-party systems there is a large area of overlapping policies near the middle of the scale, so that parties closely resemble each other.

This tendency towards similarity is reinforced by deliberate equivocation about each particular issue. Party policies may become so vague, and parties so alike, that voters find it difficult to make rational decisions. Nevertheless, fostering ambiguity is the rational course for each party in a two-party system.

A basic determinant of a nation's political development is the distribution of its voters along the political scale. Upon this factor, to a great extent, depend whether the nation will have two or many major parties, whether democracy will lead to stable or unstable government, and whether new parties will continually replace old or play only a minor role.

9

Problems of Rationality Under Coalition Governments

Introduction

IN DEMOCRATIC political systems, governmental use of coercion obtains its sanction from the consent of the governed. Various philosophic notions underlie this conception, but in practice almost every democracy regards a majority of those voting as equivalent to all of those governed. Hence every democratic government must somehow obtain the voluntary consent of a majority of voters before it can legitimately govern.

But in some multiparty systems, no party receives the votes of a majority. If so, government by one party alone amounts to the imposition of a minority's views upon the majority—clearly a violation of the basic idea behind democracy. To avoid this, the government must be made up of more than one party; i.e., it must be a *coalition* government.

Rational behavior in political systems governed by coalitions is somewhat different from that in systems governed by one party alone.

So far we have discussed only the latter because one-party government is implicit in our model. Therefore we must alter the model to study rationality under coalitions. In this chapter we make the necessary alternations and examine their implications.

Objectives

In this chapter we attempt to prove the following propositions:

1. Though rational voting is more important in multiparty systems than in two-party systems, it is more difficult and less effective.
2. In systems normally governed by coalitions, voters are under pressure to behave irrationally; hence they may treat elections as preference polls.
3. Party ideologies and policies in multiparty systems are more sharply defined than in two-party systems, but actual government programs are less integrated in the former than in the latter.
4. The parties in a coalition government are under simultaneous pressures to converge and diverge ideologically.
5. A certain amount of political irrationality is inevitable in any society.
6. The degree to which political rationality is possible and effective in a democracy depends upon how much consensus about goals exists; i.e., it depends upon the distribution of voters along the scale.

I. CHANGES IN THE MODEL

Most multiparty systems do not have winner-take-all elections in which the party gaining the most votes controls the whole government. In fact, voters do not directly elect the government at all; they elect members of a legislature, who in turn choose a government by majority vote. If, as is very likely, no one party has a majority in the legislature, then the government usually contains men from several parties. These parties combine to support the government, which thus indirectly obtains the consent of a majority of voters—the necessary prerequisite for democratic government.[1]

To study such systems, we add a legislature to our model, change the electoral structure, and allow government by a coalition of parties. Let us assume that the new electoral system works as follows:

1. Each voter votes for one party in the national election, not for any particular individual in the party.
2. Each party's national vote is totaled.
3. The total vote for all parties is counted and divided by the number of seats in the legislature to obtain the per-seat vote count, N.
4. Each party's total vote is divided by N to set the number of seats it will obtain (we are ignoring fractions here).
5. That number of men is chosen in order from a ranked list put up by the party itself before the election.
6. The legislature so constituted selects a prime minister by majority vote and approves his government department heads as a group by majority vote before they start to govern.
7. This government may contain members of more than one party.
8. Once approved by the legislature, this government has the same powers, with the same limitations, as the government described in Chapter 1. At the next election date it is dissolved and a new legislature is elected. Thus there are no intermediate votes between the initial approval of a government and the next election, either by the legislature or by the voters. Since the date of the next election is predetermined by constitutional rules, the coalition once approved, cannot be removed by adverse votes of confidence or any other peaceful means until that date arrives.

[1] The support of a majority of the legislature is not necessarily equivalent to the support of a majority of voters, because each legislator need not represent the same number of voters. In the United States House of Representatives, for example, the Congressman from the 8th District in Texas represents 807,000 people (not all of whom are voters, of course); whereas the Congressman from South Dakota's 2nd District represents only 159,000 people: figures from the 1950 Census as cited in John C. Cort, "The Dice Are Slightly Loaded," *The Commonweal*, LXII (June 24, 1955), 302–303. Sometimes legislatures are intentionally designed so that a party which receives only a plurality of votes may obtain an overwhelming majority of legislative seats. However, the electoral structure used in this chapter guarantees that a majority of the legislature is always equivalent to a majority of those voting, as is clear from the following paragraphs of the text.

These assumptions radically alter our model; hence several further clarifications are in order. First, we ignore most of the problems caused by interparty negotiations within the legislature, since they are both too complex and too empirical to be handled here.

Second, we continue to assume that voters look upon elections purely as means of selecting governments. Perhaps this seems unreasonable, because the voters in fact select a legislature, and it selects the government. Nevertheless, the purpose of elections is to create a government supported at least indirectly by a majority of the voters. Therefore rational voters will cast their ballots with only this end in mind.

This assumption precludes use of our analysis as a description of actual behavior in multiparty systems. In most such systems, at least some voters treat elections as something other than devices for selecting governments. But we define rational behavior in elections as that most efficiently designed to select the government a voter most desires from among those candidates with reasonable chances of actually governing. Therefore what is rational for some voters in reality may be irrational in our model.

For example, some political analysts believe that many French workers vote for the Communist Party purely as a protest against capitalist domination of the government's economic policy. These workers neither believe the Communists will become the government, nor do they want a Communist government. They treat the election neither as a government-selection device nor as an expression of preference, but as a social protest.

Similarly, an Italian worker may support the Communists even though he knows they are unlikely to be in the government. His vote shows merely that he would like them to govern. If elections are preference polls, his behavior is rational; in our model, it is irrational unless he is future oriented and believes his vote will help them attain office at some later date. To eliminate the latter possibility, we assume in this chapter that no voters are future oriented unless specifically designated as such.

Our third and final clarification concerns the time periods which enter into voters' decisions. In Chapter 3 we stated that voters choose future governments by comparing past records, a procedure we wish to retain in our present analysis. Thus even when a voter is making predictions of what coalitions a given party might enter and what policies each such coalition might have, we assume he is thinking about what policies each coalition *would have had* during the past election period, if it had been in power. This process may call for extensive imagination on the part of voters. It is not always obvious what policies a coalition would have had if it had been formed, when in fact it was not formed and therefore never had any policies.

However, the need for imagination is not diminished if we switch voters' contemplation to future policies. In this case, voters must sometimes guess what policies a coalition which has never existed will have if it exists in the future. Consequently, our retention of the decision-making process described in Chapter 3 does not create any added complications, and by using it, we save the reader from having to contemplate another such process. But to simplify the language of our exposition, we describe voters' decision-making as though they compared future policies of coalitions instead of present ones. The reduction of verbosity is appreciable, yet it does not lead to any misleading reasoning or false conclusions.

II. VOTER RATIONALITY UNDER COALITIONS

A. THE COMPLEXITY AND DIFFICULTY OF BEING RATIONAL

In multiparty systems such as we have described, the total vote is usually split among so many parties that none has a majority in the legislature. The rational voters therefore knows that his favorite party has very little chance of governing alone. If it is to have any part in the government, it must enter into a coalition with ideologically adjacent parties. For example, in Figure 8, party B must enter a coalition with A and C, or with C and D; otherwise it will be an opposition party.

This situation has two impacts on the meaning of voting. First, each vote helps elect at most only part of a government. Second, each vote supports a party which will have to compromise its policies even if elected; hence the policies of this party are not the ones which a vote for it actually supports. Instead the vote supports the policies of whatever coalition the party joins.

Under these conditions, a voter must know the following things in order to vote rationally:

1. What coalitions each party is willing to enter under various sets of circumstances.
2. Estimated probability distributions which show how likely each party is to enter each coalition open to it. Estimating these amounts to predicting how all other voters will vote; it is a specification of the circumstances mentioned in (1) above.
3. What policy compromises each party is likely to make in each possible coalition, i.e., what policies each coalition would adopt after it was formed. Since these compromises depend on the relative strength of the various parties in each coalition, to predict the compromises a voter must predict the outcome of the election, just as in (2) above.

Thus when a voter casts his ballot, he is in effect supporting a certain probability distribution of compromises. This distribution is itself compounded from (1) a probability distribution of the coalitions his party might enter, and (2) various probability distributions of the compromises it might make in each.

Obviously, the smaller is the number of coalitions which any given party is likely to enter, the easier it is for voters to know what a vote for that party means in terms of policy. Since some parties will enter only one coalition, the ambiguity of votes cast for them is small. Such clarity is especially true of extremist parties, because they can compromise in only one direction.

If a voter knows that his favorite party will enter only one specific coalition, he will vote for that party if he is rational, even though a vote for some other party might help elect the same coalition. This is true because the more votes his favorite party gets, the greater weight it will have in the coalition, and the more its policies will prevail therein. On the other hand, if the voter does not know what coalitions each party might enter, or what compromises it might make, he may be unable to tell which is his favorite party.

This difficulty can be shown by means of the voter distribution shown in Figure 8. Assume that the three center parties, B, C, and D, have been governing in a coalition, and another election occurs. Voter X, believing that the BCD coalition will be formed again if party C is strong enough, casts his vote for party C, because it is *per se* nearest his preference, and it has been in a coalition that is also near him. However, party C then enters a coalition with D and E, and the policies of this coalition place its net impact about where party D is. Looking back, voter X decides that if he had known what party C was going to do, he would have voted for party B. B is closer to him than D, yet the entrance of C into the CDE coalition meant that his vote supported a D position. In the next election, if he assumes C will again enter a CDE coalition, he will vote for B instead of C, although C is *per se* closer to his own position. Even if voter X thinks that B cannot win the election by itself, he may feel that his vote will pull C back towards the left and out of the CDE coalition in the future.

This example demonstrates the fact that rational voting in a multiparty system is both more difficult and more important than in a two-party system. It is more difficult because the possible outcomes are more numerous, and it may not be clear to a voter just what his ballot is supporting when he casts it. Yet each vote is more important because the range of alternative policies offered to voters in a multiparty system is likely to be much wider than in a two-party system. In the latter, both parties offer relatively moderate platforms.[2] Hence if the party a voter opposed is elected, he will probably not have to endure policies much different from those his favorite party would have implemented. But in a multiparty system, the victory of a party at the end of the scale opposite to a voter's position may usher in policies he bitterly opposes.

[2] We assume that there is only one mode in the distribution of voters and that both parties are located near it. Since the mode itself is by definition the most moderate position, both parties offer moderate programs. Under other less normal assumptions about the distribution of voters in a two-party system, the parties may offer more extreme programs, as we pointed out in Chapter 8.

The increased difficulty of voting rationally when there are more than two major parties can be further illustrated by comparing Figures 2 and 10. In a two-party system (Fig. 2), there are only two possible outcomes: A and B. Therefore a voter selects the outcome he prefers and votes for it. But in a three-party system like that shown

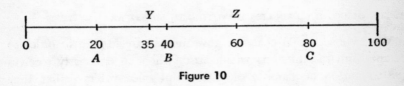

Figure 10

in Figure 10, there are at least nine possible outcomes. If we assume that the two extremist parties will never join the same government, we have five possible combinations: A, B, C, AB, and BC. But in the last two, which are coalitions between the center party and each of the extremist parties, one party might dominate the other, or they might have equal influence. Thus each coalition represents three outcomes instead of one, which means the possibilities are: A, B, C, AB, aB, Ab, BC, bC, and Bc. We can extend the number of outcomes indefinitely by increasing the measurable degrees of dominance in each coalition, but we already have enough to befuddle Y, our sample voter.

Faced with this array of possibilities, voter Y must know something about the probable outcome of the election in order to vote rationally. If only one party is going to win, he will vote for B, which is closest to him. He will also vote for B if a coalition between A and B is likely, since he would want B to be the stronger partner. But if B and C are likely to form a coalition with a net policy position of Z, it is more rational for him to vote for A than for B, since he would rather have A win alone than see such a coalition. How should he vote?

The answer to this question depends upon two factors: (1) what knowledge Y has about how other citizens are likely to vote, and (2) how men should choose rationally among alternatives with uncertain outcomes. The latter has long been a matter of interest to economic theorists, but they have arrived at no consensus on it. Therefore all we can say is that Y will follow the rather vague procedure described in the summary of Chapter 3. However, we must explore the first factor carefully because it leads to conjectural variation among voters.

B. THE OLIGOPOLY PROBLEM IN VOTING IN MULTIPARTY SYSTEMS

We have seen that coalition governments are formed in order to escape from the dilemma which arises when no one party receives the support of a majority of voters. But once voters realize they will be governed by a coalition, a feedback effect occurs and changes the nature of voting.

Rational voters no longer simply vote for the party they prefer as a sole government; instead they take into account the use of coalitions, which is itself made necessary by the scattered distribution of other people's votes. In short, every rational voter's decision depends upon how he thinks other men are going to vote. We pointed this out in Chapter 3, and we have just now seen what complications it can lead to when there is a wide diversity of political tastes.

This situation is exactly analogous to the conjectural-variation problem in oligopoly theory or the basic problem of the theory of games. Elections become games with voters seeking optimal strategies by contemplating each other's possible moves. Their predicament is reminiscent of the beauty contest analogy with which Lord Keynes pictured the stock market. The object of this contest was to pick from a group of women the ones whom the most other people picked as most beautiful; therefore, as Keynes said:

It is not a case of choosing which, to the best of one's judgment, are really the prettiest, nor even those which average opinion genuinely thinks the prettiest. We have reached the third degree where we devote our intelligence to anticipating what average opinion expects the average opinion to be.[3]

[3] John Maynard Keynes, *The General Theory of Employment, Interest, and Money* (New York: Harcourt, Brace and Company, 1936), p. 156.

Electoral systems in which similar thinking occurs exhibit conjectural variation *par excellence*. Each man's voting decision depends on what he predicts other men are predicting, and the predictions of those others are based on what they think everyone else is predicting, and so forth, *ad infinitum*.

At first glance, this situation appears both absurd and impossible to analyze. However, it does not preclude rational voting and the actual selection of governments any more than conjectural variation prevents oligopolists from selling products. Hence we need not throw out the assumption that every man views elections purely as a government-selection process. Even with this assumption, our revised multiparty model can produce governments if voters behave as we said they would in the summary of Chapter 3.

Nevertheless, we cannot make very accurate predictions as long as we retain this assumption. This inability stems from the difficulties of solving the conjectural variation problem. So far, no one has produced an acceptable answer to it. As a result, there is no way to predict what voters will do if the decision of each depends upon what he thinks all other voters are going to do, and he knows the others also make decisions this way. The outcome depends upon at what point each man cuts off the process of conjecture and counterconjecture, and, theoretically speaking, that point is not predictable.

In spite of this impasse, we can make some relevant statements about the possible outcomes of conjectural variation among voters. The most important is that voting decisions—like all decisions in real life—are made under the pressure of elapsing time, not in a timeless world of abstraction. Therefore the solution which consists of an infinite regression of calculations is impossible. Each voter has only so much time to make conjectures before the polls close on election day; he is faced with an inexorable force pushing him to make some decision. If he hesitates too long, the election will be over and he will have abstained—which is just as much of a decision as voting. Therefore he cannot escape choosing.

What choices can he make? First, he can remain "up in the air" and be so befuddled by the oligopoly problem that he stays home on election day. He is a baffled, to use the terminology of Chapter 6. Clearly, if everyone is baffled, the electoral system collapses—it fails to choose a government which has the consent of the governed. In this case, our assumption that each man views elections as government selectors leads to the end of democracy.

A second possible outcome is that each voter will decide that he is going to vote no matter what decision he has reached on election day. Having so decided, he cuts off the deliberation process at some point unpredictable by an outside observer.[4] Such truncation is encouraged by the cost of deliberation. Not only is it expensive to obtain information about party policies and what other voters will do, but also the mere act of thinking consumes time that could be devoted to other activities. Therefore men may decide to spend only so many hours weighing alternatives and to abide by whatever decision they favor at the end of this time. If all men are thus quasi-informed passives, democracy will not collapse from lack of voting. But whether the voters themselves will succeed in selecting a government or whether they will merely shift the whole problem into the legislature cannot be predicted.[5]

A third choice open to voters is refusal to contemplate what other voters are likely to do. Instead of treating the election as a government-selection process, voters choosing this method cast their ballots for the parties they would most like to see govern. They leave the actual selection of a government entirely up to the legislature. Thus the difficulty of handling conjectural variation drives citizens into treating elections as expressions of preference instead of government

[4] His actions are unpredictable in the *causal* sense; i.e., the causal steps leading to his decision cannot be stated in advance. However, if we assume that his past behavior is likely to repeat itself, then we can make statistical predictions even though we do not know why he reaches the decisions we predict. Ignorance of how men solve oligopoly problems does not, therefore, always prevent us from accurately forecasting their decisions.

[5] This method of making the voting decision may seem to contradict the procedure described in Chapter 3 because it makes no reference to the voter's party differential. Actually, as we shall see in Chapter 13, a rational voter always cuts off the process of deliberation and abides by whatever decision he has reached at the cutoff point. If at that moment he believes his party differential is not zero, he votes; if he views it as zero, he abstains. Thus the exposition here used in the text merely abbreviates the process described fully in Chapters 3 and 13.

selectors. From the point of view of our model, the complexity of behaving rationally has led them to behave irrationally.[6]

If all voters act this way, the election will express their direct preferences; so the legislature will exhibit exactly the same diversity of political opinions as the electorate. The problem of getting majority support for a government is merely shifted from electorate to legislature. Though it is not solved by this shift, it is removed from the purview of our study.

The foregoing analysis shows that voters faced with the conjectural-variation problem have at least three possible choices of action. However, there is no reason to assume *a priori* that all voters make the same choice. In fact, we believe that even in our model world, some voters make each choice; the result is a mixed electoral system. Some citizens abstain in bewilderment, others take the plunge and vote in spite of uncertainty, and still others shift their view of elections and treat them as expressions of preference. Undoubtedly a government will emerge from this process, but whether it has been rationally selected is impossible to say *a priori*.

Surprisingly enough, the more voters who are irrational from the viewpoint of our model, the easier it is for the others to be rational. Clearly, it is less difficult to predict what parties other men prefer than to predict what parties they will vote for it they are weighing each other's preferences as well as their own. Therefore the more men who merely cast ballots for their favorite parties, the easier it is for other men to predict the probable outcome of the election. And when such predictions are easier, rational men can more easily decide how to cast their own ballots *à la* the procedure described in Chapter 3.

No clear conclusion can be drawn from the preceding analysis, but we can point out a significant tendency inherent in coalition-

---

[6] Expressing their preferences directly is not the only form of irrational behavior open to voters who have decided to ignore the oligopoly problem. However, it is the most nearly rational, because it tells those who select the government—the legislators—what citizens want. Thus it is the nearest thing to direct government selection, but it is much easier for voters to carry out when the number of possible coalitions is large. Since all other forms of irrational behavior are not similarly useful as indirect aids to government selection, we do not discuss them in our analysis.

governed systems. There is a continuous pressure on voters to be irrational, i.e., to cease regarding elections as direct government-selection mechanisms. This pressure is especially strong if the number of likely coalitions is large and their policy variations extensive. Then the complexity of trying to figure out how to bring about the most favorable possible government may drive each voter into merely supporting his favorite party and leaving government selection to the legislature.

When we call such behavior irrational, we do not mean that it is unintelligent or not in the best interests of the voters. In fact, it may be the most rational thing for them to do as individuals. The only sense in which it is irrational is from the point of view of elections as direct government selectors. Obviously, if a large fraction of the electorate regards elections as means of selecting a legislature via preference polls, they are no longer rational devices for the direct selection of governments by the people.

C. THE BASIC PROBLEM: LACK OF CONSENSUS AMONG VOTERS

We have run up against a major result of lack of consensus in the electorate: voters cannot select the government which will govern them. If each votes for the party he prefers, no one party has a majority; hence no party can claim the consent of the governed. On the other hand, if each attempts to take into account the diversity of preferences, and therefore votes only after calculating how others will vote, the process of calculation becomes too complicated for him to handle.

Of course, this dire outcome is not true of every multiparty system. Where likely coalitions are few and their policies are well known, voters can treat elections as government selectors and still arrive at definite voting choices without endless conjecture. However, the paucity of likely coalitions is itself an indication that political preferences are not evenly scattered along the scale. This does not mean that there is no diversity, but that the distribution is characterized by a few large clusters rather than a wide scattering of small ones. Therefore only a few parties exist, and choices are limited.

It is where choices are many that the voters may not be able to choose their own government directly. Instead they will have to pass the buck to a legislature which has a diversified composition reflecting that of the electorate. The legislature then must face an Arrow problem: how to select a coalition government for which majority support can be obtained.

Essentially, this is merely an acute version of the problem that faces every democratic government, no matter how voters are distributed along the political scale. In all systems, the government must forge a single policy set which can somehow receive the sanction of the majority of those it governs. The United States motto, *e pluribus unum*, expresses this problem perfectly. The very nature of action forces the government to take only one stand in each situation; hence its policies must form a single set. Yet in order to govern, it must also receive the consent of a majority of citizens whose preferences are tremendously diversified.

To escape this dilemma, the government has only one resort: it must mix various policies from a variety of viewpoints, espousing many philosophic outlooks imperfectly rather than any one perfectly. This tendency is obvious in a two-party system, because in their attempt to appeal to many viewpoints, both parties adopt platforms which are ambiguous and resemble each other. The voter in such a system is faced with a rather fuzzily differentiated pair of policy sets, one of which he selects as his choice to govern him.

Such ambiguity is equally prevalent in multiparty systems, even though the parties therein tend to have sharply differentiated programs, each closely integrated around one *Weltanschauung*. Voters in multiparty systems are indeed faced with definite and well-integrated policy sets, but none of these sets will in fact govern them. Only coalitions can govern, and ambiguity and compromise are introduced on a secondary level whenever coalitions are formed. Each party's well-integrated program must be coördinated with programs of one or more other parties which are equally well integrated, but around different viewpoints. The result is a program just as non-integrated as either of those in a two-party system.

In fact, the program of a coalition government in a multiparty system is usually less well integrated than that of the government in a two-party system. This follows from the wider distribution of voters in a multiparty system; there is usually no dominant cluster around some one ideological mean. Therefore the coalition must adopt a wider spread of policies to get the support of a majority of voters than must the government in a two-party system. This is true in spite of the fact that each party in the multiparty system ostensibly stands for a much narrower spread of policies than each party in a two-party system.

Appearances are deceiving in democratic politics. The type of political system which seems to offer the voter a more definite choice among policies in fact offers him a less definite one. This system may even make it impossible for him to choose a government at all. Instead it may force him to shift this responsibility onto a legislature over which he has very little control between elections.

This paradox shows that the distribution of voters along the political scale is what determines how well integrated a government's policies are and what viewpoints predominate in them. In the last analysis, neither the number of parties nor their platforms are as important as the shape of this distribution in influencing government ideology and policy in a democracy.

III. PARTY RATIONALITY UNDER COALITIONS

Government by coalitions makes rational behavior difficult for parties as well as for voters, especially when the legislature is left with the task of choosing the government. Of course, any electoral system designed like the one in this chapter delegates some of the power of government selection to the legislators. However, if citizens' opinions are widely diversified, voters may be driven to cast their ballots purely as preference indicators, thereby leaving the whole job of designating a government to the legislature. Since their action tends to reproduce the same diversity within the legislature, the parties therein have a difficult time picking a government which a majority can support.

But we are not studying intralegislature intrigues in our analysis; hence we confine our examination of rational party strategies to those applicable after a coalition has been formed and approved. Even then, each party in the coalition is pressured by opposing forces which involve it in a conflict of desires about what policies to adopt.

The first of these forces is the desire to get along well with the other parties in the coalition. The coalition must make some attempt to solve the problems facing society; hence it must be able to act with at least a minimum degree of efficiency. True, some citizens who oppose its policies would rather see it operate inefficiently so that its policies never have any effect. But if such desires are widespread, democracy cannot produce effective governments: it degenerates into a stalemate which merely preserves the *status quo*. Since social change occurs regardless of who is in office, the gap between society's needs and government's policies eventually becomes so wide that democracy is replaced by a more effective form of government.

However, we are here discussing democracies which are governed, not paralyzed; so we assume that the electorate appreciates efficient action by the coalition.[7] To be efficient, the parties in the coalition must act in unison; hence their desire to coöperate with each other. This desire causes them to adopt similar policies; it sets up a centripetal force like that in most two-party systems. The result is a tendency towards integration of the coalition's policies around a *Weltanschauung* near the center of gravity of whatever spread of voters the coalition appeals to.

The second force can be either centrifugal or centripetal in effect. Each party wants its own policies to dominate the joint policies of the coalition; therefore it tries to win voters away from both its allies in the coalition and its opponents outside. If more voters are massed in the middle of the coalition's policy spread than are near the edges of this spread, the peripheral parties in the coalition are encouraged to move toward the middle party in policy. This convergence makes policy coördination within the coalition easier.

---

[7] In other words, we are ignoring situations like that in France, where the distribution of voters causes virtual governmental paralysis. It is questionable whether such a distribution can lead to any true government at all as long as democracy prevails if we require that a true government be able at least to attempt to solve society's major political and economic problems. This paralysis is the most serious result of lack of consensus in the electorate.

On the other hand, the coalition's peripheral parties may feel they can win more votes by moving away from the center than by moving toward it. This is true whenever the parties on either side of the coalition have more supporters than the middle party in the coalition. In this case, the desire for dominance within the coalition leads to policy divergence among the coalition's members; consequently coördination becomes more difficult.

The third force influencing parties in coalitions is centrifugal. It stems from the desire of all the parties in the coalition to maximize the chances that the whole coalition will be reëlected.[8] Therefore they wish the net impact of all of them together to be as widespread as possible; i.e., they want to appeal to as wide a range of voters on the scale as they can. They can best accomplish this by deliberately diverging from each other ideologically, thereby drawing more voters on each margin into supporting one of the parties in the coalition. However, this causes disintegration and makes coördination difficult.

All of these forces can be illustrated in Figure 8. Let us assume that a coalition government is formed of parties B, C, and D. It is logical to believe that the coalition can govern more efficiently if its members are in closer agreement about policy. Hence if these parties believe they are going to be working together for a long time, they might be encouraged to converge doctrinally towards the central position of C. They might even unify to form a single party positioned at C. However, this would be foolish politically, since it would weaken their coalition's vote-getting power.

Voter R supports party B because it is nearest him, and he believes that his vote helps keep the coalition from moving too far rightward by strengthening the power of B therein. But if B moves over to C, voter R may shift his support to A, which is closer to him than C. Therefore, in order to gain votes for the coalition, parties B and D should diverge from the central location of C. The farther from C

---

[8] This force does not always operate, because the parties in a coalition may not wish to see it reconstituted in its present form. For example, if a party feels it might win enough support to govern alone, its desire to take votes away from its present allies obliterates any tendency for it to aid the coalition as a whole. However, it is sometimes true that the members of a coalition are unlikely to attain office again except as part of that same coalition. In such cases, each party is motivated to seek reëlection for the whole coalition.

they get, the more votes they can steal from A and E; but also (1) they lose strength within the coalition to C, and (2) their greater spread makes it harder for all three parties to coöperate with each other.[9] What is the rational course for them to follow if they wish to maximize their chances for election?

Clearly, *election* in a coalition-governed system means something different from the unqualified victory it denotes in a two-party system. No one party can enjoy the prestige, income, and power that motivate politicians in our model. In fact, only certain individuals in each of the victorious parties are able to win in this sense, and their identity cannot always be predicted in advance. Yet the more votes a party wins, the more chance it has to enter a coalition, the more power it receives if it does enter one, and the more individuals in it hold office in the coalition government. Hence vote-maximizing is still the basic motive underlying the behavior of parties as corporate groups and of individuals within them.[10]

For this reason we conclude that each party in a coalition does whatever maximizes its own votes rather than what benefits the operation of the coalition *per se*. Thus in Figure 8, parties B and D might converge on C in order to take votes away from it, since they can gain more votes by moving into the densely populated center than they lose toward the extremes. However, the closer together are the three parties in the coalition, the less will be the total of their combined vote and the more likely is it that the coalition as a whole will be defeated by an extremist party. A tension is thus set up between the desire of each party to make sure the coalition gets elected on the one hand, and to raise the extent of its influence within the coalition on the other. No wonder politics is considered by many to be an art instead of a science!

[9] This argument was suggested by an example from politics in the Netherlands related by Hendrik S. Houthakker.

[10] Some parties in history have operated on a less cautious strategy and sought power on an all-or-nothing basis. Instead of accepting whatever gains they might consolidate immediately by entering coalitions, they struck boldly for complete power and disregarded petty vote-maximizing strategies. However, almost all such parties were not truly democratic, for as soon as they came into office they violated the constitutional rules set forth in Chapter 1. Therefore we feel justified in excluding them from our model.

IV. CONFLICTS BETWEEN PARTY RATIONALITY AND INDIVIDUAL RATIONALITY

In the last chapter we saw that parties in a two-party system try to be ambiguous about their policies because they want to appeal directly to a majority of voters, even though no one viewpoint is held by a majority. In contrast, parties in a multiparty system try to be relatively unequivocal about their policies, since they appeal directly only to a narrow range of voters.

However, the latter parties are extremely ambiguous about what compromises they are likely to make if they enter into coalitions with other parties. They do not wish to alienate voters clustered around their own location by admitting they will support some policie[s] from other parts of the scale if elected. Therefore each party stress[es] its own party line and plays down the compromises it must make [in] order to get into a coalition—which is the only way it can have [a] part in the government at all.

Thus clarity on one level of multiparty systems is counterbal[anced] by ambiguity on another level; whereas two-party systems a[re am]biguous throughout because they contain only one level. [In both] cases, the government itself is formed on the ambiguo[us level.] Government's real policy is also formed there, as we poin[ted out in] the previous sections of this chapter.

This conclusion raises the question of whether rational political behavior is possible for individual citizens in a democracy. Paradoxically, it seems to be rational for parties to encourage irrationality in voters. If parties are always deliberately ambiguous, how can citizens discover in them the reliability which is necessary for rational voting?

These questions are essentially a restatement of the central problem of political theory: how can social goals be developed from differing individual values?[11] We here encounter the *e pluribus unum*

---

[11] For a thorough discussion of this problem—the results of which we have mentioned elsewhere in this study—see Kenneth J. Arrow, *Social Choice and Individual Values* (New York: John Wiley & Sons, Inc., 1951).

dilemma mentioned earlier. Does it really preclude rationality in politics?

Individual rationality means pursuit of one's own goals in the most efficient manner. But men live in society and in a world of scarce resources; so when each pursues his own goals, his actions affect other men. Furthermore, these other men never have precisely the same goals that he has. Therefore, conflicts between men inevitably arise.

Politics is the system of settling these conflicts so that each individual may achieve some of his goals. All men cannot achieve all their goals simultaneously, because when one man does so, his actions prevent others from doing so; this is what *conflict* means. Thus the very nature of society places limits on individual rationality—not all individuals can achieve pure rationality at once.

In a democracy, political power is theoretically the same for all men; i.e., each supposedly has the same opportunity to achieve his goals as does every other. Thus the irrationality inevitable in any society—i.e., the inability to achieve goals perfectly—is shared by all men: no one can achieve all his goals. In short, every citizen of a democracy is necessarily somewhat irrational in the pure sense.[12]

For this reason, it should not surprise us that there is a tension between individual rationality and party rationality. Each party attempts to derive a set of social goals from the values of the individuals in society. To any individual, the party's policies represent a compromise, since the party must please many other individuals besides him. Ambiguity is a means of disguising this fact. It is a device for producing harmony where none really exists. Yet such harmony must be produced, or society dissolves into myriads of individuals in open conflict.

But even when conflict is veiled, men cannot achieve complete political rationality. Irrational elements are inevitable in any society as long as individuals have different goals. Since differences in goals are related to the very concept of individuality, we believe that irrationality can never be eliminated from society. Yet men can still

[12] This generalization does not hold for those citizens who have no selfish tendencies and whose goal structure happens to coincide exactly with the set of compromises a democracy arrives at. However, we assume very few citizens fall into this category.

act rationally in the sense we have been using: they can achieve as many of their goals as is possible, given the nature of society.

The relation their achievement will bear to pure rationality depends upon how different their goals are to begin with. The greater is the degree of consensus, the easier it is for individuals to act rationally, and the more effective such action is. Therefore the possibility of rationality depends upon the distribution of voters along the political scale. If it is unimodal and has a low variance, rationality is both easy and effective.

However, if voters are evenly distributed or massed at opposite poles, conflict tends to predominate over coöperative achievement, and society loses its vital core of harmony. In such a situation, democracy cannot produce effective government, because the premise of equal power for all leads to a cancellation of policies rather than a mutual reinforcement of them. Therefore individual rationality in politics collapses. It no longer leads to satisfactory settlements of social conflict.

Clearly, democracy presupposes consensus about goals—not perfect agreement, but something far removed from perfect disagreement. If we assume sufficient consensus exists, then rational political action is possible for individual citizens. None will ever achieve pure rationality, but by acting as efficiently as he can, each will reach more of his goals than he can in any other way.

V. SUMMARY

In some political systems, only rarely does any one party receive over half the votes cast. Hence coalitions are formed so government may still be by consent of the governed, i.e., by consent of a majority of those voting. To study such systems, we use a model in which voters elect a legislature by proportional representation and the legislature then selects a government by majority vote.

Under these conditions, each voter's ballot does not support the policies of any one party. Instead it supports the whole coalition that party joins. Thus the meaning of a vote for any party depends upon what coalitions it is likely to enter, which in turn depends upon how other voters will vote.

Consequently, each voter can make his own voting decision only after estimating what decisions others will make, so a problem of conjectural variation arises to which no solution has been found. Eventually each voter either abstains, votes after cutting off his deliberation at some unpredictable point, or decides it is easier just to vote for his favorite party. Thus some voters may be driven by the difficulty of rationally selecting a government to treat elections as expressions of preference, which is irrational in our model.

Underlying this tendency is the difficulty of getting a majority of voters to support any single set of government policies. To encompass the diversity of views in this majority, the government must adopt a nonintegrated set of policies covering a wide range on the political scale.

This is true even in multiparty systems, where parties ostensibly differentiate their ideologies sharply. But when coalitions are formed, the parties in them adopt the same widespread, nonintegrated type of program that characterizes each party in a two-party system. Thus the distribution of voters on the scale and the necessity of getting a majority of them behind one government ultimately determine government policies.

Parties in coalitions are pressured by three forces: (1) the desire to make their policies similar to facilitate efficient action, (2) the desire to make their policies different to increase the spread of voters supporting the coalition, and (3) the desire of each to do one or the other of the above to increase its weight in the coalition. During elections, all parties also try to be as ambiguous as possible about how they will compromise if they enter various coalitions. This makes individual rationality difficult, but if there is sufficient consensus in the electorate, democracy can function efficiently even though society can never achieve pure rationality.

10

Government Vote-Maximizing and Individual Marginal Equilibrium

---

Introduction

BECAUSE government behavior follows a rule different from that which regulates the actions of private firms or individuals, government's methods of allocating its resources are not the same as those employed in the private sector. Yet government allocation has a tremendous impact upon the private sector—even upon the allocation methods which private agents use.

In this chapter we show how government's use of the vote-maximizing principle affects (1) the profit-maximizing and utility-maximizing processes which traditional economic theory ascribes to private economic agents and (2) the probability that a perfectly competitive economy will reach a Paretian optimum position.

Objectives

In this chapter we attempt to prove the following propositions:

1. Since there are some collective goods and nonmarket interdependencies in every society, even a perfectly competitive economy cannot achieve a Paretian optimum without government action.
2. Although a democratic government undertakes actions which yield future utility pay-offs, it has no discount rate of its own because it seeks to maximize only present votes.
3. Government often deliberately avoids moving society to a Paretian optimum by forsaking actions which make some persons better off and none worse off.
4. Democratic societies never reach Paretian optimum positions unless by accident, even if the private sector embodies perfect competition.
5. Very few citizens in a democracy attain marginal equilibrium in their dealings with the government.
6. Even if a democratic government were technically able to allocate its costs according to the benefit principle, it would not do so.
7. Democratic governments generally act in favor of low-income citizens and against high-income citizens, unless this tendency is offset by the political effects of uncertainty.
8. The more effective democracy is economically, the greater is the degree of government intervention in the free market.

I. RESOURCE ALLOCATION IN A FREE MARKET

A. PLANNING IN THE PRIVATE SECTOR

Rational resource allocators in the private sector follow the general rule of applying inputs to those activities with the highest net marginal rates of return, thereby maximizing total net returns. Although this rule is put into action by individual firms and consumers, each looking at only a narrow range of possible resource uses, it is made true for the market as a whole by competition among these individuals.

However, returns are not always immediate, i.e., within the present action period. Hence a problem of allocation between present-paying and future-paying investments must be solved as well as one of allocation among different present uses. This means that the quantity to be maximized, whether utility, profits, or welfare, can no longer be viewed as a simple present total. Instead it is seen as a stream of many incomes, each associated with a different time period, beginning with the present and stretching into the future.

All future incomes are subject to discounting when compared to present ones, and the rate of discount is compounded as the income's accrual period becomes farther away from the present. This allows present and future net pay-offs to be compared in homogeneous units. The rational planner allocates his current resources to those uses whose net pay-offs have the highest present values. By so doing he obtains the largest possible quantity of present value units—whether utility, profits, or welfare. Therefore, this is the best method of allocating resources for any private planning agency.

There are three things especially to be noticed about this familiar planning procedure. First, it requires extremely accurate and detailed information about present and future costs and pay-offs for all relevant resource uses. In other words, it implies that the particular part of economy concerned is a minor version of the certain world we have discussed before. Whenever uncertainty is present, planning will only roughly approximate the process described, chiefly because fewer resource uses will be considered than the large number theoretically possible.

Second, the planning agent deals in terms of some homogeneous quantity, such as utility, profits, or welfare. This is more a manner of speaking than a description of what actually happens, but it is a necessary manner of speaking. Any possible act is an alternative to every other possible act that makes use of the same scarce resources as the first. Therefore, because all acts use time, they can all be viewed as alternatives to each other. Naturally, every planning unit must choose to carry out some acts and to reject their alternatives, since it has limited resources.

To make this choice, it must somehow compare alternatives. Such comparison can be logically structured as the appraisal of the cost of and return from each action in terms of some common denominator. The planning agent chooses that combination of actions which (1) does not exceed the resources at its command and (2) results in the largest net income in units of the common denominator. This is *rational* planning, whether the planner be a housewife, a monk striving for a spiritual life, a government, or a profit-seeking entrepreneur. Thus the concept of some homogeneous measuring unit is necessarily implied by rational planning in a world of scarce resources.

Third, the fact that future pay-offs are discounted in rational planning does not explain what causes the discount rate to be what it is. In our model, there are three reasons why future income is discounted when compared with present income:

1. The course of future events is less certain than that of present events; therefore an allowance for risk must be added to future income.[1]
2. People prefer present enjoyment to prospects for future enjoyment; therefore they must be induced to abstain from the former by a bonus added to the latter.
3. If the current profit rate is positive, a continuous reinvestment of present returns will cause a build-up of capital; therefore a present investment that pays off only once in the distant future must do so at a higher rate than those which pay off sooner. Thus it can compensate for the capital build-up possible with the latter.

The last reason can be clarified by an example. If the present profit rate is 10 percent per annum, $100 can be parlayed into $121 at the end of two years. Consequently, an investment which absorbs $100 now but does not pay off until two years from now must pay at 21 percent to provide a return equal to annual reinvestment of current profits. Thus every return accruing two years from now must be discounted before comparison with returns accruing in one year, or immediately.

---

[1] This is only one of several possible ways to treat risk in economic planning. We use it here because it fits into our model more easily than its alternatives.

These three causal factors are the bases for the liquidity preference, time preference, and marginal productivity theories of interest respectively. In our model, the discount rate consists of the sum of (a) the risk discount, which is a specific allowance for each particular investment's riskiness, and (b) the time preference rate or the rate necessary to compensate for reinvestment at the current profit rate.[2] This rule establishes the discount rate for any given planning agent.

The existence of a positive discount rate means that every planning agent in the economy is *biased* in favor of action which pays off in the short run and against action which pays off in the long run. Because we accept the causes of the discount rate as real factors, we consider this a rational bias. Therefore all politicians will be shortsighted in their planning no matter how intelligent and disinterested they are, since everyone is short-sighted to some extent and would be considered irrational if he were not.

Every planning agent in the private sector uses a discount rate appropriate to its own circumstances, and there is no *a priori* reason for these rates to be the same. Thus at first glance it appears that profit rates will not be equalized throughout the economy. In some parts of the economy, it seems, investments paying 20 percent at the end of two years will be made, and in others investments paying 40 percent will be rejected.

However, a closer look reveals that the mobility of capital tends to make profit rates the same everywhere, allowing slight variations for risk. For example, if A owns an investment opportunity with a future pay-off which he discounts to below the current interest rate, he can sell it to B, whose risk discount is lower, and B will undertake it. If B has no funds, he may borrow from C at the current interest rate, buy the opportunity from A, and get a large enough return to pay off C and still have a profit left. Such capital movements continue until the subjective discounted marginal profit rate is the same on all margins, including those involving future pay-offs. At this

[2] In competitive equilibrium, these two alternative rates are equal to each other at the margin; hence we need not specify which of the two should be used in computing the discount rate. It should also be noted that investments with immediate returns are discounted for risk only.

point, no reallocation of resources among present uses, or from present-paying to future-paying uses, or vice versa, can make anyone better off.

Thus capital flows rationalize the market, in the sense that they allow any risky investment to be made if it pays off enough to survive any investor's discount rate, even if that investor has no direct interest in the particular activity he finances; e.g., even if a butcher's savings finance a faraway gas station. This process is extremely important because it insures that all the highest-paying investments are made and the lowest-paying ones are not made—i.e., it makes resource allocation rational.[3]

The mechanism that effects this rationality is a market in which each individual can buy or sell personal prerogatives. For example, a man who owns a strategic corner lot can either build on it himself, sell it, or rent it to someone who can make more profits from it than he can. Workers can sell their personal time and labor, and consumers can sell the use of their savings to banks. In fact, anybody can sell anything he has except himself as a person.

These sales continue until no sale can make both buyer and seller better off. At this point, if we assume the usual competitive conditions, the market has reached a Paretian optimum; i.e., no transactions between private parties can make someone better off without harming someone else. Attainment of such a position is possible only because all economic agents are free to sell their prerogatives if they wish and, conversely, to buy those of others if they so desire and can afford it.

Our stress on this exchangeability stems from the fact that in politics a man cannot sell his vote or buy votes from others. This prohibition differentiates government planning from private planning in a significant fashion, as we shall see.[4]

[3] Of course, such rationality is guaranteed only if capital is perfectly mobile, which is never actually the case. However, we will not discuss this qualification in detail because we do not wish to become entangled in capital or monopoly theory here. Our only purpose is to establish that, at least in theory, a relative mobility of resources based upon marketability of prerogatives can lead to efficient allocation.

[4] In our discussion of the private sector, we have spoken of "economic activity" in a general sense that refers to both production and consumption, since both pro-

B. OBSTACLES TO THE ATTAINMENT OF A PARETIAN OPTIMUM BY A FREE MARKET

The object of the preceding analysis is to show how a perfectly competitive economy automatically moves toward a Paretian optimum. However, we have ignored two important obstacles to the attainment of such an optimum: collective goods and nonmarket interdependencies.[5]

A collective good is one which provides indivisible benefits; i.e., as soon as it exists, everyone is able to benefit from it regardless of whether he himself has paid for it and regardless of how many others are also benefiting from it.[6] For example, provision of national defense is a boon to every citizen; even if one citizen paid for it solely out of his own pocket, all the others would gain from it. Where citizens are numerous, each man finds it advantageous to refuse to pay for such indivisible benefits. Instead he assumes that other men will bear the costs and he will still benefit. But in a free market, everyone makes the same assumption, so no one bears any of the costs and none of the benefits are forthcoming.

This situation means that voluntary action cannot produce a Paretian optimum in a large society when collective goods exist.

---

ducers and consumers (theoretically) make rational plans in the manner set forth. Government also plays these two roles, and in each it produces utility because its actions add to citizens' utility incomes. In analyzing the private sector, economists usually assume that profit-making firms engaged in production are likely to plan their activities more precisely than consumers. However, in our model world we need make no such distinction—nor do we in reference to governments, which we treat as being fully rational in all their economic (and other) roles.

[5] We are ignoring many other such obstacles besides the two mentioned, but only these two are directly relevant to the analysis in this chapter.

[6] Not all collective goods can benefit every member of society; they may be able to benefit only a certain subset of members who have access to them. For example, Central Park in New York City does not provide any direct benefit to a resident of South Dakota who never leaves home. Therefore when we refer to "everyone" in the subsequent argument, we mean everyone who has access to the collective good in question. Furthermore, there may be some limit to the number of citizens who can enjoy a collective good at once; e.g., the more people who occupy Central Park at the same time, the less enjoyment each gets—at least after some finite point. Where such a limit exists, the good is not perfectly collective; it also contains some elements of private goodness. For a discussion of this point, see Paul A. Samuelson, "Diagrammatic Exposition of a Theory of Public Expenditure," *Review of Economics and Statistics*, XXXVII (November, 1955), 356.

According to traditional general equilibrium theory, each individual shifts his resources from one margin to another until the rates of return on all margins are identical. This maximizes his total utility.

In the diagram, all margins of activity are categorized into the groups that give rise to rates of return commonly utilized in economic analysis. Each arrow depicts a direction in which resources can be allocated, and has a marginal rate of return corresponding to it.

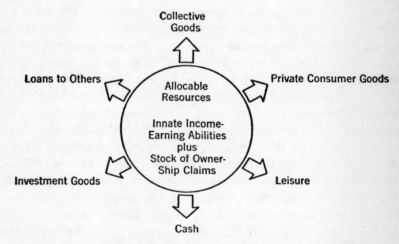

Figure 11. Diagrammatic representation of individual marginal equilibrium

The relevant markets and rates of return are as follows:
1. Goverment action in any or all markets—marginal return from government action.
2. Consumer products market—marginal return from consumption.
3. Labor market—marginal disutility of labor.
4. Hoards—marginal liquidity preference.
5. Capital goods market—marginal efficiency of capital.
6. Money market—interest rate.

The diagram shows the indispensable role of government in aiding individuals to achieve marginal equilibrium, and, therefore, maximize total utility. This role is usually ignored in general equilibrium theory, which often considers only rates 2 to 6. The implications of its inclusion are discussed in the text.

Everyone would be better off if some central agency coerced each individual to bear his share of the cost of such goods, since his share of the benefits (we assume for the moment) is larger than the cost he would pay. If no such agency exists, then society arrives at a position where transactions between private parties would make at least some people better off and none worse off, but these transactions do not occur. Clearly this is a suboptimal position.

As we pointed out in Chapter 1, this state of affairs led Paul Samuelson to conclude that one of the proper roles of government in the economy is to provide collective goods and pay for them by coercing its citizens to give up resources.[7] Since such coercion makes each citizen better off than he would be in a free market, and since each citizen is rational, everyone will agree to be coerced. Hence government action embodies voluntary coercion which allows society to reach a Paretian optimum even though collective goods exist.

However, as we shall see later, it is sometimes irrational for the government to move the economy into a Paretian optimum position. In analyzing such cases, it is important not to blame the failure to reach a Paretian optimum solely upon the government. True, government's nature prevents it from moving society to an optimum position, but the nature of the collective goods involved prevents the free market from doing any better. Responsibility for the ensuing suboptimal position is therefore shared by both factors.

The second obstacle to attainment of a Paretian optimum in a perfectly competitive market has been described by Tibor Scitovsky as follows:

Equilibrium in a perfectly competitive economy is a situation of Paretian optimum, except when there is interdependence among the members of the economy that is direct, in the sense that it does not operate through the market mechanism. In general equilibrium theory, then, direct interdependence is the villain of the piece and the cause for conflict between private profit and social benefit.[8]

[7] Paul A. Samuelson, "The Pure Theory of Public Expenditures," *Review of Economics and Statistics*, XXXVI (November, 1954), 387–389.

[8] Tibor Scitovsky, "Two Concepts of External Economies," *Journal of Political Economy*, LXII (April, 1954), 143–151. Professor Scitovsky is not unaware of the impact of collective goods upon a Paretian optimum, but he assumes complete divisibility in his discussion, thus eliminating all effects of indivisible benefits.

As Professor Scitovsky and other theorists have pointed out, non-market interdependence sets up utility flows which do not affect market prices. When such flows exist, the free market—which allocates resources strictly according to the signals formed by prices—may fail to carry out certain rearrangements of resources which would improve the lot of some citizens at no others' expense. Thus the market fails to reach a Paretian optimum.[9]

In some cases, government action may counteract the effects of nonmarket interdependence and bring about certain unequivocally good reallocations that a free market would not produce.[10] For example, if A owns a glue factory located in a residential neighborhood, the government can levy taxes on the surrounding residents and use the resulting funds to bribe A to move into an industrial area. If the value of each piece of property in the residential neighborhood consequently rises, then everyone is better off, even though coercion was needed to produce the change.

This change would not occur in a free market for two reasons. First, no one neighbor could afford to bribe A, since his own gain from A's departure would be smaller than the bribe necessary. Second, assuming the neighborhood is a large one, no voluntary association of neighbors could be formed to bribe A because its members could not force each other to pay. As a rational man, each is motivated to let the others bear the cost of the bribe while he shares in the benefits; hence no costs are borne and no benefits accrue. In other words, the desire of each individual to get a large net benefit rather than a small one prevents any individuals from getting any benefit at all. What each needs is a guarantee that all the others

[9] This problem is discussed at length in William J. Baumol, *Welfare Economics and the Theory of the State* (London: Longmans, Green and Co., 1952). Baumol also analyzes the relation of indivisible benefits to government activity and reaches the same conclusion concerning voluntary coercion that we mentioned earlier. See especially pp. 90–94 and 140–142.

[10] An unequivocally good act is one which makes at least one person better off without making anyone worse off. Such acts are not the only ones society may judge to be good. In fact, some actions which are not unequivocally good may be judged superior to those that are. However, only unequivocally good acts can be deemed good on economic grounds alone; all other good actions require ethical justification.

will pay their shares if he pays his but no one will pay if he does not. Government coercion provides that guarantee.

When the government can carry out unequivocally good acts which a free market would leave undone, the social benefits from government action are obvious. In fact, whenever collective goods and certain nonmarket interdependencies exist, a Paretian optimum can be reached only if government intervenes in the free market. However, a government intervention under such conditions does not always produce a Paretian optimum. Furthermore, government intervention in our model is not limited to instances in which it performs unequivocally good actions that the free market would not perform. The government may also intervene in ways which are not unequivocally good—in fact, its acts can conceivably prevent the attainment of a Paretian optimum which the free market (with some government help) might otherwise reach. We will encounter all of these types of government action as our analysis proceeds.

II. GOVERNMENT PLANNING AND INDIVIDUAL MARGINAL EQUILIBRIUM

A. THE RELATION BETWEEN GOVERNMENT AND DISCOUNTING

Unlike private planning agents, governing parties are never interested *per se* in future returns from action; they are always concerned only about the next election and the votes they receive therein. Hence no government aims at maximizing a stream of incomes composed of separate incomes for each of many periods. Rather it always organizes its actions so as to focus on a single quantity: its vote margin over the opposition in the test at the end of the present election period.[11]

[11] Some political parties (especially newly founded ones) are more interested in future elections than in present ones because their chances of gaining office are greater in the future. However, a governing party has already gained office; hence its primary concern is retaining its position, i.e., winning the next election. This conclusion also applies to parties in coalition-governed systems. The only exception occurs when the government feels defeat in the next election is preferable to abandoning some principle. Under our hypothesis, governing parties view principles purely as expedients; hence this situation can come up only if the

Such preoccupation with the present does not mean that the government ignores all activity which comes to fruition after the next election. On the contrary, governments are vitally concerned with the effects their actions have upon the future utility incomes of voters, since voters often decide how to vote on the basis of the prospects for such future income. But a government cannot trade present votes for future votes the way a voter can trade present income for future income. Therefore government has no discount rate of its own to apply to its own income—an income measured in votes. Discounting enters government planning only indirectly because the government, in order to know how to please its supporters, must calculate at what rates they discount their future utility incomes.

As we have already mentioned, in a competitive equilibrium, every voter discounts his future income at the same rate as every other voter because the market tends to equalize marginal rates of return both interspatially and intertemporally. Consequently, a dollar invested at any place or with a pay-off accruing at any moment brings precisely the same net effective return as a dollar invested at any other margin. In this situation of marginal equilibrium, no individual can gain by reallocating his own resources, and no two individuals can gain by trading with each other. A Paretian optimum is reached, as mentioned earlier.

In such an equilibrium, the marginal returns which are equalized are money returns, or utility returns associated with the allocation of money. Thus the structure underlying the equilibrium is the distribution of money income. Once this is given, the market allows each individual to allocate his income so that his dollar-spending yields equal utility returns on all margins.

Since government's actions usually involve the collection and allocation of large amounts of money, these actions are clearly of great importance in the attainment of any equilibrium such as that de-

party in power feels that some principle will be very valuable in winning elections subsequent to the impending one, even though it causes defeat in the latter. We believe that this situation is rare in politics; therefore we retain the view that only the next election matters to the incumbents. We are indebted to Professor Kenneth Arrow for pointing out this possibility.

scribed. But the government's handling of money is based on signals it receives from citizens as owners of votes, not as receivers of money incomes. This is true because the government is interested primarily in a nondollar currency—votes—which is distributed quite differently from the way money income is distributed.

As we saw in Chapter 4, government seeks to equate vote pay-offs on all margins of behavior, not dollar or utility pay-offs. By means of economic and other actions, it tries to manipulate both present and future utility pay-offs to voters in a way that will win their votes. Furthermore, in pursuing this vote-seeking course, it enjoys an asymmetry of power in its relations with money-seekers and utility-seekers. Government can impose its decisions about manipulating money and utility upon these agents by force; whereas they cannot do the reverse. Therefore if conflicts arise between government's quest for marginal vote pay-off equilibrium and private agents' quest for marginal utility pay-off equilibrium, the former always takes precedence over the latter.

Furthermore, this asymmetry of power cannot be directly counterbalanced by economic pressure from money-owners. The government can operate freely in the currency which interests money-seekers, but money-seekers cannot operate freely in the currency which interests the government.[12] This is a result of a legal prohibition against any exchange of ownership rights between private holders of the two currencies. No citizen is allowed to trade his political privileges for increased economic rights, or vice versa; i.e., no one can legally buy or sell votes for money. This prohibition holds no matter how in-

[12] By *money-seekers* we mean both seekers after money (firms) and seekers after utility (individuals). Ultimately, all men seek utility rather than money or votes, but this is a mere tautology, since we defined utility as a common denominator of what men seek. The basic relationship in the private market is that men use money to acquire goods which give them utility incomes. Therefore the distribution of money income determines the relative power of command over those resources which yield utility income. It does not determine the distribution of utility income; to assume so would be to make interpersonal comparisons of cardinal utility by equating units of money with units of utility. Nevertheless, for purposes of our discussion here, we will assume that the distribution of money income is the key factor in shaping the actions of men in their pursuit of utility income. This fact plus the need for verbal simplicity justify, we feel, our treating both utility and money under the heading of *money*.

different a citizen who needs money urgently feels about party policy, or, conversely, how indifferent a citizen who desperately wants political influence feels about money.

B. HOW GOVERNMENT ACTS MAY PREVENT A PARETIAN OPTIMUM IN A CERTAIN WORLD

From the foregoing analysis, it is clear that whether or not society ever reaches a Paretian optimum is entirely dependent upon government action. In the first place, even a perfectly competitive market cannot reach an optimum position without government intervention if collective goods or certain nonmarket interdependencies exist. Since both exist in any organized society, government can always prevent a Paretian optimum by failing to take the necessary optimum-furthering actions (i.e., the unequivocally good acts a free market would not undertake by itself). We call this failure *negative blocking*.

Second, even if government carries out the required optimum-furthering actions connected with collective goods and nonmarket interdependencies, it may still block attainment of an optimal position by carrying out some other optimum-distorting action. Its ability to do so is inherent in the powers of government described above. Such prevention we call *positive blocking*. It consists mainly of deliberate redistributions of income, which we discuss later in the chapter. For the moment, let us focus our attention upon whether or not government is likely to do any negative blocking.

At first glance, we would expect a rational government never to indulge in negative blocking. Since any optimum-furthering acts government performs make everyone better off (or some better off and none worse off), it hardly seems likely that government could win votes by failing to carry out such acts.

However, this conclusion is false. There are in fact several reasons why a democratic government might engage in negative blocking. The first is the technical impossibility of handling indivisible goods in such a way as to reach an optimal position. As we shall see later in this chapter, the very nature of collective goods prevents the government from allocating their costs and benefits so that no re-shuffling could make anyone better off without harming someone else.

True, our later analysis shows that government could move society to a Paretian optimum if it could infallibly judge every individual's income-earning potential, measure his benefits and costs cheaply, directly, and without error, and pass individually discriminatory laws. Under these conditions, it could cover its costs by making with each person an individual bargain that left him in marginal equilibrium in his dealings with government. But we may regard this outcome as a practical impossibility for two reasons: (1) the conditions it presupposes go beyond even the assumption of perfect knowledge in traditional theory, since government must be able to read minds infallibly, and (2) though these conditions are necessary for achievement of an optimal position when collective goods exist, they are not sufficient, since government might engage in negative blocking even if they exist.

Therefore the existence of collective goods or nonmarket interdependencies practically precludes achievement of a Paretian optimum even in the certain world of traditional economic theory. However, in order to demonstrate the other factors which might prevent society from reaching such an optimum, let us momentarily assume that all the technical obstacles to it can be overcome. This makes attainment of an optimum strictly a political problem.

The political parties in our model are not interested *per se* in making society's allocation of resources efficient; each seeks only to get elected by maximizing the number of votes it receives. Therefore even if the government has the ability to move society to a Paretian optimum, it will do so only if forced to by competition from other parties. Otherwise it is indifferent about whether society is at an optimal position; hence such positions will be attained only by accident—a highly improbable occurrence.

Thus the crucial issue is whether interparty competition always forces the government to move society to a Paretian optimum. If the preferences of individual citizens are sufficiently diverse, the answer is no. To prove this assertion, we construct an example based upon the following assumptions:

1. A given society is in position X at period T_1.
2. Position X is a suboptimal position, because some persons would gain and none would lose by a perfectly feasible move to position X', which is an optimum.
3. Because the move from X to X' involves collective goods, only government can bring it about.
4. There are two parties in this society: party A is now in office and party B is the opposition.
5. Party A must always commit itself on any issue before party B.
6. In the election at the end of T_1, both parties are called upon to reveal their proposals for society's position in T_2, and they are judged by voters solely on the basis of these proposals (i.e., not on their past records as described in Chapter 3).

Under these conditions, it is clear that party A cannot support position X if it wishes to be reëlected. If it does, party B will support position X', and all voters will either abstain because they are indifferent between X and X' or vote for B because they are better off at X'. Since no one prefers X to X', party A will get no votes. Let us assume that party A supports X' in order to forestall this catastrophe. What will party B do?

Its strategy depends upon the degree of consensus among the citizenry. For instance, assume that a majority of citizens prefer position Z to either X or X', though a move from X to Z is harmful to a minority. If party B supports Z, then it can defeat party A, even if Z itself is a suboptimal position. In this case, competition for votes does not move society into an optimal position.

However, this argument implies that party B has more information than party A. If party A also knows that a majority prefer Z to X', it will certainly not support X'. Furthermore, if Z is a suboptimal position, party A will not support Z either, since then party B could support the optimal position dominating Z and win the election.[13] To prevent this outcome, party A supports that dominant position, which we call Z'. Thus it appears that competition forces the party which commits itself first to support a position that is both optimal and undominated by any other positions—a position the opposition obviously cannot better.

But such undominated optima do not always exist. It is true that every suboptimal position is dominated by some optimal one that can be reached from the former by an unequivocally good move, assuming all such moves are feasible. But it is possible that every optimum is itself dominated by some other position, which may or may not be an optimum. This outcome is a result of extremely disparate preferences among voters; it is a form of Arrow problem.

In fact, since our example depicts what is essentially a one-issue election, we can illustrate it by employing the same scheme of preference rankings that we used in Chapter 4. Assume that there are three citizens in society—P, Q, and R—and three suboptimal positions—X, Y, and Z—each of which is dominated by a corresponding optimum—X', Y', and Z'. Every citizen prefers each optimum to its corresponding suboptimal position, but they do not rank the optima in the same way. Their preferences are as follows:

	Citizens		
Ranking:	P	Q	R
First	X'	Y'	Z'
Second	X	Y	Z
Third	Y'	Z'	X'
Fourth	Y	Z	X
Fifth	Z'	X'	Y'
Sixth	Z	X	Y

In this case, every optimum is dominated by a suboptimal position: X' by Z, Z' by Y, and Y' by X. Therefore even in a world of

[13] One position *dominates* another if (1) a majority of citizens are better off in the first and realize it, (2) that majority have the power to move society from the first to the second, and (3) the process of moving is both technically possible and not a cause of enough disutility to the majority favoring it to offset their benefits.

perfect certainty, with no technical obstacles to achieving a Paretian optimum, a two-party democracy would not necessarily arrive at one. No matter what stand the incumbents took, the opposition could defeat them by taking a suboptimal stand, because a majority would prefer the latter to the former.

Furthermore, similar preference structures are likely to exist in any society which has a per capita income above the subsistence level, i.e., in which nearly everyone produces an output in excess of what is necessary to keep him alive. In such societies, there is always some redistribution of income which would benefit a majority at the expense of a minority. Of course, not every such redistribution is acceptable even to the majority who benefit by it, because it may have long-range or nonmarket repercussions which offset their gains. Nevertheless, it still seems likely that some acceptable reallocation of government taxes and benefits would make a majority better off at the expense of some minority, no matter what tax-benefit structure is extant.

What conclusion can we draw from this reasoning about whether society will always reach a Paretian optimum? The answer depends upon the validity of our assumption that the incumbents must take a stand before the opposition has done so. If it is true, the opposition can defeat the incumbents with either an optimal or a suboptimal position; hence whether society arrives at a Paretian optimum is largely a matter of chance. And because the total range of possible social states includes many more suboptimal than optimal positions, the odds are that society will not attain a Paretian optimum in a two-party system.

But if all the parties in a political system reveal their policy sets (each of which is equivalent to a social position) simultaneously, then each party will always choose an optimum to espouse. By doing so, it minimizes the number of other positions that can dominate its choice; therefore it increases its chances for victory. For instance, in the example we have given, if party A chooses suboptimal position X, it can be defeated by X', Z, and Z'. If it chooses optimal position X', it can only lose to Z and Z'. Therefore every party selects a Paretian optimum to espouse, and society arrives at such an optimum no matter which party wins the election, as long as the winner carries out its promises.

We can summarize what we have said in this section as follows:

1. Unless we make very unrealistic assumptions about government's knowledge of men and events, technical difficulties almost always prevent society from reaching a Paretian optimum whenever collective goods exist by forcing government to engage in negative blocking.

2. Even if we make the assumption of superperfect certainty necessary to overcome these technical difficulties, society will not always reach a Paretian optimum.

   a. It will do so only by chance in a two-party system if the opposition party can wait to reveal its proposals until after the incumbents have done so.

   b. It will do so systematically in a multiparty system or a two-party system if all parties must reveal their proposals simultaneously and the winner always carries out its proposals when in office.

C. EFFECTS OF UNCERTAINTY UPON ATTAINMENT OF AN OPTIMAL POSITION

It is clear from the preceding analysis that when collective goods exist, society attains a Paretian optimum only under very special conditions. One of these conditions is the prevalence of perfect certainty. We have accepted this condition partly because it is a cornerstone of traditional general equilibrium analysis, and partly to illustrate certain forces that would be at work even in a certain world. Now let us introduce uncertainty and see what happens to our conclusions.

In the first place, when uncertainty exists, the private sector is not likely to reach a Paretian optimum even if there are no collective goods or nonmarket interdependencies. Most of the reasoning of general equilibrium theory regarding the efficiency of perfect competition is based upon the assumption of certainty. When it is dropped, so is the conclusion that a perfectly competitive economy automatically reaches a Paretian optimum.

Second, uncertainty is the main technical obstacle which prevents government from handling collective goods so as to reach a Paretian optimum, assuming the private sector has somehow done so regarding private goods. As we shall show later, if the governing party knew the innate abilities and utility functions of every citizen and could make instantaneous and costless calculations concerning them, it could design a tax-benefit system that would not leave any of its citizens in marginal disequilibrium. In other words, it could eliminate negative blocking if it wished to do so. But when perfect knowledge is absent—as in fact it always is—the government cannot help but negatively block attainment of an optimal position.

The third effect of uncertainty is quite similar to the second: because no party knows which social states are optimal or in what way various states dominate each other, interparty competition does not guarantee a Paretian optimum even when all parties reveal their proposals at once. Each party is forced to guess about both optimality and dominance, and the odds are that no party's guess is actually an optimal position. Since each knows this, the general incentive even to seek optimal positions is reduced, further lowering the probability that they will be achieved. In addition, uncertainty reduces the ability of the winning party to carry out its promises completely; hence even if it espouses an optimum-producing policy set, it may not be able to effect an optimum.

Finally, uncertainty may cause citizens to oppose giving government the powers necessary to achieve optimal states because they fear the use of such powers will create a precedent which might be employed against them in the future. For example, assume there exists a society at present in position J, which is a suboptimal position because specific unequivocally good acts involving collective goods could move society to optimal position K. But the government in this society is not at present empowered to make the direct income transfers and individual assessments necessary to carry out these acts. To reach K, the citizenry must alter government's rules of procedure (by majority vote, we assume) so as to give it these powers.

But once government has made use of these powers to move from J to K, there is no guarantee that it will not use them again in the future to move from K to some other state. True, it is a democratic government; so it will always move to a state preferred to K by a majority. But its moves may not always be unequivocally good; i.e., they may be at the expense of a minority. For instance, assume that the whole society consists of citizens D, E, and F, and that D and E both favor moving from state K to state L, though this move injures F. Citizen F would like to move from K to M, a change which also benefits E but harms D.

Under these conditions, if the proposed move from J to K sets a precedent by giving government powers it can subsequently use again, both D and F may oppose this move even though everyone is made better off by it. Uncertainty makes each unwilling to risk setting a precedent which a majority may use against his interests later. Therefore society remains at a suboptimal state because most of its citizens oppose allowing government to exercise the powers necessary to reach an optimum. In such cases a form of temporal indivisibility—the inability of citizens to separate completely what is done at one moment from what can be done at later moments—causes a vote-maximizing government to prevent a Paretian optimum by negative blocking.

The preceding analysis shows that uncertainty makes attainment of a Paretian optimum highly unlikely, especially when collective goods and nonmarket interdependencies exist.[14] Uncertainty causes suboptimal outcomes partly because it prevents full integration of the two different distributions that influence the allocation of resources in the economy: the distribution of votes and the distribution of money income. The latter is the key ordering factor in optimal arrangements of economic activity. Each agent disposes of its given money income in such a way as to equate the discounted net

[14] The effects of uncertainty are not entirely negative, however. It also prevents the Arrow problem from causing virtual chaos, as we have pointed out before. For instance, in the society we described in the preceding section, no stable policy could be maintained if certainty prevailed, because a majority would always prefer some policy other than the one being carried out. Only uncertainty can prevent this outcome. See footnote 11 in Chapter 4.

rates of utility return on all its margins of action. The interlocking of all these income allocations determines the whole structure of the economy, which is therefore rooted in the original income distribution.

As soon as we admit into this picture a government like the one in our model, a second distribution sharply competes with the distribution of money income for influence over the economic scene. This is the distribution of votes—by assumption in our model an equal distribution among all adults. Government's actions are ordered according to this political distribution, yet these actions have a vital role in determining the structure of the economy. Therefore a basic dualism appears among the forces shaping economic activity. The pattern of activity which emerges results from a struggle and compromise between those who own the quantities in these two distributions.

There are other distributions in society which are important to economic activity besides those of income and votes. However, most of these soon come under the influence of the distribution of money income or become a part of it. Athletic talent, for example, is distributed in a way not closely correlated, as far as we know, with either money income or votes. Yet it can be marketed and its possessors' services bought and sold. Therefore it soon comes under the sway of the distribution of money income, and those who have such talent take their place in that distribution. The same is true of the distribution of rights of access to valuable minerals, of great scholastic minds, and of most other things with any significant economic relevance—except the ownership of votes.

If enough certainty prevails to rule out the type of political influence described in Chapter 6, money is powerless to influence votes. Here the disparity between the distribution of money income and the distribution of votes is most sharply seen. How it can cause the government to refuse to carry out an optimum-furthering action can be shown by an example. Let us assume there are only three voters: A, B, and C. Voters A and B are satisfied with government's present role in society and oppose any further allocation of private funds to government activity via taxes. Voter C, however, wants the government to spend $1,000 more in cutting down the trees in the public park opposite his house, since these trees are shading his flower garden. Being a fanatical gardener, he is even willing to pay the $1,000 himself because he regards the net result as worth at least $2,000 to him. But he cannot run out and chop down the trees himself because they are public property; nor can he pay the government to do it because the government is interested in votes, not in money.

However, as a result of C's clamor, the government makes inquiries and discovers that A and B are nearly indifferent about the whole matter, but not quite: they rank "shade" just barely above "no shade" in their preference orderings. Therefore the government leaves the trees just as they are, although C urgently wants them removed and A and B just barely want them to remain.

If vote-selling were allowed, C could pay A and B each $100 plus the increase in his taxes—i.e., a total of $433 apiece—to vote for removal of the trees. In this case, removal of the trees would make everyone better off than leaving them there. Neither A nor B (we assume) cares about shade to the extent that he cares about $100, and C obtains a result worth $2,000 to him at a cost of only $1,200. However, the law prohibits the sale of votes, so rationality requires that A and B vote for shade. If we make the crucial assumption that this is the only political issue, government simply follows the majority, leaving C frustrated and an obvious Paretian optimum unattained.

Welfare economists might argue that the government should tax C more than the cost of removing the trees, place no taxes on A and B, and pay A and B subsidies—thus indirectly buying their political support for the measure. This would make everyone better off. However, this solution implies that the government can make individually discriminatory bargains with voters; whereas in fact uncertainty precludes such bargains for two reasons.

First, lack of knowledge about the preferences of individual citizens makes it technically impossible for the government to discriminate either accurately or inexpensively. Second, fear of setting a precedent may prevent voters from allowing government to discriminate individually even if it could. If individual discrimination were possible in our example, A and B could vote to tax C and pay themselves subsidies without removing the trees. This maneuver would make the majority even better off than the legitimate use of the compensation principle suggested above, though a minority would suffer. However, as we explained before, A and B may refuse to take advantage of this possibility because each fears doing so would set a precedent that could be used against him later by a majority that does not include him. Thus all three citizens oppose government's integrating the distributions of votes and money income by means of individual discrimination. Here again, uncertainty prevents society from reaching a Paretian optimum.

This blocking of marginal equalization is not restricted to present-paying activities, as the following example shows. Assume that two voters, X and Y, want government to finance two different future-paying investments. Both investments pay off at the same date but not at the same net discounted marginal rate of return in utility computed against the marginal tax dollars going into them. Citizen X regards the investment he favors as paying off at 2,000 percent, though this rate would decline if more resources were shifted there. In contrast, citizen Y sees his project as having a return of 2 percent. However, these two rates of return cannot be directly compared because they are not computed on the same utility function. Each citizen calculates the return on his favorite government project by means of his own utility function, and, as we here assume, each feels the project desired by the other is worthless.

A single planning agent—the government—must allocate resources to these two uses. But the government does not appraise these investments by their utility pay-offs, since it has no utility function. Rather it evaluates then on a vote pay-off function, and because each citizen has one vote, the two investments may very well have equal marginal rates of return in its eyes. If so, it cannot rationally shift resources from the 2 percent investment to the 2,000 percent one.

If free trading were allowed, citizen X, whose pay-off rate from government action is 2,000 percent, would pay citizen Y to allow government to transfer all its funds to the investment X preferred until its rate of return fell to 2 percent. X could easily compensate Y for the loss Y would sustain in this transfer and still be much better off himself. But this means X would be paying Y to shift his political influence; in effect, X would be buying Y's vote. Since such bribery is illegal, he cannot resort to it. Yet Y will not shift his influence voluntarily if, in his eyes, the 2,000 percent return is really a less-than-2 percent return because he sees little benefit in this particular government project.[15]

Thus the prohibition of buying and selling votes blocks operation of the marginal-return-equalizing principle both intertemporally and intratemporally. As a result, government is constantly engaging in activities with diverse rates of return; so arbitrage could always make both buyers and sellers of voters better off. Yet government has no incentive to make them better off by shifting resources without any sale of votes; hence it engages in negative blocking and prevents a possible Paretian optimum from being attained. Would not society as a whole be better off, therefore, if the buying and selling of votes were legal? Would not a Paretian optimum then be possible, whereas now it is impossible? [16]

D. A HYPOTHETICAL VOTE-SELLING MARKET

Before answering these questions, we must first examine the peculiar character of the value of voting to an individual—a topic which will come up again later. In any large-scale election, a rational voter knows that the probability that his vote will be in any way decisive is very small indeed. Given the behavior of all others, his

[15] In reality, a great deal of bribery occurs in democratic political systems, though usually not with cash pay-offs. The whole "boss" system, in which citizens agree to vote as the boss directs in return for favors he does them, is a form of bribery, i.e., of vote-selling. In fact, the main idea behind our model is that voters will reward politicians who please them by voting for those politicians. Nevertheless, even in the real world there is no organized vote-selling market like the wheat market or the stock market, and the lack of such a market has the main effects discussed here. Therefore we will omit from our model world localized influence markets like those in "boss" systems.

[16] These two questions are not necessarily identical; i.e., making society as a whole better off and achieving a Paretian optimum are two distinct acts which do not always coincide.

vote is thus of almost no value to him at all, no matter how important it is to him that party P beat party Q. Consequently he will be willing to sell his vote for a very low price if vote-selling is legal, since money is definitely of value to him. In other words, every rational voter has a low reservation price on his vote. Nevertheless, this does not mean votes would be cheap in an uncontrolled market; their price depends upon demand as well as supply.

To explore this matter further, let us assume for the moment that (1) there is no legal restraint on the purchase or sale of votes and (2) some kind of negotiable vote certificates are printed up and distributed one to each voter before each election. What will happen?

No one voter has much political power—that is why there is a low reservation price. But any voter who can buy up a large number of votes can strongly influence the government's policy in any area of interest to him. As a result, those desiring such power and possessed of vote-buying capital funds will form a demand for votes. Others not so desirous, or not so endowed with funds, will act as vote-suppliers. It is even possible that there will be keen competition among vote-demanders, so that the price of votes will be driven well above the reservation price of a majority of citizens. If this happens, most low-income citizens will not be able to afford to be buyers but will instead become sellers.

Thus no matter which of the competitors finally accumulates enough votes to control government policy, the winner will almost always be a possessor of high income or large capital. In short, if an open vote market exists, government policy will be dictated by high-income groups, even if there is severe competition within these groups for dominance over specific policies.

Presumably, low-income citizens will eventually get tired of being discriminated against by government policy. To counteract high-income domination, they may attempt to form large collective-bargaining units exactly as in the labor market—in fact, they might make use of those collective-bargaining units which already exist in the labor market. Then the individual voter will no longer feel that his vote is worthless, since he can join a group and, by doing so, raise the probability that his vote—seen as the vote of the whole group—

will be decisive. Thus he will be rewarded for the casting of his vote collectively not by payment in money, as he was when he sold his vote, but by payment in policy, effected when low-income bargaining centers attain enough power to influence the government.

In this hypothetical world, it is always more rational for a voter to sell his vote than to vote—whether collectively or individually—as long as he is indifferent about what policies government adopts. It is also more rational for him to sell his vote if he regards the votes of all other voters as given. Therefore it is not easy to persuade men to continue combining their votes, each contributing his own to the group, after the group has become so large that the defection of any one man is *per se* trivial. The history of the labor movement and even of large cartels proves how difficult this is. Either defection must be punished, or men must be taught to view such situations emotionally and morally instead of statistically; e.g., each member must regard his behavior not as unique to him but as an example which others are going to follow. Otherwise the group will not hold together under stress.

Let us assume that this obstacle is overcome and low-income bargaining groups emerge in the vote market. They soon enter into competition with high-income receivers for the control of peripheral votes, perhaps by purchasing votes with funds collected as dues, perhaps by making policy promises. Political parties either become superfluous institutions or else enter the vote market themselves and become partisan to low- or high-income interests.

Thus the vote market evolves towards an unstable balance of power between two sets of groups: (1) high-income groups, whose funds give them initial dominance, and (2) emergent low-income collective-bargaining centers, which may eventually gain a numerical edge. As long as the high-income groups succeed in buying any votes at all, they have more political influence than they would have had if vote-selling were illegal. But this influence has been purchased by the sacrifice of income; so the low-income recipients who sold their votes are better off financially because of the bribes they received. The only unequivocal losers are low-income citizens who did not sell their votes but tried instead to influence policy. They have no greater incomes and less political power than they had before vote-selling was legal.

Low-income citizens as a group have traded political influence for money income. In order to get back as much political influence as they had prior to the legal sale of votes, they have to (1) band together in a collective bargaining combination to which every low-income recipient belongs and (2) give up the money income which the bribes provide them. If this money income gives them more utility than a return to their original degree of political influence, it is clearly foolish for them to quit selling their votes. However, they should still sell them via collective bargaining so as to get the maximum money for them. Otherwise vote-buyers can play each seller off against the rest and capture all the rent in the market, just as in the labor market.

However, if policy control is more important to low-income receivers than the money they can get by selling their votes, then their best course is to get vote-selling prohibited. By this one stroke, they can prevent the high-income groups from making any inroads whatever on their political influence. When each man controls only one vote and can neither purchase more nor sell his own, political power equality is achieved among individuals—at least in a certain world. Such equality naturally benefits low-income groups because of their numerical preponderance. Therefore enforcing the equality of franchise and the prohibition of vote-selling is the most efficient way for low-income groups in society to assure themselves of having influence over government policy.

With this conclusion in mind, let us return to the question of whether vote-selling will produce a Paretian optimum. It is true that in many situations an indigent vote-seller and a wealthy vote-buyer would both gain if the former could sell his vote to the latter. However, in almost every such instance, their gain is someone else's loss. For example, take the case of the shade trees discussed earlier in this chapter. A and B oppose cutting down the trees and C desires it. If C could bribe both A and B, he could get the trees cut down and everyone would be better off. But if bribery is legal, it is obviously cheaper for C to bribe just B instead of both A and B. Both B and

C gain—B by the bribe and C because he now controls enough votes to have the trees removed—but A loses. He gets neither shade nor increased income—in fact, his taxes go up to pay for the removal he opposes. Yet it is irrational for C to bribe A too, since doing so costs C more but gives him no additional benefits. If C were somehow compelled to bribe either both A and B or neither, then C could not improve his own position at the expense of someone else. But such compulsion is incompatible with a free market because only purely voluntary transactions can be made therein.

In the terminology of welfare economics, a movement can be unequivocally called good if it makes someone better off and no one worse off. Clearly, introduction of a wide-open vote-selling market will not cause such a movement, since the transactions therein will almost inevitably make someone worse off. Therefore we cannot say that society would necessarily be better off if such a market were made legal.[17]

There are conceivable conditions under which a vote-selling market would make everyone better off even though everyone tried to minimize costs and maximize returns. These conditions are as follows:

1. No vote-seller receives a bribe smaller in utility value to him than the utility loss he experiences from the total alterations in policy which occur from the operation of the market.
2. No vote-buyer pays in bribes an amount larger than the gains he experiences from the alterations in policy mentioned in (1).
3. Everyone who is neither a vote-seller nor a vote-buyer experiences no loss in utility because of the alterations in policy mentioned in (1).

[17] It is true that making vote-selling legal might be good for society even though some persons would lose from it. However, its goodness can be judged only by means of interpersonal welfare comparisons, i.e., specifically ethical judgments. Because all citizens do not use the same ethical principles in making such comparisons, the goodness of legalized vote-selling is essentially a matter of opinion. Our opinion is that it would not be good for society, a view which seems to predominate in most democracies, since there is almost no political agitation for making vote-selling legal and considerable agitation against sales of votes whenever they are detected.

In order that these conditions prevail, we believe that (a) all vote-sellers would have to bargain collectively and (b) all vote-buyers would have to agree on what policy changes were to be introduced by means of purchased votes. In short, the vote-sellers would form a single group which would trade its political influence to a cartel of vote-buyers.

However, in our opinion it is extremely unlikely that such a giant bilateral monopoly would form in a free market, particularly since various vote-buyers have quite different policy preferences. Only if government somehow intervened to compel all vote-sellers into one group and all vote-buyers into another would this situation occur. Obviously, the market would no longer be a wide-open one. Furthermore, such control over politics by the governing party would violate the terms of the constitution specified in Chapter 1; government would be shutting off its citizens' freedom of political action. True, prohibition of vote-selling also limits that freedom. But such prohibition does not imply any specific dictation of policy to all those desiring political influence, as would compulsory membership in a vote-buying cartel. Therefore we reject the possibility that a vote-selling market could make some citizens better off and not injure others without destroying political freedom.

Our conclusion is that the slightest degree of uncertainty prevents a democratic government from carrying out all the optimum-furthering actions that are necessary to bring about a Paretian optimum in even a perfectly competitive economy. Because it lacks perfect knowledge about voters' abilities and utility functions, a vote-maximizing government inevitably prevents individual marginal equilibria from occurring. Therefore arbitrage in the form of certain political bargains could make everyone better off, or some better off and none worse off. But these bargains cannot be made. Free enterprise cannot make them because they involve collective goods or nonmarket interdependencies or both. Hence influencers offering political bribes always find it more profitable to injure some affected citizens than to bribe all of them. Realizing this, a majority of citizens unite to make bribery illegal because uncertainty causes each to fear he may be in the injured minority. Nor could government force these bargains to be made, even if it knew what they were, because by doing so it would jeopardize political freedom. In short, a Paretian optimum is never reached in a democracy.

E. THE IMPACT OF INDIVISIBILITY AND ITS TECHNICAL CAUSES

In preceding sections of this chapter, we pointed out that certain indivisibilities connected with government operations create technical obstacles to attainment of a Paretian optimum. However, we postponed further discussion of these obstacles until later; now we wish to analyze them in detail. The first step is a reëxamination of the individual's utility income from government activity, which we first discussed in Chapter 3.

Each voter receives a *total* utility income from government activity, and a *marginal* income from the marginal government dollar. He also pays a total cost in utility via taxes and restraints, and bears the marginal cost of the last tax dollar (or loss of income from restraint or inflation). Since a rational man remains in a given society as long as his total utility income from governmental and nongovernmental activities therein exceeds the total cost to him of all such activities, there is no reason why his total income from governmental acts alone need exceed or even equal the total cost to him of those acts.

Similarly, there is no *a priori* reason why any citizen's marginal gain from government action need equal his marginal loss from that action. In the private market, this is not true; a rational man regulates his whole economic life by equating marginal returns with marginal costs (which are really foregone returns at other margins), thus maximizing his net income. This is possible because he can control his behavior at the margin with precision by altering it slightly in either direction. In other words, each of his endeavors is—at least in theory—divisible and can be augmented or diminished by any desired degree.

Government, however, assigns to its citizens obligatory costs which the citizens can vary only within narrow limits.[18] Furthermore, it

---

[18] For example, a man can reduce his working time to avoid income taxes, or save to avoid sales taxes, or shy away from luxury-taxed goods.

provides services in a manner unrelated to what each individual has contributed to their financing. Therefore only by the most incredible coincidence is a man ever in perfect marginal equilibrium in his dealings with government. Normally we can expect every man's marginal gain from government action to be unequal to his marginal loss; hence he is usually getting a net marginal bonus from the government or suffering a net marginal drain to it.

In a free, divisible market, neither of these outcomes could long prevail. A rational man who was suffering a net drain at some margin would reduce the flow of resources to that margin. This would eventually raise the marginal return there to the level of marginal cost, assuming that the law of diminishing marginal returns held there. Or if he were enjoying a net gain at some margin, he would transfer more resources there until marginal return was driven down equal to marginal cost. In either case, his reaction would increase his total net income.

However, the government does not engage solely in voluntary transactions with each citizen, as do private firms. Like many such firms, it deals with categories of persons by means of uniform rules applied to all persons within each category, but its "customers" are required to be in certain categories whether they like it or not. Thus a private manufacturer of pencils may set up the rule that "everyone who buys my product pays $2.69," but nobody has to buy his product. Such freedom is absent from government rules like "everyone in Minnesota who receives taxable income pays 5 percent of it to the state treasury."

Though it could be argued that no one need receive taxable income, it is difficult to survive in a market economy without doing so. On the same basis, one might even argue that a compulsory poll tax was really voluntary, since no one is forced to be alive. However, such sophistry denies the possibility of coercion, which is certainly a real force in the world as well as in our model.

At the opposite extreme is the contention that there is just as much coercion in the private sector as in the public sector. In our economy, one cannot survive without entering into *some* transactions with entrepreneurs unless one is a hermit. Therefore every non-hermit is compelled to buy from and sell to private firms just as forcibly as he is compelled to pay income taxes.

Although there is a large grain of truth in this argument, the type of compulsion exercised in the public sector is quite different from that in the private sector. In the latter, one must deal with *someone*, but the particular agents involved and the extent of each deal are left to the discretion of the individual. He can move in and out of various transactions and markets, marginally altering his position in each. Thus he can carry out the marginal-equation process previously described.[19]

This is not true in the public sector, where each citizen must deal with the government and must do so in ways specified by the government, not the citizen. True, he can attempt to equate marginal cost and marginal return of all the categories he is in seen as a unit by intentionally moving in and out of some of them. But so many categories are imposed upon him that areas of possible movement are too limited to insure marginal equilibrium.

This situation results from the indivisibility of government action, which in turn has two important technical causes: (1) the nature of the benefit flow from certain government actions and (2) the difficulty of measuring benefits. We will discuss these in order.

As we pointed out earlier in this chapter, the chief activities of government yield certain indivisible benefits. Since everyone is a potential gainer from these benefits regardless of who pays for them, they cannot be allocated to individuals. Therefore, as we explained before, government must coerce its citizens to pay for such benefits, which usually derive from fundamental services of government like police protection, a court system, and defense. Obviously, such coercion eliminates the possibility of free bargaining.

However, this indivisibility of benefit flow does not account for the extent of spending upon these activities or for the allocation of their

---

[19] Here we are assuming that perfect competition exists in the private sector and that all commodities therein are perfectly divisible. These assumptions are implicit in all our discussions of the private sector (except for collective goods) in this chapter. We make them both for simplicity's sake and because they are the usual premises behind general equilibrium models in economics.

costs, nor does it mean that benefits received by all are necessarily equal. Expenditure for national defense from air attack no doubt benefits everyone to some extent, but it benefits people living in cities near defense plants much more than those living in the desert by themselves. Some citizens may even feel that the marginal defense spending being done is a net loss to them because of overmilitarization of national life, too much noise from jet planes, etc. Also, the fact that government extracts costs from its citizens by coercion does not explain how much it takes from each citizen.

This cost-allocation problem might be easier to solve if it were possible to measure an individual's benefit income accurately. But much benefit income from government action is purely psychic—i.e., it does not accrue in dollar-receipt form but is consumed directly. Since interpersonal comparison of psychic incomes is impossible, a man's benefit income cannot be measured and compared with the benefit incomes of others for cost-allocation purposes. Nor can government find out how much each citizen benefits from its actions by asking him, "How much would you pay rather than lose X service?" Because many government services yield large consumer surpluses, nearly every citizen is receiving a greater total benefit from the existence of government than he could provide for himself by spending his whole income for this purpose alone. Also contributing to this result are the great economies of scale inherent in many government activities.

Even inventing a method of measuring benefits would not remove all the obstacles to allocating costs via the benefit principle. The government would still have to enter into negotiations with each citizen to discover the size of his benefit income, just as it now does in regard to his money income. If these negotiations were very expensive, the costs might invalidate any gains the citizens could achieve by reaching marginal equilibrium in their relations with government.

Since at present no device for measuring benefits exists, the government cannot allocate costs in proportion to benefits even if it wishes to do so. And the indivisibility of benefits prevents it from selling government services in a free market on a *quid pro quo* basis.

For these technical reasons, government must forego any thoughts of helping its citizens attain individual marginal equilibrium in their interaction with it.

F. INCOME DISTRIBUTION AS A CAUSE OF BLOCKED MARGINAL EQUILIBRIUM

Even if the technical problems involved in measuring individual benefits and conducting low-cost individual negotiations could be solved, there is no reason to suppose each individual would attain marginal equilibrium in his dealings with government. In fact, the government's best interest would probably lie in deliberately refusing to make the individual bargains necessary for reaching such equilibrium.

Each individual maximizes his own utility income, *ceteris paribus*, when the utility loss caused by his marginal tax payment, or by the marginal inflationary movement in case of deficit financing, is equal to the utility gain yielded by the marginal benefit he receives from government action. Under these conditions, the individual is, in effect, purchasing government services out of his money income, given the latter. He is using this given money income in the most efficient possible way; i.e., he is getting the largest utility income from it that he possibly can.

But government need not regard everyone's money income as given because it has the power to redistribute incomes. In our model, it makes use of this power whenever doing so helps it maximize votes. Clearly, in a society where every citizen has one and only one vote, the best way to gain votes via redistribution is to deprive a few persons of income—thereby incurring their hostility—and make this income available to many persons—thereby gaining their support. Since the pretax distribution of income in almost every society gives large incomes to a few persons and relatively small incomes to many persons, a redistribution tending toward equality accomplishes the very political end government desires. Thus the equality of franchise in a democratic society creates a tendency for government action to equalize incomes by redistributing them from a few wealthy persons to many less wealthy ones.

But government does not continue this process until all citizens have the same income after taxes have been subtracted from and government benefits added to the original income of each. It does not do so for three reasons, all of which are related to uncertainty.

In the first place, the government cannot devise a system of taxes and benefits which redistributes income without causing any feedback or incentive effects. One of the axioms of rational behavior is that every individual seeks to avoid costs and gain returns if he can. Therefore whenever the government announces a set of rules governing taxation and benefit distribution, every citizen allocates his resources so as to escape taxes and gain benefits in so far as is feasible. Of course, as we pointed out in the preceding section, he cannot maneuver as freely in regard to government rules as he can in regard to rules in the private sector, since the former are compulsory. Nevertheless, as long as any movement away from penalties and toward rewards is possible, such movement will be made.

If the government knew precisely how every citizen would react to any proposals it made, it could conceivably plan a tax-benefit structure that would redistribute income from rich to poor without causing either a drop in total output or an upset in individual marginal equilibria. For example, it might impose a tax on each person's innate income-earning ability rather than his actual money income. Such a tax has all the advantages of both a poll tax and an income tax and neither of their major disadvantages. It resembles a poll tax because no one can escape it by reallocating his resources; hence it has no optimum-upsetting effect at the margin. Yet like an income tax, it can discriminate between individuals and be used for redistribution of income. Thus perfect knowledge of every individual's income-earning potential would enable the government to rig its taxes and benefits so that after each citizen had responded to the announced schedules, he would find that his marginal gain from government action was equal to his marginal loss in taxes, even though the taxes were imposed upon him and income had been redistributed in the process. However, the slightest degree of uncertainty—such as inability to read minds or to judge income-earning potentials infallibly—

makes the necessary omniscience totally unfeasible.[20] In reality, any large-scale tax-benefit structure at all prevents a Paretian optimum, and any redistributive effects have some repercussions on total output.

In practice, this means that any attempt to tax money incomes and distribute benefits in such a way as to bring about post-government-action equality would have serious repercussions on the economy's total output. Formerly high-income citizens would convert much of their time from money-income earning to leisure-income enjoying, thus reducing per capita nonleisure output. Even low-income citizens feel that the total output produced by an ultimately unequal income distribution would be much larger than that produced by an equal one—so much larger that their less-than-proportional shares of the former would be absolutely greater than their equal shares of the latter. Therefore opposition to complete income equalization is nearly universal; so the vote-maximizing government in our model respects it.

There are two other ways in which uncertainty prevents the government from redistributing incomes until they are the same for all men. First, uncertainty allows low-income citizens to believe that someday they too may have high incomes; hence their desire to "soak the rich" is mitigated by the hope that they themselves will be rich.[21] Second, uncertainty creates more and less influential voters; i.e., it alters the distribution of voting power to one that is not equal. Usually voters with the highest incomes also have the most

[20] It is doubtful whether an acceptable definition of "income-earning ability" can ever be framed even conceptually. The judgments involved concern interpersonal comparisons that are really ethical in nature rather than economic or psychological; hence a scientific basis for consensus may be impossible. This fact emphasizes the inability of any real-world government to impose a redistributive tax structure that does not rule out attainment of a Paretian optimum. We are indebted to Kenneth J. Arrow for pointing out the theoretical possibilities and practical weaknesses of this type of taxation.

[21] This type of thinking by low-income citizens might be construed as irrational and hence out of place in our model. However, to appraise its rationality thoroughly is a difficult task involving analysis of subjective vs. objective probabilities. Although we cannot attempt such a task in this study, we regard such thinking as important enough at least to be mentioned. Its rationality has been discussed at length by Milton Friedman in "Choice, Chance, and the Personal Distribution of Income," *Journal of Political Economy*, LXI (August, 1953), 277–290.

political power, since in an uncertain world they can use their financial resources to create influence for themselves.

The first of these impacts weakens the natural "Robin Hood" tendency of a democratic government, and the second sets up a counterforce that may completely overshadow that tendency. If it does, rational government action may even redistribute income from the poor to the rich.

III. RECAPITULATION AND CONCLUSIONS

In this chapter we have examined what happens to an individual marginal equilibrium when we add a vote-maximizing government to the general allocation model of traditional economic theory. Our conclusion is that no private agent is likely to reach the marginal equilibrium regarded as normal by traditional theory. Several conditions in our model prevent most agents from equating their marginal returns from government action to their marginal cost thereof. These conditions are as follows:

1. Equal distribution of votes among citizens, which may be considerably offset in conditions of uncertainty by an unequal distribution of influence biased in favor of high-income receivers.

2. Unequal distribution of incomes arranged so that a few persons receive very high incomes relative to the great majority of persons.

3. The ability of the government to force its citizens to give it some of their resources via taxation or inflation or both.

4. The fact that government acts to maximize votes but its actions have repercussions on individual utility incomes. Although individuals' actions, which are aimed at maximizing utility, include a voting decision, individuals cannot coerce the government the way it can coerce them.

5. Technical indivisibilities of government operation caused by the nature of certain benefits government provides, and the impossibility of measuring individual benefit incomes objectively.

6. Prohibition of purchase or sale of voting rights, but allowance of purchase or sale of most other personal prerogatives, particularly property rights.

7. Government's lack of perfect knowledge about the utility functions and innate abilities of its citizens, and their lack of perfect knowledge about future events. This condition partly underlies both (5) and (6) above.

Traditional economic theory posits that each planning agent will allocate its resources so as to equate returns at all the margins. However, as the foregoing conditions imply, government prevents private agents from acting freely at certain margins; therefore it keeps them from reaching the equilibrium posited in traditional theory. Furthermore, individuals cannot bargain with each other for political influence. Hence the market mechanism is eliminated as a means of evading government blockade of the marginal equation process.

Also, the vote-maximizing goal of government causes it to act in favor of the most numerous income groups—low-income receivers. Therefore it tends to redistribute income away from high-income groups by its allocation of costs and services.

These reflections and the conditions preceding them lead us to the following general conclusions:

1. Democratic government policies tend to favor low-income receivers as a class rather than high-income receivers.
2. Consequently, because the free market produces a highly unequal distribution of income, the more effective democracy becomes politically, the greater is government interference with the normal operation of the economy.
3. Uncertainty and costliness of information redistribute political power so as to offset the economic leveling tendency of democracy. This causes a reduction in the amount of government interference with the natural income-distribution process.
4. Therefore, the greater the degree of uncertainty in politics, the more likely government is to be smaller—in terms of actions and size—than it would be in a perfectly informed democracy.[22]

---

[22] This conclusion does not hold for extreme degrees of uncertainty. When extreme uncertainty exists, social action becomes impossible because no plans can be made. Men react to such chaos by instituting strong governmental control to reduce uncertainty to tolerable levels, though this control is not always vested in the official agencies of government. Thus as uncertainty increases, government

5. Rational government planning may simultaneously maintain enormously varying rates of discounted utility return at the margins of action. This is true because government balances the utility margins of different individuals against each other on its own vote margins.

6. As a result, the economy is always at a suboptimal position in Paretian terms. An optimum position could be reached in theory by means of certain political bargains, but in practice they cannot be made without jeopardizing the political freedom guaranteed by the constitution.

These outcomes all result from perfectly rational behavior on the part of both private planning agents and the government, given their several ends.

IV. SUMMARY

In the private sectors of the economy, resources are allocated to those uses of highest net marginal return. This process continues until net returns at the margin are equal in all directions, both for each planning unit and for the economy as a whole. So concludes the general reasoning of traditional economic theory.

A vote-maximizing government, however, upsets this marginal equilibrium by imposing certain obligatory costs upon some decision-makers and making subsidized benefits available to others. These decision-makers cannot return to marginal equilibrium by negotiating with each other because vote-selling is forbidden. Furthermore, technical indivisibilities prevent governments from remedying this situation by either (1) selling all government services in a free market, thus giving each citizen the same maneuverability he has in the private sector, or (2) entering into personal bargaining with private decision-makers. Finally, the difference between the distribution of votes and the distribution of incomes gives government an incentive

---

control will at first decrease because of the augmented influence of high-income laissez-faire groups. Even this conclusion is not universally valid, but in all systems, government control eventually increases greatly when the degree of uncertainty reaches intolerable proportions.

to maintain net drains and gains at individual utility margins via income redistribution. This imparts a "Robin Hood" tendency to its behavior, unless uncertainty augments the political power of high-income groups.

One result of this marginal upset is that a rational government may simultaneously carry out projects with widely varying rates of utility return without reallocating its resources from the lowest returns to the highest. This means there will always be a possible Paretian optimum which cannot in practice be reached.

All of these results stem from the government's desire to equalize returns on its vote-income margins rather than on voters' utility-income margins. Since government can use force to implement its desires but private decision-makers cannot, utility equilibrium must give way to vote equilibrium whenever conflicts occur.

Part III

Specific Effects of Information Costs

11

The Process of Becoming
Informed

Introduction

TRADITIONAL economic theory assumes that un-
limited amounts of free information are available to decision-makers.
In contrast, we seek to discover what political decision-making is like
when uncertainty exists and information is obtainable only at a cost.
A basic step towards this goal is analysis of the economics of becoming informed, i.e., the rational utilization of scarce resources to obtain
data for decision-making. Though this process does not exist in a
"perfectly informed" world, we shall see that in any realistic model it
radically affects the whole decision-making procedure.

Objectives

In this chapter we attempt to prove the following propositions:

1. In an uncertain world, rational decision-makers acquire only a
   limited amount of information before making choices.
2. All reporting is biased because the reporter must select only some
   of the extant facts to pass on to his audience.
3. A rational citizen keeps properly well-informed by systematically

exposing himself to a particular set of information sources he has chosen for this purpose.

I. THE ROLE OF INFORMATION IN DECISION-MAKING

A. THE DECISION-MAKING PROCESS AND ITS COSTS

To make rational decisions, a man must know (1) what his goals are, (2) what alternative ways of reaching these goals are open to him, and (3) the probable consequences of choosing each alternative. The knowledge he requires is contextual knowledge as well as information, both of which are usually necessary for each of the above aspects of decision-making. Even choosing goals requires information, since only his ultimate goal—his picture of the ideal social state—exists independent of his knowledge of the current situation. Most of his other goals are means to this ultimate end; hence choosing them requires information as well as ideals.

For purposes of our present analysis, we make two simplifying assumptions about information: (1) contextual knowledge and information can both be treated as information, since acquiring both is costly, and (2) no false information is published by any sources. The latter does not mean that facts cannot be manipulated so as to give false impressions; it only means that all factual statements can be accepted as correct without further checking, though their significance may be equivocal.

In our model, citizens who are not members of the government must make two important political decisions: (1) how to vote, and (2) what ways—if any—to exert influence directly upon government policy formation. The difference between decisions made for these two purposes is discussed in detail in Chapter 13. In this chapter, we assume all political decisions are made in the same way; therefore we can illustrate them all by analyzing the voting decision.

To show how the cost of information impinges upon this decision, we first translate the logic of voting as described in Chapter 3 into a series of discrete steps. Like most breakdowns of unified dynamic processes, ours may appear somewhat arbitrary, but we believe it provides a useful tool free from distortions which cause false conclusions. The main steps of rationally deciding how to vote and then voting are as follows:

1. Gathering information relevant to each issue upon which important political decisions have been (or will be) made.
2. For each issue, selecting from all the information gathered that which will be used in the voting decision.
3. For each issue, analyzing the facts selected to arrive at specific factual conclusions about possible alternative policies and their consequences.
4. For each issue, appraising the consequences of every likely policy in light of relevant goals. This is a value appraisal, not a strictly factual one.
5. Coördinating the appraisals of each issue into a net evaluation of each party running in the election. This is also a value judgment personally tailored to the goals of the voter himself.
6. Making the voting decision by comparing the net evaluations of each party and weighting them for future contingencies.
7. Actually voting or abstaining.

Every one of these steps except the last can be delegated to someone other than the voter himself. If such delegation occurs, additional steps must be added to allow for transmission of the conclusion of these other agents to the voter, or from one agent to another. For example, if a voter relies on an expert to appraise the facts regarding atomic energy policies, there is a cost involved in transmitting the expert's opinion to the voter. Also, the expert himself may have had to pay for the gathering of data by others. Thus the cost of transmission may intervene between any steps; if so, it must be added to the cost of the steps themselves in computing the total cost of making the decision.

Of what does this cost consist? By definition, any cost is a deflection of scarce resources from some utility-producing use; it is a foregone alternative. The main scarce resource consumed in the steps above is the time used for assimilating data and weighing alternatives, but many other resources may also be involved, particularly in the gathering and transmission steps. We divide all these costs into two major classes:

1. *Transferable costs* can be shifted from the voter onto someone else. We separate transferable costs into three types:
   (a) *Procurement costs* are the costs of gathering, selecting, and transmitting data.
   (b) *Analysis costs* are the costs of making factual analysis of data.
   (c) *Evaluative costs* are the costs of relating data or factual analyses to specific goals; i.e., of evaluating them.
2. *Nontransferable costs* must be borne by the voter himself. Theoretically, every cost except that of going to the polls can be passed onto others, but we assume, unless otherwise specified, that step (6) is always performed by the voter himself; hence he must bear at least a minimal cost of assimilating information or judgments.

Clearly, the fewer steps the voter performs himself, the fewer costs he bears directly. However, he can shift the steps described onto others and still bear their costs indirectly by paying the others to perform these steps; e.g., a voter may hire someone to make expert decisions for him on foreign policy.

At first glance, it may appear irrational for a voter to delegate some of these steps to others, since every such delegation removes him one degree from the reality which his decision concerns. Insofar as gathering, selecting, and analyzing facts are concerned, it is clear that delegation is very often rational because it allows the voter to make use of economies of scale and the expert knowledge of specialists. But the rationality of delegation is not so obvious in the case of value judgments like those of steps (4) and (5). The issues raised by such delegation are discussed in detail in the next chapter.

B. THE NECESSITY AND NATURE OF SELECTION PRINCIPLES

In a perfectly informed world, information is available to any decision-maker in unlimited amounts at zero cost, and he need not consume time in making use of it. Therefore the problem of selecting the most relevant information never arises: a planner can use all the data that have any bearing whatsoever on his decision, no matter how colossal their number. But in our model, as in the real world, regardless of how many data are available, the amount a rational decision-maker can employ for any one decision is strictly limited because (1) the human mind, even when abetted by calculating machines, can encompass only a limited amount of information at once, and (2) assimilating and evaluating data take time, which is especially scarce in decision-making because of the pressure of events. These conditions impose the necessity of selection upon all decision-makers, who must choose from the vast supply of data that exist only a limited number to use in their decisions.

Furthermore, as we saw in the previous section, there are costs connected with acquisition or use of information besides the time involved. Naturally, this fact increases the pressure upon decision-makers to reduce the number of data they use. And because this pressure exists throughout the decision-making process, an economic problem arises at each of the aforementioned steps: how much information (including judgments) should be sent on to the next step? True, the necessity of selection is intrinsic only to the first step, since it is possible to carry everything that is gathered through all the other steps without further culling. However, this practice would eliminate the great economy of continuously reducing the quantity of data transferred up the ladder of decision. The dramatic size of such economy is demonstrated by those executives who demand that all the data for each decision they make be reduced to one typewritten page, no matter how many volumes were originally considered relevant.

Thus from the basic economic nature of becoming informed emerges the necessity of selection among data. Immediately there arises the crucial question of how to decide which data to select and which to reject. The question is crucial because the answer chosen determines what type of information is used in making decisions and therefore shapes the decisions and their effectiveness. Furthermore, at every stage except (6), selection can be carried out by someone other than the decision-maker. Obviously, whoever carries it out has a potentially enormous influence upon decisions even if he does not make them himself.

The preceding analysis shows that information is necessarily gathered by means of certain *principles of selection:* rules employed to determine what to make use of and what not to. Different persons use different rules, but everyone must use some rule—even random selection follows a rule. Therefore all information is by nature biased because it is a selection of data from the vast amount extant, others of which could have been selected.[1] As Karl Mannheim said:

> History as history is unintelligible unless certain of its aspects are emphasized in contrast to others. This selection and accentuation of certain aspects of historical totality may be regarded as the first step in the direction which ultimately leads to an evaluative procedure and to ontological judgments.[2]

Since information is essentially short-run history, this statement applies fully to the process of becoming informed, which has as its end the evaluative procedure of making decisions. Because evaluation begins with emphasis upon—i.e., selection of—certain data in contrast to others, all such selection is evaluative to some extent. In short, there is no such thing as purely objective reporting of any situations or events.

II. HOW SELECTION PRINCIPLES ARE CHOSEN RATIONALLY

Because of the division of labor, most citizens in modern democracies do not gather for themselves the information they need for political decision-making. Thousands of specialized agencies gather, interpret, and transmit such information, making it available to the citizenry in a tremendous variety of forms, from television broadcasts to encyclopedias. But since the resources any citizen can devote to paying for and assimilating data are limited, he finds himself in a

[1] We have deliberately used the word *biased* to denote this inherent characteristic of reporting, in spite of its emotionally pejorative associations. When we speak of reporting as biased, we are not implying that the data therein are false, since we have assumed all data are accurate, nor that the reporter is immoral, since bias cannot be avoided. We only mean to convey that the selection and arrangement of facts in any report are inevitably tinged by the viewpoint of the reporter.

[2] Karl Mannheim, *Ideology and Utopia*, Harvest Book Series (New York: Harcourt, Brace and Company, 1955), pp. 93–94.

situation of economic choice: from among these many sources of information, he must select only a few to tap.

The object of this choice is creation of a *system of information acquisition* which provides him with data that are both (1) chosen by means of selection principles in accord with his own and (2) comprehensive enough to enable him to make the decisions he faces. We will deal with the breadth of information required later. Here our analysis concentrates upon how the selection principles used are chosen and tested.

We concluded earlier that every observer reporting an event must select some facts to pass on and others to omit; hence his reporting is inherently biased. His method of selecting facts depends upon the objectives he has in making the report; e.g., a Russian doctor would report the death of Stalin in one way, a British political scientist in another, and the Vatican newspaper in another. Even within the borders of political reporting, methods of selection differ widely according to the political philosophies of the reporters, their intelligence, their experience at reporting, and such other variables as their flair for the dramatic.

When citizens rely on others to report events to them, rationality decrees that they select those reporters who provide them with versions of events that closely approximate the versions they would formulate themselves were they expert on-the-spot witnesses. To accomplish this, they must choose reporters whose selection principles are as nearly identical with their own as possible. Then the reporters' inevitable biases will aid their decision-making rather than hinder it.

This leaves two questions unanswered: (1) how can citizens choose their own selection principles rationally? (2) how can they be sure that those who report to them always use these principles or near facsimilies of them?

A man's selection principles are rational if application of them provides him with information that is useful for making decisions which will help bring about the social state he most prefers. Obviously, because men prefer widely varying social states, no one set of selection principles suits all men. Nevertheless, these principles are means which deal with empirical phenomena; hence it should be possible for any citizen to test various sets of them to discover the one most rational for him—i.e., most useful in attaining his ends.

A rational voter chooses his selection principles by experimentally sampling the reporting of several different information sources simultaneously. His sampling should cover reporters with widely different selection principles; e.g., a man might read the New York *Times*, the *Daily Worker*, and the Chicago *Tribune* and compare their reports. Next he makes hypothetical decisions on the bases of each reporting source's output. Then, as the real situation unfolds, he evaluates the outcomes each of his hypothetical decisions would probably have led to. The selection principles which consistently lead him to make decisions with outcomes closest to his favorite social state are the principles it is most rational for him to use. Admittedly, this testing process is imperfect because much of it is necessarily hypothetical, and therefore subject to great error. Nevertheless, in our model it is the most rational choice mechanism available.

After the rational citizen has chosen that set of information-selection principles he believes best for his purposes, he finds out what reporting agencies also have these principles. However, this does not end his researches, since he must occasionally check up on these agencies to make sure they are not deviating from the principles he wants. For this purpose, he must upon occasion compare their reports with those of other agencies which also share his own principles. For example, a man might simultaneously consult the New York *Times*, the New York *Herald Tribune*, and the *Christian Science Monitor* to see how each covered some set of events. Thus he reduces the probability that any one agency can deviate without being discovered.

III. THE QUANTITY OF INFORMATION IT IS RATIONAL TO ACQUIRE

Some people obtain information as an end in itself. They receive enjoyment from knowing that Gregory Peck had dinner at the Stork Club last night, or that St. Teresa of Lisieux has caused fifty miracles.

All such information procured solely for the edification it provides we call *entertainment information*, no matter how serious its content.

However, most information is used as a means to some decision-making end. As with all means, the usefulness of this information and the manner in which it is selected depend upon the end it serves. We classify all the decisions requiring this kind of information into three types: production decisions, consumption decisions, and political decisions. Therefore all nonentertainment information can be classified as either *production information, consumption information,* or *political information,* or any combination of these, depending upon how it is used.

For all three types of decision-making, the basic rule for deciding how many data to acquire is the same. The information-seeker continues to invest resources in procuring data until the marginal return from information equals its marginal cost. At that point, assuming decreasing marginal returns or increasing marginal costs or both, he has enough information and makes his decision. The example we use in our analysis is the application of this principle to the voting decision a citizen makes, assuming he follows the decision procedure set forth in Chapter 3.

The making of any decision presupposes that the decision-maker already possesses a certain minimum of information. At the very least, he must realize that he has a decision to make and be aware of its general context. Thus before he can make a voting decision, a voter must acquire information about the date of the election, the number of parties running, their names, voting procedure, etc. We assume that the continuous stream of free information present in all societies has already given the voter this minimum before he starts detailed calculations about how much information to acquire.[3]

Three factors determine the size of his planned information investment. The first is the value to him of making a correct decision as opposed to an incorrect one, i.e., the variation in utility incomes associated with the possible outcomes of his decision. The second is the relevance of the information to whatever decision is being made. Is acquisition of this particular bit of knowledge likely to

[3] See Chapter 12, Section I.

influence the decision one way or another? If so, how likely? To answer these questions, a probability estimate must be made of the chances that any given bit of information will alter his decision. This probability is then applied to the value of making the right choice (the *vote value* in our example). From this emerges the return from the bit of information being considered, i.e., the marginal return from investment in data on this particular margin.

The third factor is the cost of data. The marginal cost of any bit of information consists of the returns foregone in obtaining it. A comparison of the estimated marginal cost and estimated marginal return of any bit determines whether this particular bit should be acquired. When such comparisons have been made for all bits, the data to be procured are determined. Since we discuss both returns from and costs of information in greater detail in the next two chapters, we will not enlarge here upon this brief description of the decision-making process.

Our brevity may cause the disparity between real behavior and the procedures in our model world to appear striking, since few actual decision-makers seem to behave in the manner indicated. However, the acts we described are implicit in any rational decision-making which requires information, even if casual observation fails to confirm this fact. Furthermore, as we shall see, many rational citizens obtain practically no information at all before making political decisions; hence their behavior may differ greatly from what we have described and still be rational. Therefore our model world is not as far removed from reality as it seems.

IV. THE NEED FOR FOCUSING ATTENTION

The first step in determining the value of being correct is discovery of what outcomes are possible and what the differences between them are. In our example, this task requires immense effort. Since rule by each party forms an outcome, any differences between the way one party would run the government and the way its opponents would is relevant, including trivial differences in administering obscure agencies. Of course, these differences are not equally relevant, but it is impossible to know which ones are most revelant without first knowing what all of them are. Obviously, the cost of discovering the latter is prohibitive to the average voter.

To escape this dilemma, voters need a device for the *a priori* focusing of their attention upon only the most relevant data. Such a device will allow them to avoid the staggering difficulty of knowing everything the government has done during the election period and everything its opponents would have done were they in office. This device should focus attention only on the following *differential areas of decision:*

1. Areas of decision in which opposition parties contest the policies of the incumbents and offer alternative policies.
2. Areas of decision in which the presently governing party changed the government's method of reacting to, or handling, situations, i.e., changes in policy or competence of performance as compared with preceding governments.
3. Areas of decision in which the situations to which the government must react are markedly different from those extant under preceding governments. This knowledge allows comparison of what the government did with what preceding governments would have done.

Knowledge of the first of these areas (contested policies) is necessary and sufficient for computing the current party differential; knowledge of the last two (new policies and new situations) is necessary and sufficient for computing its future-orienting modifiers. Hence if voters focus on these areas and ignore all others, rational vote-casting is vastly simplified.

Through the division of labor, a set of agencies has arisen which provides information dealing mainly with these differential areas. Furthermore, this information is often given to voters either free of charge or at a very low cost, because many of the agencies which provide it are subsidized by persons other than those who receive the information. We will analyze these agencies in detail in Chapter 12.

V. CHARACTERISTICS OF A RATIONAL INFORMATION SYSTEM

Every rational citizen eventually constructs for his political usage a system of information acquisition. It consists of a limited number of information sources, a part of whose data output he selects to use in political decision-making. As explained, he is forced to rely on a rather crude process of trial and error experimentation to construct this system, but if it emerges as a truly rational one, it will have the following characteristics:

1. The data reporters in it use principles of selection as nearly identical to his own as possible.
2. It is broad enough to report anything of significance in the differential areas, yet narrow enough to cull out data not worth knowing about. In short, it focuses his attention on facts germane to his decision-making.
3. It provides him with enough information about each issue for his decisions, given his desire to invest in information.
4. It has sufficient internal plurality so that its parts can be used as checks upon each other's accuracy and deviation from his own selection principles. To be effective as mutual checks, information sources must be independent as well as nominally separate; e.g., a radio station and a newspaper which both use only Associated Press reports do not really check each other.

The creation and maintenance of such a rational system naturally absorbs scarce resources, the cost of which must be balanced against the returns from the information obtained. Therefore the extent of the system depends a great deal upon the nature of these returns, which we analyze in Chapter 13.

VI. SUMMARY

Decision-making is a process which consumes time and other scarce resources; hence economy must be practiced in determining how many resources shall be employed in it. This fact forces decision-makers to select only part of the total available information for use in making choices. The principles of selection they use depend upon the end for which the information is a means, but some principles are inherent in every report; so all information is biased by its very nature.

In a complex society, information which is used by one citizen is often gathered, transmitted, and analyzed by others. If the user is to know what his information really means in terms of his decision-making, he must be sure these others have the same principles of selection he has, or know how their principles differ from his.

Even choosing one's own selection principles is difficult, but by a process of trial and error, each rational citizen finds a set that best serves his political ends. He must check his data sources occasionally so as to detect any deviation from these principles.

Each citizen decides how much information to acquire by utilizing the basic marginal cost-return principle of economics. The marginal return from information is computed by first weighing the importance of making a right instead of a wrong decision. To this value is applied the probability that the bit of information being considered will be useful in making this decision. The marginal cost is the opportunity cost of acquiring this bit of information. Much of this cost can be shifted from the decision-maker to others, but the time for assimilation is a nontransferable cost. The decision-maker continues to acquire information until the marginal return equals the marginal cost to him.

To avoid surveying all the extant data, decision-makers seek information sources which focus their attention upon certain relevant areas of knowledge. Each selects a few gatherers and transmitters and molds them into a personal information-acquisition system. To be rational, this system should have the proper bias, be well-focused, provide adequate but not superfluous data, and contain some internal plurality.

12

How Rational Citizens
Reduce Information
Costs

Introduction

RATIONAL citizens in an uncertain world are under great pressure to cut down the quantity of scarce resources they use to obtain political information. In this chapter, we examine their methods of reducing data costs to discover how effectively these methods work and what impact they may have upon the distribution of political power in our model democracy.

Not all the behavior we will describe follows necessarily from our original axioms; some derives in part from a few new assumptions we make in this chapter. These postulates are added to make the model more relevant to the real world. However, it should not be construed as a replica of the real world, nor should our analysis of it be viewed as a description of actual processes of communication. Formulating a comprehensive theory of communications and propaganda requires exploration of the extensive research in these fields—a task we cannot undertake in the present study. Though we believe our model offers possibilities as a foundation for such a theory, our purpose in using it here is much less grandiose.

Objectives

In this chapter we attempt to prove the following propositions:

1. Society's free information stream systematically provides some citizens with more politically useful information than it provides others.
2. Certain specialists in the division of labor act automatically to reduce data costs drastically and to focus citizens' attention on the areas most relevant to their political decision-making.
3. Even when the returns from making correct decisions are infinite, rational men sometimes delegate part or all of their political decision-making to others; hence they may be totally uninformed about politics.
4. In any society which contains uncertainty and a division of labor, men will not be equally well-informed politically, no matter how equal they are in all other respects.
5. Any concept of democracy based on an electorate of equally well-informed citizens presupposes that men behave irrationally.

I. THE FREE INFORMATION STREAM

A. THE NATURE AND SOURCES OF FREE INFORMATION

Every society provides its members with a constant flow of free information about a variety of subjects. This practice results from the face-to-face contacts in all cultures and the need for close personal coöperation in production, leisure activities, the rearing of children, and political action. It may also have psychological roots in the inquisitiveness of man and his need for personal relationships with others. The breadth of topics covered by this stream varies among cultures and within any one, but we can reasonably assume that in democratic societies there is no ban on the free circulation of political data. Hence the free information stream is a potentially significant factor in our model.

Before we see just how significant it is, we must explain what we mean by "free" information. None of the information a man receives is completely costless. Merely perceiving it takes time; and if he assimilates it or thinks about it, these acts take more time. Thus unless the opportunity cost of this time is zero, which is unlikely, he must sacrifice a scarce resource to gain information. This sacrifice is a nontransferable cost. However, there are many other costs connected with information that are transferable: most of the costs of gathering, selecting, transmitting, analyzing, and even evaluating data can be shifted onto others.

When we speak of free information, we mean information which is given to a citizen without any transferable cost. The only cost he must bear consists of the time he spends absorbing and utilizing it. This cost varies tremendously, depending on the nature of the data. For example, the time a man spends heeding the sharp warning "Look out!" when he steps off a curb is minute compared to the time he uses reading the President's Economic Report, though the former may have infinitely higher returns than the latter.

Citizens in a democracy normally receive free political information in the following ways:

1. The governing party publishes large amounts of information as an intrinsic part of its governing activities.

2. All political parties, including the one in power, put out partisan information for the purpose of influencing voters.

3. Professional publishers distribute some information that is wholly subsidized by advertisers (e.g., throwaways, television programs).

4. Interest groups publish information gratuitously in order to persuade citizens to accept their viewpoints.

5. Other private citizens provide free data in the form of letters, conversations, discussion groups, speeches, etc.[1]

[1] Empirical research indicates that this source is probably the most important one politically even in technologically advanced nations like the United States. We can therefore assume it has always been the most significant, since earlier societies were without the alternative means of communication available today. For an extensive discussion of this subject, see E. Katz and P. F. Lazarsfeld, *Personal Influence* (Glencoe, Illinois: The Free Press, 1955), and P. F. Lazarsfeld, B. Berelson, and H. Gaudet, *The People's Choice* (New York: Columbia University Press, 1948).

6. Entertainment sources sometimes yield political information as a surplus benefit from what is intended as an entertainment investment (e.g., the newsreel in a motion picture theater). Some citizens also seek straight political information purely for its entertainment value because they enjoy political rivalry and warfare. Any strictly political values they get are consumer-surplus by-products of the entertainment.
7. Similarly, information acquired in the course of making production or consumption decisions may have political value. Since this value is incidental to the purpose for which the data is obtained, it can be regarded as a free benefit.

Free political information from these sources is of two types: *accidental* and *sought-for*. Accidental data are by-products of the non-political activities of a citizen; they accrue to him without any special effort on his part to find them. Thus their cost in time is ordinarily much lower than that of sought-for data. Sources (5), (6), and (7) produce mainly accidental data; whereas data from sources (2), (3), and (4) are usually ignored by the citizen unless he is specifically looking for political information. Source (1) produces both types.

Not all citizens receive the same amount of free data, nor are those who do receive the same amount equally able to make use of it. Anyone with time to spare can acquire endless amounts of sought-for data, but variations in the quantity of accidental data received can result from several other factors as well. In fact, systematic variations in amount of free information received and ability to assimilate may strongly influence the distribution of political power in a democracy.

Prior to exploring these variations, we should point out that the main role of free information in our model is acting as a floor for all types of rational calculations. It is the basis for preliminary estimations of such entities as the party differential, the marginal return from information, the marginal cost of information bits, and the cost of voting. By using whatever free information he has at hand, the rational citizen can guess how large each of these items is and thus determine whether to obtain more information before making his political decisions.

Since free information is also the chief instrument for each person's acculturation, it actually plays a much more significant role than the one mentioned above. Furthermore, this role is directly related to politics, because the type of acculturation a society provides its members partly determines whether democracy will be successful therein. However, so as to avoid any excursions into anthropology, we consider only the more superficial political uses of free information in our study.

B. THE AMOUNT OF FREE DATA CITIZENS RECEIVE

The factor most important in determining how much free information a man can fruitfully receive is his ability to bear the nontransferable costs inherent in all information. For this reason, the amount of time he can spend informing himself is paramount. Men of leisure or men whose work schedule includes time for absorbing information have the greatest opportunity to assimilate free data. Though there is no reason to suppose free time correlated with income, the ability to overcome a second cost—that of access to free-information channels—definitely rises with income. Actually, the information received over television and radio stations is not free because of this initial access cost. But once the entry fee has been paid, information can be obtained at a marginal cost of almost zero.

Another factor influencing the amount of free information a man receives is the nature of his informal contacts, both at work and during leisure hours. The kind of data a man obtains through these contacts varies with his social class and with the percentage of his contacts that cut across the lines of social class. The president of a giant firm often receives information of national political significance in chats with his colleagues; whereas a dishwasher may never hear politics discussed at all.

The type of entertainment information men seek further affects the amount of free political data they receive. For example, a man who reads history as a hobby may discover many politically pertinent data accidentally. Since readers of many inexpensive entertainment-oriented publications gain similar benefits, it is hard to say whether this access to free data varies with income.

Finally, the extent to which government action directly affects men determines the amount of free information they receive as a part of the governing process. Men who deal with the government in business, or are members of it, are automatically informed about at least some of its politically relevant decisions.

In the last part of this chapter, we discuss ways in which these variations and variations in the ability to use free information may affect the distribution of political power in our model democracy.

II. HOW ATTENTION IS FOCUSED BY INFORMATION PROVIDERS

As we pointed out in the last chapter, political decision-making in a large-sized democracy cannot be undertaken without fantastic costs unless (1) information is gathered for the many decision-makers by a few specialists and (2) the information each citizen receives is prefocused upon the differential areas of decision. Both of these general conditions must prevail before individuals can begin reducing their personal data costs to match their personal returns from information.

In most modern democracies, the division of labor delegates these functions to a set of expert information-providers. By specializing in procuring information, these agencies reduce the per unit cost of data tremendously and thus make it possible for individuals to buy information—though usually not without subsidy. And by selecting for presentation only data within the differential areas, they solve the problem of focusing attention. There are four major types of information-providers in our model other than private persons, whom we assume to be nonspecialists ultimately dependent for data upon the specialists we discuss. Since each type has different motives for its actions, we will treat them separately.[2]

[2] Though some nonprofit, nonpolitical organizations (e.g., colleges and universities) also put out data, most of these data reach citizens through one of the four channels mentioned; hence we do not treat these groups as a fifth type of information source.

A. PROFESSIONAL DATA-GATHERERS AND PUBLISHERS

Professional information gatherers and promulgators transmit only differential area information because that is what consumers want, and their aim is to make profits by pleasing their customers. "News" implies by its very name that it concerns changes in the situation worth knowing about. Of course, the fact that publishers focus on the kind of data consumers want does not mean they always use the political selection principles consumers want. However, they do relieve consumers of the overwhelming burden of surveying everything before picking out the few things that are sufficiently relevant to merit consideration.

B. INTEREST GROUPS

Because their primary concern is influencing current government policy, interest groups usually focus their information output upon policies that seem about to change. They do this whether they favor or oppose changing these policies. Thus they do not waste resources publicizing dead issues but concentrate upon the very items that are most relevant to citizens' political decision-making. Of course, there are some exceptions to this rule. Nevertheless, most data disseminated by interest groups concern events in the differential areas, in part because the agitation of such groups helps decide what matters lie within those areas.

C. POLITICAL PARTIES

Number one on the list of every party's objectives is the winning of elections. All the information it issues bears upon this goal and is therefore relevant to political decision-making. It is true that parties occasionally pass out irrelevant data as a deliberate smoke screen to cover up unfavorable facts or to increase the ambiguity of their stands.[3] Furthermore, each party traditionally produces a large output of sanctimonious platitudes praising the flag, motherhood, and the home. However, most of every party's emanations are either

[3] See Chapter 8 for a detailed discussion of such ambiguity.

attacks on its opponents or defenses of itself, so it emphasizes the very elements from which party differentials are formed.

D. THE GOVERNMENT

Besides the usual information output of a political party, the government must distribute large quantities of data as an intrinsic part of governing. These data include administrative directives, promulgations of new laws, announcements of its research findings, and other notices it gives its citizens in the course of its operations. The vast majority of these data are shaped solely by the necessities of administration and are not political in nature. Nevertheless, they provide important evidence for citizens who are making political decisions, because they tell these citizens what policies the government is carrying out. Since any changes in policy must be especially well-girded with instructions to those affected, a great deal of this information is focused upon differential areas of action.

However, this advance is likely to be submerged in the tremendous deluge of information which governments produce. Only by maintaining a purely superficial contact with government can a citizen gain any focusing benefits from it, since he will then hear only of major policy changes. But this superficiality may cause him to overlook more significant but less publicized data put out by the government. Altogether, it is doubtful whether the nonpolitical information provided by governments aids in focusing citizens' attention on the differential areas. Only if it is filtered through professional reporting agencies will the chaff be separated from the grain enough so that the total volume is not overwhelming. In this case, of course, the focusing is done by these agencies, not by government itself.

III. HOW RATIONAL CITIZENS REDUCE THEIR DATA COSTS

A. THE PROBLEM AND ITS BASIC SOLUTIONS

Even when most of his political data are prefocused on areas of general relevance, the rational man in politics must take further steps to increase his efficiency. Therefore he seeks (1) to expend no more time and money obtaining political information than its returns warrant and (2) to receive as many data as possible from whatever resources he does use. In the next chapter we discuss the probable size of returns from political information. For now let us assume that our sample citizen, voter A, expects a given return, X; his problem is to keep his information costs down to X and still maximize his knowledge.

To illustrate the main approaches to this problem, let us assume that A is currently investing more than X in political information and desires to cut down his investment. He can do so in one or more of the following ways:

1. Reduce the quantity of information he is receiving, i.e., absorb fewer bits and therefore use fewer resources in procuring and assimilating them. This method has the disadvantage of diminishing the amount of knowledge going into A's decisions, thereby increasing the probability that they will be incorrect ones.
2. Receive the same amount of information but reduce its procurement costs by
   a. Utilizing more free information, or
   b. Accepting subsidies for these costs whenever possible, or
   c. Doing both of the above.
3. Maintain the same information flow into his political decisions but delegate part of the making of those decisions to others by
   a. Using expert advice to reduce analysis costs, or
   b. Employing others' explicit value judgments to reduce evaluative costs, or
   c. Doing both of the above.

The first of these alternatives needs no elaboration, but because the others are somewhat more complicated, we will examine them more closely.

B. THE SHIFTING OF PROCUREMENT COSTS

If a man does not wish to delegate any more of the analysis and evaluation of facts to others than he has already, his means of cutting the cost of political decisions are limited. In fact, if we assume he cannot learn to think faster and does not want to use fewer data, all he can do is try to get the same information as before at less expense. This can be done in two ways.

The first is to use more free information. As we saw earlier, free information in our model society comes from a variety of sources, which can be divided into two classes: persons and nonpersons, the latter composed mainly of mass media. Thus, for example, a man can get more free data by conversing more often with his well-informed friends or by reading the newspapers in the library more thoroughly. Both acts reduce the costs he pays for information if he substitutes the data he gets in these ways for other data for which he used to pay.

Which type of free data source is a rational man likely to use most? Personal contact with others who have already obtained data has the advantage of producing several other types of utility, such as pleasure in their company and ability to steer the discussion so as to gain more precise information. Also, it is usually easier to contact relatively well-informed persons than to locate free literature or broadcasts, which are scattered in many places. Finally, nonpersonal free data are often wholly subsidized by sources interested in promulgating their own viewpoint. Thus information issued by political parties, favor-buyers, representative groups, and other influencers is chosen strictly by their own selection principles, which are unlikely to coincide with those of any one citizen. In contrast, it is often relatively easy for a man to find someone he knows who has selection principles like his own.

For all these reasons, our *a priori* expectation is that rational citizens will seek to obtain their free political information from other persons if they can. This expectation seems to be borne out by the existing evidence.[4]

The second way to cut procurement costs is to utilize partially subsidized information. In modern democracies, most mass media of communication are subsidized either by commercial advertisers or by government; hence nearly every rational citizen who obtains much

---

[4] See Katz and Lazarsfeld, *op. cit.*; and Lazarsfeld, Berelson, and Gaudet, *op. cit.*

information receives some that is subsidized. Ultimately, the subsidies are paid by purchasers of advertised products or taxpayers. But since the recipients need not be identical with the persons who pay, we can treat the former apart from the latter.

The major drawback of using partially subsidized data is the same as that of using wholly subsidized data: the selection principles embodied in the data may differ from those of the decision-maker in such a way that he may be led into wrong decisions. As we saw in the last chapter, this danger is inherent in all data selected by someone other than the decision-maker, whether subsidized or not. However, its acuteness is greatest in subsidized data because the decision-maker cannot force the provider to conform to his own principles if the provider's income is partly furnished by men with other principles. As in any market where a large number of small-scale consumers are served by a few large-scale producers, no one consumer has enough bargaining power to influence the producers. Hence whenever information is provided to consumers at low cost because of either mass production or subsidies or both, each consumer gains financially only by sacrificing control over the selection principles behind the information. Unless his own selection principles coincide with those of the data providers, this sacrifice may completely offset his economic gain.

We cannot describe the exact effects of subsidies or mass marketing of data without making a detailed analysis of the whole communication structure of society. For reasons stated in the introduction to this chapter, the present study is no place for such an undertaking. Hence we must limit ourselves to the conclusion that subsidies may cause some distortion in the distribution of political power, but we cannot specify its nature *a priori*.

C. DELEGATION OF ANALYSIS AND EVALUATION AS A MEANS OF REDUCING COSTS

In any highly specialized society, many areas of decision pose literally incomprehensible problems for those who are not experts therein. Yet nonexperts often must have opinions concerning the aptness of policies followed in these areas in order to make important political choices. For example, the nature of national defense in an atomic age is a crucial political problem both for survival of the nation and for proper allocation of its resources. But the issues involved are so complex that almost everyone who does not specialize in them must rely for his opinions upon those who do.

The division of labor creates this problem but also solves it, since citizens can buy the generalized opinions of experts in each area at a much lower cost than they would incur by manufacturing comparable opinions themselves. This saving is so enormous that rational political action in a large-sized democracy is impossible without a shifting of factual analysis onto specialists.

But how can the inexpert citizen know whether the experts' analyses are accurate? Fortunately, professional standards in most areas of specialization provide an independent check upon expertness which the layman can use in picking an expert to consult. Even the experts disagree among themselves, but most recognize certain standard methods of procedure as valid. If a specialist hews to these standards and shows ability besides, he will develop a reputation in his profession which nonexperts can use as a check upon his reliability. This check is by no means infallible, but it sharply reduces the uncertainty which nonexperts would face without it.

Though shifting analysis of facts onto experts reduces the cost of such analysis tremendously, some cost still remains. It must be paid by the citizen himself (in coöperation with the other citizens buying the same information) unless he can pass it onto subsidizers or gain access to expertness through the free information stream. Reducing the cost of expertise is thus exactly the same as reducing the cost of procurement, which we discussed previously.

Unfortunately, the nature of evaluation prevents development of any objective check upon accuracy similar to professionalization among experts. Evaluation is a process of judging means in the light of ends; thus the ends are all-important. But political ends vary from person to person, with no objective standards available to choose among them. Of course, as we pointed out in the last chapter, even selection and analysis of facts are partially evaluative, but at least some objective standards of procedure can be framed for them.[5] Since this cannot be done for explicitly evaluative acts, rational decision-makers must be extremely careful about delegating the evaluative steps of their decisions to others. Evaluative delegation is therefore less likely to occur in our model than delegation of analysis, which is in turn less likely to occur than delegation of procurement.

To be rational, an evaluative delegator must personally determine whether the agent he selects (1) has goals similar to his own, (2) possesses more data than he himself does, and (3) has powers of judgment that are, at worst, not so inferior to his own that they offset the advantages of better information. These conditions need not hold for all areas of the agent's decisions, only for those in which the delegator plans to trust the agent's judgment. For example, A can disagree with B about racial segregation and yet rationally delegate to B an evaluative decision about foreign policy, where A and B agree on goals.

In order to discover whether to trust a prospective agent's judgment, a rational decision-maker must first investigate the agent by checking the latter's past judgments. This means that evaluative delegation—like all rational delegation—often involves a cost of selecting agents. We can divide the agents selected into three groups: (1) *persons* with whom the delegator has face-to-face contacts, (2) *interest groups*, including political parties, with whom the delegator has identified himself on one or more issues, and (3) professional evaluation *experts* who make their living by selling their judgments to others (e.g., political columnists, commentators, and editorial writers). Each decision-maker may make use of several agents of any or all types. For example, a man might accept the views of the American Medical Association, a farm-owning friend of his, and Walter Lippmann in their various areas of specialization, and then balance all these evaluations together himself in deciding how to vote. To save time, his wife might delegate her voting decision entirely to him. These acts are all highly efficient ways to cut down data costs and still make judgments based on extensive information.

[5] In this case, *objective* means very widely agreed upon among specialists and others whose welfare is concerned.

Is there any *a priori* reason to expect one type of agent to be more often employed than others in the real world? Actually, the frequency distribution of consultation cannot be determined without empirical investigation, but we suspect persons are more often used as evaluators than other agents. Our reasoning here is exactly the same as that given earlier to support our view that persons are the most widely used source of free information.

D. THE RELATION OF DELEGATION TO THE RETURNS FROM INFORMATION

The preceding analysis leads to a rather striking conclusion: it may be rational for a man to delegate part or all of his political decision-making to others, no matter how important it is that he make correct decisions. To prove this assertion, let us assume an extreme case in which one citizen, S, must decide which of several contending parties will govern the whole nation during the next election period. What is the most rational way for him to go about making this choice?

Clearly, S cannot be expert in all the fields of policy that are relevant to his decision. Therefore he will seek assistance from men who are experts in those fields, have the same political goals he does, and have good judgment. Furthermore, if S knows that T, whom he trusts, has general political goals similar to his own and better judgment than S himself, then it is rational for S to delegate the final decision to T if the latter has information equal to S's. In short, S's most rational course is to make no decisions himself except deciding who should make decisions; any other course is irrational even if S's life depends upon whether the right choice is made.

In this case the returns from information are very large indeed, yet rationality still demands delegation of evaluation as well as of procurement and analysis. Not only will such delegation assure the best possible decision, but also it will reduce S's costs enormously—hence he has a double motivation for it.

Nevertheless, under normal voting conditions, citizens in our model cannot rationally regard the contending parties in an election as possible agents for delegation. If they eschew thinking about policies and select a party because its personnel are well-informed and have good judgment, they are acting irrationally. This is true even though in the real world such delegation of evaluation to parties or candidates is probably common and may even at times be rational.

The crux of the matter lies in the assumption of common goals necessary for rational delegation. According to our hypothesis, party officials are interested only in maximizing votes, never in producing any particular social state *per se*. But voters are always interested in the latter. Therefore a rational voter who is not a party official himself cannot assume members of any party have goals similar to his own. But without this assumption, delegation of all political decisions to someone else is irrational—hence political parties can never be the agents of rational delegation.

There is only one exception to this rule: if a voter believes a certain party will seek to maximize votes by catering to the desires of a specific interest group or section of the electorate, and if his own goals are identical with the goals of that group or section, then he can rationally delegate all his political decision-making to that party. However, he must investigate policies in order to discover any such identity between his own goals and those of a large group to whom a party might cater. This type of delegation thereby requires him to incur some of the costs of information about policies anyway.

IV. THE DIFFERENTIAL POWER IMPACT OF INFORMATION

A. VARIATIONS IN ABILITY TO USE POLITICAL DATA

Given the total amount of political information a man receives, his ability to use it depends primarily upon three factors: (1) the time he can afford to spend assimilating it, (2) the kind of contextual knowledge he has, and (3) the homogeneity of the selection principles behind the information with his own selection principles.

Since we have discussed (1) already in Part I of this chapter, we will examine only (2) and (3) here.

Education is the primary source of contextual knowledge. However, it need not be formal education, since training on the job can be just as effective as training in school. Thus a man's formal schooling and the type of job he has have an important bearing upon his ability to make meaningful use of current data. They shape not only his contextual knowledge in general, but also his specific decision-making ability. We cannot state *a priori* what kinds of occupations have the greatest carry-over into making political decisions; this can be determined only by rather complex empirical studies. All we can say is that (1) the division of labor will definitely produce differences among men in so far as their ability to use data is concerned and (2) to the extent that formal education makes decision-making more efficient, the children of high-income groups, who usually get better educations than the offspring of low-income citizens, tend to have an advantage.

If the selection principles behind the data a man receives are not homogeneous (i.e., similar or identical) then he may encounter different versions of the same occurrences, even if all the individual facts reported are true *per se*. Thus a citizen who gives equal weight to articles in the *Daily Worker* and the *Freeman* may find himself bewildered by opposite interpretations of the same events. Similar confusion may result if a man receives information only from sources whose selection principles differ from his own, e.g., a laborer who cannot afford to read anything except the only daily newspaper in his city, which is controlled by a conservative publisher. The conflicts which arise in both these situations tend to paralyze decision-making by creating uncertainty. Again, it is difficult to generalize about the impact of this factor without empirical investigation. A tentative conclusion might be as follows: since the mass media of communication in many democracies are owned or dominated more by high-income interests than low-income ones, low-income citizens are more likely to receive data selected by principles conflicting with their own than are upper income groups. We do not know how great an effect this conflict has. However, it contributes to the general advantage of high-income groups produced by the necessity of bearing costs to obtain political information.

B. THE COST OF INFORMATION AND EQUALITY OF POLITICAL INFLUENCE

One fact stands out clearly from all the analysis in this chapter: in any society marked by an extensive division of labor and the presence of uncertainty, the cost of information is bound to be different for different men. Hence the amount of data it is rational for one man to acquire may be much greater or much smaller than the amount it is rational for another man to acquire. This conclusion is valid even when the returns from information are identical for all.

If our model world were populated by rational individuals with equal intelligence, equal interest in government policies, and equal incomes, they would nevertheless not be equally well-informed politically. In fact, many of them might know almost nothing about politics because they delegated their decisions to others. The division of labor always places men in different social locations with varying access to and needs for information, and lack of perfect knowledge prevents each from communicating his specialized knowledge to the others without cost. Therefore we may conclude as follows:

1. Any concept of democracy based on an electorate of equally well-informed citizens is irrational; i.e., it presupposes that citizens behave irrationally.
2. The foundations of differential political power in a democracy are rooted in the very nature of society.

Furthermore, to be at all realistic, we must add to the aforementioned differentiating forces the unequal distribution of income. All information is costly; therefore those with high incomes can better afford to procure it than those with low incomes. As we have seen in previous chapters, this fact further distorts operation of the principle of political equality—the principle that lies at the heart of democratic theory.

V. SUMMARY

Every society provides its members with a stream of information free from transferable costs. In modern democracies, though not all citizens receive the same amount of free political data, they all use whatever they have to make preliminary estimates of whether it is worthwhile to acquire more information.

A necessary prerequisite to rational political action is the prefocusing of attention upon the differential areas of decision. This end is accomplished by the providers of political information acting for various reasons of self-interest. To reduce his personal data-procurement costs, the rational citizen can start using more free information, which he will probably obtain from other persons rather than mass media. Another method of reducing costs is to accept subsidized information, although by doing so the citizen may lose some control over the selection principles behind the information.

In complex cultures, an essential part of political decision-making is delegation to others of several steps in the process. Nearly all data procurement and much factual analysis are done by specialized agencies rather than decision-makers themselves. By utilizing such agencies, citizens can cut their costs enormously.

Evaluative decisions are more difficult to delegate because there are no professional standards by which to recognize experts. Delegators must therefore select only agents whose goals are similar to their own and whose information is more extensive than their own. Evaluation delegation is most likely to be made to other persons rather than interest groups or professional experts. This is sometimes rational even when the returns from information are very high, though political parties cannot be treated as agents for rational delegation in our model.

Even if men received the same amount of data, not all could use it with equal efficiency. In fact, the division of labor and the presence of uncertainty guarantee that rational men will be politically informed to different degrees. Thus the foundations for inequalities of power are inherent in democratic societies, even though political equality is their basic ethical premise.

13

The Returns from Information and Their Diminution

Introduction

CITIZENS acquire political information for two main reasons: (1) to help them decide how to vote, and (2) to form opinions with which they can influence government policy formation during the period between elections. The voting decision is made in view of the policies that government has pursued during the election period. It is the voter's reaction to whatever government has already done. The opinion-forming decision is designed to influence the formation of government policy during the election period; it is not a *post facto* reaction to government decisions but an active moulder of them.

Of course, voting itself is a device to influence the future policies of government by selecting governors who have made specific promises. It has also already influenced past policies because the government's action was conditioned by how it thought men would vote. Therefore, from the government's point of view, there is not much difference between these two uses of information. But from the citizen's point of view, the differences are vast, as we shall see.

In this study, we ignore all motives for obtaining political information other than the two mentioned above. Some citizens find exhilaration in arguing about politics or following campaigns; others gain social prestige at cocktail parties from appearing well-versed in current affairs. We classify information obtained for all such purposes as entertainment information, no matter how political its contents may seem.

Objectives

In this chapter we attempt to prove the following propositions:

1. The citizens who care most about which party wins a given election have the least need of information; whereas those for whom information is most useful do not care who wins the election.

2. For a great many citizens, acquisition of any nonfree political data whatever is irrational, as is acquisition of much free political data, even during election campaigns.

3. Most citizens in a democracy do not vote on the basis of their true political views. Therefore, democratic government may fail to provide the majority of its citizens with all the benefits they could obtain from it.

4. Only a few citizens can rationally attempt to influence the formation of each government policy; for most, it is irrational to know anything about formulation of even those policies which affect them.

5. In general, the economic decisions of a rational government in a democracy are biased against consumers and in favor of producers.

6. Inequality of political power is inevitable in every large society marked by uncertainty and a division of labor, no matter what its constitution says or how equal its citizens are in every other respect.

I. ACQUIRING INFORMATION FOR VOTING

A. THE ROLE OF THE PARTY DIFFERENTIAL

Why does a rational man vote? In our model, voting is a means of selecting the best possible government from among the parties competing for the job. Therefore a rational man votes because he would rather have one of these parties in office than any of the others. The margin of his preference is his *party differential*, as explained in Chapter 3; it forms the basic return upon which the marginal return of investing in information is calculated.

Let us assume temporarily that only one citizen is voting; so his ballot decides which party will govern. In this case, his party differential represents to him the cost of voting wrongly, or, looking at it the other way around, the reward for being right. To "be right" here means to select the party which will actually give the citizen a higher utility income from its acts in office than any other party; whereas to "be wrong" means to select some other party and thus lose the utility margin which the best party affords.

Clearly, if a voter is indifferent about which party governs him—i.e., if his party differential is zero—he has nothing to gain from being informed. If he makes a mistake and votes for the wrong party, he will not suffer any loss of utility. There really is no "wrong" party for him; so the potential return on any political information he obtains for voting purposes is zero. But because time is spent in absorbing any data, the cost of political information is never zero. Apparently, men with zero party differentials are irrational if they invest in any political information to help them make their voting decision.

But how does a voter know what his party differential is if he has not invested in information? Just to find out whether or not it is zero, he must obtain some data. In fact, discovering one's party differential is identical to making a normal voting decision—the former is simply our terminology for the latter.

Here we encounter the fact that in the uncertain world of our model, as in the real world, making a voting decision is a dynamic act. We must therefore analyze it as a process occuring in time and consisting of discrete steps. The first step is estimation of one's party differential, either (1) by means of the free information which one absorbs in daily living, or (2) by means of data obtained in an exploratory investment made just for this purpose.

The preliminary estimate of the party differential is the basic return upon which subsequent calculations are built. It is the estimated cost of being wrong, derived without serious consideration of the cost and returns of making the estimate. From this point on, however, the costs and returns of all data must be weighed and information procured only if its expected return exceeds its cost.

B. INFORMATION BITS AND THEIR USE IN DECISION-MAKING

A rational voter is interested only in information which might change his preliminary voting decision, i.e., the decision indicated by his first estimate of his party differential. Though all information is costly, only this information provides returns in terms of a better decision or increased confidence in the present one. Hence this is the only type of data it is rational to acquire.

To discover whether a given bit of information might change his mind, the voter compares it with his estimated party differential. The information which the bit contains can be translated into a positive, negative, or zero change in the utility income he expects if one of the parties is elected. This change directly affects his party differential, since the latter is the difference between the utility income he expects if the incumbents are reëlected and the one he expects if their rivals win. If there is a reasonable chance that the party differential he now has will be completely negated by the change this bit indicates, he acquires the bit.

However, it is extremely difficult for the citizen to estimate what change in his party differential he can expect from a given bit of information. Because bits are not independent of each other, the order in which they are acquired is crucial. For example, assume that bit X will tell the voter whether or not party A is secretly run by subversives, and bit Y whether it favors a high or low tariff on cheese.

Clearly, the value of bit Y depends entirely on the content of bit X, since if party A is subversive, its policy on the cheese tariff is irrelevant. Hence bits cannot be evaluated singly but must be considered in sets. The exact method of consideration to be used is a statistical problem we cannot discuss here. However, from now on, whenever we refer to a *bit* we mean a *set of bits* considered as a unit.

Another difficulty is conversion of a bit's expected value into its expected pay-off. All a voter really knows about each bit before acquiring it is (1) a list of its possible values, (2) the probability associated with each value, and (3) its cost. This knowledge is really a set of subjective estimates based on whatever information he has already acquired. From it he can calculate the expected value of the bit and its variance, which he weighs against its cost and his party differential in deciding whether to acquire it.

To clarify this process, let us assume that citizen Z has estimated his party differential at 50 units and is then confronted by a single bit. It costs 10 units to acquire and has the following probable values:

0.5 probability of being   100.0 units
0.4 probability of being   −10.0 units
0.1 probability of being   −100.0 units

Its expected value is therefore 36, which means that it is unlikely to change his mind; in fact, it will probably increase his party differential. However, there is a 10 per cent chance that it will shift his position from favoring one party by 50 units to favoring its rival by 50 units. Thus if he fails to buy the bit and its value is in fact −100, he incurs a loss in utility income of 40 units by voting for the wrong party (assuming his vote decides the election).[1] This example shows that he must consider the entire distribution of each bit rather than just its expected value when appraising it.

The purpose of this detailed analysis is to show how a bit's expected pay-off varies in relation to its expected value and variance. The *expected pay-off* of a bit is the amount of utility a voter is likely to save by changing his decision as a result of receiving the data in

[1] His loss is 40 instead of 50 because he must deduct the cost of buying the bit from the gain he would obtain by voting correctly.

the bit. If a bit is not likely to change his decision, its expected pay-off is zero, even if its expected value is not zero. When a bit's expected pay-off outweighs its cost, he will buy it; otherwise he will not. Clearly, the size of any bit's expected pay-off depends upon the size of the estimated party differential to which it is applied as well as upon the bit itself. For a bit with given variance and given expected value, the larger is a voter's party differential, the smaller is the bit's expected pay-off, and the less likely he is to buy the bit.

In other words, the more a voter originally favors one party over another, the less likely he is to buy political information, *ceteris paribus*.[2] If he has a strong preference to start with, it takes a great deal of adverse information to change his mind. Only a series of bits with value ranges including high negative values can possibly do so. Since such a series is unusual in most political campaigns, rational citizens who have strong preferences at the beginning of a campaign will probably not use many data issued during it. Except for whatever free information they absorb accidentally, they are likely to remain uninformed.

On the other hand, a voter who is indifferent to begin with may also feel apathetic about becoming informed. True, his incentive to acquire information is larger than that of a highly partisan voter, since almost any bit may cause him to switch his vote from one party to the other. But unless new data reveal a very large change in some expected income, it does not really make much difference to him who wins. Therefore it is irrational for him to acquire many costly bits unless they have either large expected values or high variance relative to his original party differential. Only such data can raise his party differential so that he is no longer indifferent about voting correctly.

---

[2] Most empirical studies reach exactly the opposite conclusion. They show that the more partisan a man is, the better informed he is likely to be. In our opinion, this finding indicates that people inform themselves in proportion to their interest in the outcome, not in proportion to the usefulness of data in deciding how to vote. If so, men's well-informedness will vary directly with the size of their party differentials. From the point of view of elections *per se*, this behavior is irrational unless the data is used to persuade others; i.e., unless the well-informed voters are agitators. See P. F. Lazarsfeld, B. Berelson, and H. Gaudet, *The People's Choice* (New York: Columbia University Press, 1948).

We therefore conclude that (1) information is relatively useless to those citizens who care which party wins and (2) those citizens for whom information is most useful do not care who wins. In short, nobody has a very high incentive to acquire political information.

C. WHY THE PARTY DIFFERENTIAL MUST BE DISCOUNTED

Throughout these considerations, we have assumed that each citizen behaved as though his vote alone determined the election. But in fact, hundreds, thousands, or even millions of other citizens are also eligible to vote; so each man's ballot is only one drop in a vast sea. The probability that his vote will decide the election, given the votes of all others, is extremely small, though not zero. Its size varies depending upon how the others are likely to cast their ballots. For example, if a community is almost evenly divided between staunch Republicans and die-hard Democrats, any one man's vote has a greater chance of deciding a local election than if the community is 85 percent Republican. Or if 95 percent of the voters in an area stay away from the polls, the probability that any one vote among the other 5 percent will be decisive is much greater than if 100 percent voted, *ceteris paribus*.

But no matter what conditions prevail, every rational voter realizes that he is not the only person voting. This knowledge radically alters his view of the importance of his own vote. If he is the only voter, the cost to him of voting incorrectly is measured by his party differential, because an incorrect vote elects the wrong party. But in fact there are multitudes of other voters. Therefore the party which eventually wins will probably be elected no matter how he casts his ballot, as long as the other citizens vote independently of him. Thus the cost of his making a mistake cannot be measured by his party differential, since this mistake may not alter the outcome.

Instead he must discount his party differential greatly before arriving at the value of voting correctly. This *vote value* is compounded from his estimates of his party differential and of the probability that his vote will be decisive. Since the vote value measures the possible cost to him of being inadequately informed, it is from the vote value, not the party differential, that information relevant to voting derives its worth. We must therefore substitute the vote value, which is nearly infinitesimal under most circumstances, for the estimated party differential in all the calculations outlined above. The result is an enormously diminished incentive for voters to acquire political information before voting.

Although we cannot make *a priori* predictions of just how small this incentive is, it seems probable that for a great many citizens in a democracy, rational behavior excludes any investment whatever in political information *per se*. No matter how significant a difference between parties is revealed to the rational citizen by his free information, or how uncertain he is about which party to support, he realizes that his vote has almost no chance of influencing the outcome. Therefore why should he buy political information? Instead he is likely to rely purely on the stream of free information he receives in the course of his nonpolitical pursuits. He will not even utilize all the free information available, since assimilating it takes time.

This conclusion is not equivalent to saying that all politically well-informed men are irrational. A rational man may buy political information because (1) he wishes to influence the government's policies, (2) his prediction of how other voters will act indicates that the probability is relatively high that his own vote will be decisive, or (3) he derives entertainment value or social prestige from such data. Nevertheless, in so far as voting is concerned, we believe that it is rational for a great part of the electorate to minimize investment in political data. For them, rational behavior implies both a refusal to expend resources on political information *per se* and a definite limitation of the amount of free political information absorbed.

D. THE IMPACT OF INDIVISIBILITY

This view of rationality conflicts sharply with the traditional idea of good citizenship in a democracy. Indeed, the whole concept of representative government becomes rather empty if the electorate has no opinions to be represented. If so, how can we defend our conclusions?

It is not possible in this study to explore fully the contrast between traditional ethical models of democracy and our own model. However, we can indicate a tentative explanation for the conflict mentioned above. It arises from the simultaneous truth of two seemingly contradictory propositions: (1) rational citizens want democracy to work well so as to gain its benefits, and it works best when the citizenry is well-informed; and (2) it is individually irrational to be well-informed. Here individual rationality apparently conflicts with social rationality; i.e., the goals men seek as individuals contradict those they seek in coalition as members of society.

This paradox exists because the benefits men derive from efficient social organization are indivisible. For purposes of this discussion, let us assume that everyone benefits in the long run if government is truly run "by consent of the governed"; i.e., if every voter expresses his true views in voting.[3] By his "true" views, we mean the views he would have if he thought that his vote decided the outcome.

But in fact his vote is not decisive: it is lost in a sea of other votes. Hence whether he himself is well-informed has no perceptible impact on the benefits he gets. If all others express their true views, he gets the benefits of a well-informed electorate no matter how well-informed he is; if they are badly informed, he cannot produce these benefits himself. Therefore, as in all cases of indivisible benefits, the individual is motivated to shirk his share of the costs: he refuses to get enough information to discover his true views. Since all men do this, the election does not reflect the true consent of the governed.

Furthermore, the usual remedy for such situations cannot be applied in this case. Normally, individuals receiving indivisible benefits give powers of coercion to a government, which then forces each of them to pay his share of the cost. In this way all gain, as we have

---

[3] This assumption is false because those who are in the minority may gain if the majority fail to express their true views in elections. Therefore our argument holds only for those who stand to gain by the better working of democracy. However, since by definition they constitute a majority (if we ignore Arrow problems), the argument is not without significance.

explained before. But in a democracy, government cannot force people to become well-informed for the following reasons:

1. There is no reliable, objective, inexpensive way to measure how well-informed a man is.
2. There is no agreed-upon rule for deciding how much information of what kinds each citizen should have.
3. The loss of freedom involved in forcing people to acquire information would probably far outweigh the benefits to be gained from a better-informed electorate.

In the face of these obstacles, most democratic governments do little more than compel young people in schools to take civics courses.

The foregoing reasoning suggests that democratic election systems always operate at less-than-perfect efficiency. The tension which exists between individual and social rationality prevents the governed from expressing their true consent when they select a government. As the analysis proceeds, we shall discover other reasons why no democracy can perfectly achieve its ideals in an uncertain world.

II. ACQUIRING INFORMATION IN ORDER TO INFLUENCE GOVERNMENT POLICY

A. HOW DATA DERIVE VALUE FROM INFLUENCE

When the government in our model formulates policy, it does so expressly to please as many voters as it can, as explained in Chapter 4. But no voter is pleased by a particular policy unless he prefers it to the alternatives that could have been chosen. And in order so to prefer it, he must be informed about the situation in which this policy decision is being made. Therefore political information is useful to voters because it enables them to have specific preferences, which in turn influence government policies that affect them.

Of course, the people who have opinions in advance about government decisions are not the only ones affected by them. Hence government cannot take account only of their reactions in making its decisions. Nevertheless, since government operates in a fog of uncertainty, it is sure to pay more attention to desires it can perceive than to those which remain obscure. This tendency is especially strong whenever the government is uncertain about the factual outcomes of various policy alternatives, as well as their impacts upon citizens' votes. For example, a government may know that its citizens do not want a given labor dispute to disturb peace and prosperity. However, it may be uncertain about which side's proposals will lead to the most tranquil outcome. Even though many people other than the well-informed are affected by its settlement of the dispute (assuming it has jurisdiction), it must rely upon the latter to tell it what the effects will be. Therefore the well-informed have a strong influence in determining what policy government will follow.

In our model, the government does not care whether the utility incomes of its citizens are affected by its behavior; it is interested only in their votes. Hence it is concerned about their utility incomes only when those incomes affect their votes. But the government does not always know whether voters can trace their utility-income changes to government action, even when government action in fact causes those changes. In other words, government may not know how much its citizens know about how its policies affect them. By looking at these several levels of knowledge, we can classify the various degrees of attention which government will give to a citizen's desires as follows:

1. If government does not know how a given decision affects a citizen's income, it obviously cannot take account of his interests. Therefore it has to ignore him in making the decision.
2. If the government knows that the citizen's income is unaffected by a particular decision, it ignores him in making the decision.
3. If the government knows that a citizen's income is affected but that he cannot trace the effects specifically to government action, it ignores him.
4. If government knows that a voter's income is affected by its policy but does not know whether the voter is aware of this, it may try to make some adjustment in case he is.
5. If government knows that a citizen's income is affected and also knows that the citizen is aware of this, it gives full consideration to the impact of its policies upon him. Even in this case, how-

ever, it may still tactically ignore his wishes in an attempt to please other voters.

All these degrees of knowledge depend upon the information which (1) citizens have about how government policies affect them, (2) governments have about which citizens are affected, and (3) governments have about which citizens know they are affected. Clearly, the more information a citizen has, the more influence over government policy he is likely to exercise—provided he informs the government what his preferences are. Conversely, the less a citizen knows about policy alternatives, the fewer specific preferences he can have, and the more likely it is that government will ignore him in making decisions.

Information thus derives value from the influence it enables its possessors to wield in the formation of government policy. The quantity of this value is the return on information which must be balanced against its cost in deciding whether to buy the data in question. Again we utilize the principle of equating marginal return with marginal cost, and again we have to view investment in information as a process to be analyzed sequentially.

However, we must first take a closer look at how information derives its value from influence. Let us assume that citizen X is interested in the policy government adopts in economic area A, from which X obtains his income. Even if X does nothing at all *re* influence—fails to inform himself and fails to communicate with government—government is going to pursue some policy in area A, assuming that "hands off" is a form of policy. We call this policy a_1. On the other hand, if X is fully informed about area A, he will desire a certain policy, a_x, which benefits him more than any other policy.

If a_1 and a_x are identical, then citizen X need not influence the government at all to maximize his gain from policy in area A. In fact, any investment he makes in order to exercise influence there is wasted. However, as we saw in discussing voting, citizen X cannot know whether a_1 and a_x are identical until after he has made some investment in information. Therefore he must utilize free information, or make some exploratory data investment, to form a preliminary estimate of the natures of a_1 and a_x and the utility-income difference between them. Let us call this margin the *intervention value* in area A. It is the maximum gain which X would make if he himself could set policy in that area, altering it from what it would be without his intervention to what he would most like it to be.

Citizen X's intervention value depends upon what influence other citizens are likely to exert in area A. Obviously, if X does not intervene in area A, those who do intervene will set government's policy there. Thus a number of citizens simultaneously trying to appraise their own intervention values in area A resemble a number of oligopolists pondering each other's policies. Each must estimate what the others are going to do before he can calculate what is rational for himself, and each knows the others are similarly trying to weigh his own probable actions. We make no attempt to offer any general solution to this problem of mutual conjectural variation. However, each citizen must somehow solve the version of it facing him before he can decide upon his most rational data investment.

In practice, even when X becomes informed about area A, his influence does not necessarily control government policy there. The government may not be aware that X cares what policy it adopts in area A. Even if it knows what X's preferences are in this area, government may not follow them because it is also trying to please other voters. As a matter of tactics, it may compromise with X's desires or ignore them altogether. Thus in order that X have any influence on policy in area A, the following conditions must be fulfilled:

1. X must have specific preferences in area A. To do so, he must be informed about what alternatives exist there.

2. The government must be aware that X has preferences and know what they are. This means there must be communication from X to the government.[4]

[4] The government may cater to X's desires even if it is not certain (1) that he has any or (2) what they are. Thus if it feels a large group of voters might be affected by some policy in such a way as to alter their votes, this feeling may influence its decision. In this case, there is no cost of communication, and the voters need not actually be informed (i.e., the government can be mistaken). However, the influence exerted in such cases is much smaller than that exerted as described in the text, *ceteris paribus*.

3. The government must be moved by its awareness of X's preferences to alter the policy it would have followed in the absence of
such awareness. It is true that X may be trying to persuade the
government to retain its present policy, but unless it was about
to change this policy, X's action is superfluous.

The policy which actually emerges after X has communicated his
opinions to the government we shall call a_2; it embodies whatever
influence X has had. If a_2 is the same as a_1, X has had no influence
at all. If a_2 differs from a_1 but is the same as a_x, then X has prevailed
in area A. Finally, if a_2 is better for X than a_1 but worse than a_x,
then X has had partial influence. In all cases, the amount of X's influence is measured by the utility-income difference between a_1 and a_2.
We shall call this difference X's *opinion impact*, since it represents
the actual gain he incurred by becoming informed and letting government know his preferences. Only when X prevails is his opinion
impact as large as his intervention value.

From this analysis we can see two discouragements facing the influencer. First, if it is not obvious what policy would benefit him most,
he may have to make a costly investment in information to find out.
Even then, great uncertainty about the outcomes of various policies
may still plague him. Second, even if he knows what policy he prefers, he never knows the extent of his influence upon the actual government decision until after it is made. Hence his opinion impact
is always a prediction based on what other pressures he believes
government is under.

Similar difficulties are encountered by voters trying to decide how
much data to buy, as we saw earlier in this chapter. In fact, the intervention value here is precisely analogous to the party differential in
our previous analysis, just as the opinion impact is analogous to the
vote value. Thus the intervention value measures the maximum possible gain X can get from information about area A; whereas the
opinion impact measures this gain discounted to account for the
influence of other citizens. The opinion impact is also the basic return on which the marginal return from information bits is computed.

This computation is exactly analogous to finding the marginal return on information used for voting, and the same reasoning applies to it. Furthermore, the same cost-return balancing process is employed in deciding what bits of information to purchase. Therefore we need not repeat our analysis of these procedures.

B. THE COST OF COMMUNICATION

In spite of these similarities, there are significant differences between acquiring information in order to vote and acquiring it in order to influence policy-making. In the first place, voters automatically communicate their decision to government in the act of voting, but influencers must transmit their opinions to government by specific act in order to get results. Like all acts, this one uses scarce resources; i.e., it is costly. The amount of this *cost of communication* depends upon the position of the citizen in society. If he happens to be Vice-President of the United States, it will be low; if he is a laborer in a mining town, it may be very high.[5]

Whatever size this cost is, someone must pay it. However, the one who pays need not be the citizen himself. If his interest in a policy area stems from his business, he can charge the costs of transmitting his views to his firm, which will probably deduct them from its taxable income. Thus the firm and the government bear the cost, not the citizen.[6] But no matter who pays, whatever part of the cost falls on the influencer must be counted as part of the marginal cost to be balanced against whatever marginal return there is from being informed. This cost varies depending upon to whom in the government a citizen communicates his views, because it is more expensive to reach some officials than to reach others. Of course, the opinion impact also depends upon whom the influencer contacts. Both these factors must be accounted for in deciding how much information to buy for purposes of influencing policy.

[5] The reception his communication receives depends upon whether or not he is an influential voter, as described in Chapter 6. However, for the moment we wish to keep his communication position analytically separate from his political influence.

[6] The firm is really its owners, who thus bear part of this cost. The government, of course, passes its share of the cost onto taxpayers or sufferers from inflation, depending upon how it is financing itself.

C. WHY INFLUENCERS ARE BETTER INFORMED THAN VOTERS

There is a second important distinction between the two types of return from information: almost everyone at least considers voting, but relatively few citizens ever consider exerting influence in any particular area of policy. As we have seen, a voter's party differential is subject to heavy discounting because of the great number of other voters. In contrast, an influencer's intervention value may suffer hardly any discount because only a small number of others are interested in the policy he wants to influence. Perhaps many people are affected by this policy, but since most of them do not realize in advance the source of these effects, they cannot seek to alter policy pursued at that source.

Such ignorance is not the result of mere apathy; rather it stems from the great cost of obtaining enough information to exert effective influence. Each influencer must be acquainted with the situation at least well enough to be in favor of a specific policy. True, many people voice strong policy preferences without benefit of much information, and the ballots these people cast are just as potent as those of the well-informed. Nevertheless, the government knows that its behavior in a given policy area will affect many people who show no immediate interest in that area. Consequently, it must be persuaded that these presently passive citizens will not react against whatever policy an influencer is promoting. A would-be influencer has to be knowledgeable enough to carry out this persuasion.

Thus formulation of policy requires more knowledge than choosing among alternatives which others have formulated. As a result, influencers need more information about the policy areas they operate in than even the most well-informed voters; hence their data costs are higher. The complexity of these areas often forces influencers to become experts before they can discover what policies best suit their own interests. And because many influencers with different goals are competing with each other for power, each must (1) produce arguments to counter any attacks upon him, (2) assault the others' contentions with data of his own, and (3) be informed enough to know what compromises are satisfactory to him.

In contrast, a voter need find only the differential impact on him of a few alternatives formulated by others. He does not have to examine all the possible alternatives, since not all are open to his choice—though all are open to the choice of a policy-maker. Also, a voter need not be well-informed enough to think of compromises, since either one party or the other will win (except in the case of coalition governments). In addition, unless he is trying to persuade others to vote his way, he does not have to argue with opposing forces, so he is under no competitive pressure to become informed.

The gist of this analysis is that influencers are specialists in whatever policy areas they wish to influence; whereas voters are generalizers trying to draw an overall comparison between parties. Specialization demands expert knowledge and information, especially if competition is keen, but most men cannot afford to become expert in many fields simultaneously. Therefore influencers usually operate in only one or two policy areas at once. This means that in each area, only a small number of specialists are trying to influence the government.

Naturally, the men who stand most to gain from exerting influence in a policy area are the ones who can best afford the expense of becoming expert about it. Their potential returns from influence are high enough to justify a large investment of information. In almost every policy area, those who stand the most to gain are the men who earn their incomes there. This is true because most men earn their incomes in one area but spend them in many; hence the area of earning is much more vital to them than any one area of spending. Furthermore, the cost of data purchased in order to influence government policy in an area of production can often be charged to a business firm or labor union. These corporate units can, in turn, deduct the cost from their taxable incomes. Also they may be large enough to gain economies of scale in data consumption through intensive specialization in relevant policy areas.

For all these reasons, producers are much more likely to become influencers than consumers. The former can better afford both to invest in the specialized information needed for influencing and to pay the cost of communicating their views to the government. This conclusion even applies to business firms, since their revenue nearly always comes from fewer policy areas than their cost inputs. However, almost every man is both a producer and a consumer at different moments of his life. Therefore we must rephrase the above conclusion as follows: men are more likely to exert political influence in their roles as income-receivers than in their roles as income-spenders, whether acting as private citizens or as members of a corporate entity.

This conclusion is of great importance because from it we can deduce (1) the pattern of information investment which any particular citizen is likely to make, (2) which citizens are likely to be well-informed on any given policy area, and (3) what pressures upon government are likely to be strongest in any area. Clearly, the cost of acquiring information and communicating opinions to government determines the structure of political influence. Only those who can afford to bear this cost are in a position to be influential.

A striking example of this fact is the failure of consumers-at-large to exercise any cogent influence over government decisions affecting them. For instance, legislators are notorious for writing tariff laws which favor a few producers in each field at the expense of thousands of consumers. On the basis of votes alone, this practice is hardly compatible with our central hypothesis about government behavior. But once we introduce the cost of information, the explanation springs full-armed from our theory. Each producer can afford to bring great influence to bear upon that section of the tariff law affecting his product. Conversely, few consumers can bring any influence to bear upon any parts of the law, since each consumer's interests are spread over so many products. In fact, most consumers cannot even afford to find out whether tariffs are raising the price they pay for any given product. Yet without such knowledge they cannot have policy preferences for the government to pay attention to.

Under these conditions, government is bound to be more attentive to producers than consumers when it creates policy. This is true even though (1) government formulates policy so as to maximize votes and (2) more voting consumers are affected by any given policy than voting producers. As a result, such devices as tripartite industrial control boards with representatives from labor, management, and consumers are doomed to failure.[7] The consumer representative never has effective forces behind him comparable to those of labor and management. Hence these boards practically always seize any opportunities for labor and management jointly to exploit consumers.[8] Even giant labor unions acting for their members' interests as consumers have to spread their influence across too many products to be truly effective as counterweights to producers in each field. Economically speaking, government policy in a democracy almost always exhibits an anticonsumer, proproducer bias. And this bias in our model exists not because the various agents concerned are irrational, but because they behave rationally. This fact has tremendous implications for economic predictions in almost every field, though we cannot explore them here.

Actually, all of these deductions follow directly from the role of information in the division of labor. In a specialized society, every man is naturally better informed about the area of his specialty than about other areas. This has two effects: (1) because his income derives from this area, the returns to him on information useful for influencing policy in it are high, and (2) because he is already familiar with the area, the cost to him of becoming well-informed about it is low. Thus by its very nature, the division of labor creates a few men in each policy area who can rationally afford to influence government policy there, and makes it irrational for most men to do so. This outcome occurs even if all men are equal in intelligence, wealth, income, and interest in government activity.

The foregoing analysis explains why only a few men try to exert influence in each area, even though many could actually gain by doing so. Most potential gainers cannot afford to discover where influence would profit them. They are forced to leave the field to a few specialists in each area; consequently each of the specialists need discount his intervention value relatively slightly when subtracting the influence of other men. As noted, this conclusion does not apply

[7] For this point we are indebted to Professor Melvin W. Reder.
[8] A similar argument is presented in Henry C. Simons, "Some Reflections on Syndicalism," *Economic Policy for a Free Society* (Chicago: University of Chicago Press, 1948).

to voting. The cost of voting is so small that multitudes can rationally afford to do it; hence each voter must discount his own impact heavily to account for the huge number of his fellows.

D. DISPARITY OF INFLUENCE AND THE DISTRIBUTION OF POWER

In the last chapter, we showed that the division of labor and uncertainty inevitably cause men to be informed to different degrees; now we have proved that this inequality of information always results in a corresponding inequality of influence over government policy formation. This conclusion emphasizes once more the inherent inequality of political power in democratic societies.

Democracy is often defined as "government by consent of the governed." We can further define "government by consent of the governed" as "decision-making in which the decider makes each choice on the basis of the preferences of those affected by it and weights the preferences of each in proportion to the degree to which he is affected." [9] Though this complex definition is still ambiguous, it is clear enough to compare with the method of weighting preferences used by the rational government in our model.

The comparison shows that the cost of information prevents our model government from ever functioning by consent of the governed in a pure sense. This does not mean that government makes decisions without considering the desires of the people affected by them; on the contrary, it is extremely sensitive to the wishes of the electorate. Nevertheless, because of the very structure of society, each government decision cannot result from equal consideration of the wishes of men who are equally affected by the decision.[10] When we add to this inherent disparity of influence the inequalities of power caused by the uneven distribution of income, we have moved a long way from political equality among citizens.

[9] Actually, this definition is both outside the purview of our study (because it is an ethical definition) and incomplete (because it ignores the problem of how to translate individual preferences into social choices). However, we believe it is adequate for the limited use to which we put it. Therefore we make no attempt to defend it in detail.

[10] Decisions made with equal consideration for those affected equally need not provide them with equal benefits. "To consider" here means "to take cognizance of" rather than "to act in favor of."

This conclusion by no means implies that democracy cannot work, or that it is without benefits, or that it embodies only sham equality. A contrast between our model and a model of, say, a communist government would probably show that democracy is relatively successful at achieving political equality. Nevertheless, our model does tend to verify the following assertion: even if a society's rules are specifically designed to distribute political power equally, such equality will never result in an uncertain world as long as men act rationally. In short, perfect political equality is irrational when uncertainty exists, unless there is no division of labor, in which case it is irrelevant.

III. SUMMARY

Political information is valuable because it helps citizens make the best possible decisions. Therefore the primary measure of its value is the margin of utility income by which the outcome of the best decision exceeds that of the worst one. However, every rational citizen discounts this margin when deciding what data to acquire because his voice is only one among the many that make the decision.

For voting purposes, a citizen's basic return on information is his party differential. From it he calculates the expected pay-offs of various sets of information bits. Before being compared with the cost of data, these returns must be drastically reduced to accord with the infinitesimal role which each citizen's vote plays in deciding the election. As a result, the returns are so low that many rational voters refrain from purchasing any political information *per se*. Instead they rely upon free data acquired accidentally.

In order to influence government policy-making in any area of decision, a citizen must be continuously well-informed about events therein. Unlike a voter, he cannot deal merely with *post facto* differentials. The expense of such awareness is so great that no citizen can afford to bear it in every policy area, even if by doing so he could discover places where his intervention would reap large profits. If he is going to exercise any influence at all, he must limit his awareness to areas where intervention pays off most and information costs least.

These are the areas of his production specialization, since his income flows from them and he already knows a great deal about them.

Because each rational citizen can handle enough information to be influential in only a few—if any—policy areas, there are relatively few influencers operating in each area. Thus discounting to allow for the existence of other citizens is much less drastic for influencers than for voters, though it may still be significant.

In general, it is irrational to be politically well-informed because the low returns from data simply do not justify their cost in time and other scarce resources. Therefore many voters do not bother to discover their true views before voting, and most citizens are not well enough informed to influence directly the formulation of those policies that affect them. These results demonstrate that true political equality is impossible even in democracies as long as (1) uncertainty exists, (2) there is a division of labor, and (3) men act rationally.

14

The Causes and Effects
of Rational Abstention

Introduction

CITIZENS who are eligible to vote in democratic
elections often fail to do so. In fact, some citizens never vote, and
in some elections abstainers outnumber voters. In this chapter we examine the conditions under which abstention is rational and attempt
to appraise its impact upon the distribution of political power.

Throughout this analysis, we assume that every rational man decides whether to vote just as he makes all other decisions: if the returns outweigh the costs, he votes; if not, he abstains.

Objectives

In this chapter we attempt to prove the following propositions:

1. When voting is costless, every citizen who is indifferent abstains
   and every citizen who has any preference whatsoever votes.
2. If voting is costly, it is rational for some indifferent citizens to
   vote and for some citizens with preferences to abstain.
3. When voting costs exist, small changes in their size may radically
   affect the distribution of political power.

4. The cost of information acts in effect to disenfranchise low-income groups relative to high-income groups when voting is costly.

5. Voting costs may also disenfranchise low-income citizens relative to wealthier citizens.

6. It is sometimes rational for a citizen to vote even when his short-run costs exceed his short-run returns, because social responsibility produces a long-run return.

I. PARTICIPATION IN ELECTIONS WHEN VOTING IS COSTLESS

When the cost of voting is zero, any return whatsoever, no matter how small, makes it rational to vote and irrational to abstain. Therefore, whether abstention is rational depends entirely on the nature of the returns from voting.

A. WHY ONLY THOSE CITIZENS WHO ARE INDIFFERENT ABSTAIN

In the last chapter we pointed out that a citizen's reward for voting correctly consists of his vote value, i.e., his party differential discounted to allow for the influence of other voters upon the election's outcome. If the citizen is indifferent among parties, his party differential is zero, so his vote value must also be zero. It appears that he obtains no return from voting unless he prefers one party over the others; hence indifferent citizens always abstain.

However, this conclusion is false, because the return from voting *per se* is not the same thing as the return from voting correctly. The alternative to voting *per se* is abstaining; whereas the alternative to voting correctly is voting incorrectly—at least so we have viewed it in our analysis. But an incorrect vote is still a vote; so if there is any gain from voting *per se*, a man who votes incorrectly procures it, though a man who abstains does not.

The advantage of voting *per se* is that it makes democracy possible. If no one votes, then the system collapses because no government is chosen. We assume that the citizens of a democracy subscribe to its principles and therefore derive benefits from its continuance; hence they do not want it to collapse.[1] For this reason they attach value to the act of voting *per se* and receive a return from it.

Paradoxically, the size of this return depends upon the cost of voting. When voting costs are zero, the return from voting *per se* is also zero, but when voting is costly, the return from voting *per se* is positive. The second of these assertions we discuss later; now let us examine the first one.[2]

Democracy cannot operate rationally if everyone is indifferent about who wins each election. Of course, not everyone has to have a party preference, but someone must if the election is to be a meaningful act of choice. Therefore we assume throughout this chapter that (1) at least one citizen is not indifferent, (2) no tie votes occur, and (3) indifference does not reflect equal disgust with the candidates but rather equal satisfaction with them.[3]

When the cost of voting is zero, everyone who is not indifferent votes, because his return from doing so, though small, is larger than zero. Therefore citizens who are indifferent know that the election will work and democracy will continue to function even if they abstain. This conclusion holds even when the vast majority of the electorate is indifferent; in fact, only one man need vote. The parties running still must cater to the interests of the whole electorate, because (1) they do not know in advance who will be indifferent and (2) once elected, they know that the citizens who were indifferent may vote in the future. Thus parties compete with each other to attract the potential votes of men who previously abstained as well as the actual votes of those who voted.

As a result, men who are indifferent about who wins have nothing to gain from voting, so they abstain. Hence when the cost of voting is zero, every citizen who is perfectly indifferent abstains. However,

---

[1] This assumption does not mean that all citizens receive the same benefits from democracy, nor does it preclude their opposing the majority on any or all issues. Rather it implies that (1) every citizen receives some benefits and therefore (2) the loss he sustains when the majority cause something he dislikes to be done is partly offset by the benefit he receives from operation of majority rule *per se*.

[2] Since voting costs in reality are never zero, this discussion is merely a preliminary to our later analysis.

[3] The third assumption is discussed in detail later.

the above reasoning does not apply when voting is costly, as we shall see later.

B. THE NATURE OF INDIFFERENCE

In our model, indifferent voters never influence the outcome of elections.[4] Yet their interests are still catered to by each party, because competition forces parties to seek potential as well as actual votes. This fact raises the question of whether indifference has any political significance at all.

Indifferent voters are those who cannot see any net difference in the utility incomes they expect from each party if it is elected. Therefore it seems reasonable *a priori* that they should have no influence on who wins. However, this conclusion can be questioned on two counts.

First, are indifferent voters equally pleased by all parties or equally repelled by them? When a large portion of the electorate is indifferent—as often seems to be the case in reality—the rationality of elections as government-selectors depends upon the answer to this question. If indifference reflects equal disgust with all candidates and a strong preference for some noncandidate, the election is bound to produce a government repugnant to many citizens. On the other hand, if indifference indicates high but equal satisfaction with those running, only the citizens who vote against the winner will be displeased by the outcome.

Essentially, this argument raises an issue with which we dealt briefly in Chapter 8: How are the candidates for each election chosen? To avoid discussing it further here, we assume that every political viewpoint which has a significant number of supporters is represented by some party running in the election. Thus indifference in our model is not caused by equal loathing for all the candidates but reflects ambivalence of a less pejorative nature.

The second question raised by indifference is whether indifferent

---

[4] This conclusion holds even though some indifferent voters cast ballots when voting is costly, since they do so at random and their ballots therefore cancel each other. See Section II of this chapter.

voters really have zero party differentials or merely lack information. In the last chapter we saw that most voters do not acquire enough information to discover their true preferences, since each knows his vote is of small significance. Perhaps a great many voters who are not indifferent would cease to be so if they found out their true views. However, the cost of information makes further research irrational. Since this cost is harder to bear for low-income citizens than for high-income ones, the incidence of falsely indifferent voters may be higher among the former than among the latter. If so, uncertainty imposes a bias on the distribution of political power. It causes a disproportionate number of low-income citizens to refrain from influencing election outcomes.

The validity of this argument rests upon the following proposition: the more information a citizen receives about the policies of each party, the less likely he is to be indifferent. Unless this proposition is true, there is no reason to believe that men who know their true preferences are less likely to be indifferent than those who do not.

In our opinion, the proposition is false. The amount of information a man has necessarily affects the confidence with which he holds his decisions, but it does not necessarily affect their nature. If everyone had 100 percent information, some citizens might still be indifferent.[5] Therefore indifference is not merely an illusion caused by lack of data; so we cannot argue *a priori* that increases in data will tend to eliminate it. However, more information does raise the confidence of each citizen in his decision, *ceteris paribus*, because it moves him closer to being 100 percent informed. For this reason, the more data a man has, the less he must discount his estimated return from voting correctly.

[5] It is conceivable that indifference might not exist in a perfectly informed world, but only if preferences are discontinuous. Therefore most economists assume indifference is a real state of mind, even though it cannot easily be detected in behavior. To show the reasoning behind this view, let us assume that a rational consumer faces three bundles of goods: A, B, and C. He prefers A to B and B to C. Now assume that bundle A is continuously varied in composition so that it gradually comes to resemble bundle C, though in such a way that it is never identical to B. Since the consumer prefers it to B at the start and B to it at the end, somewhere between, he must be precisely indifferent between it and B: so runs the argument. We accept it.

When the cost of voting is zero, it makes no difference how much each citizen discounts his estimated party differential as long as the rate is less than 100 percent, since even a tiny net return causes him to vote. Thus information costs do not increase abstention among low-income groups relative to high-income groups. But when voting is costly, the fact that poorer citizens cannot afford as much information as their wealthier neighbors does create a bias. For example, assume that the distribution of voting costs and of real voting returns is the same for both groups.[6] Because less affluent citizens discount their returns more, fewer of them will vote. Thus lower confidence among low-income groups has no political repercussions when voting is costless but becomes quite important when voting costs are introduced into the model.

II. PARTICIPATION IN ELECTIONS WHEN VOTING IS COSTLY

A. VOTING COSTS AND THEIR BEHAVIORAL EFFECTS

Heretofore we have assumed that voting is a costless act, but this assumption is self-contradictory because every act takes time. In fact, time is the principal cost of voting: time to register, to discover what parties are running, to deliberate, to go to the polls, and to mark the ballot. Since time is a scarce resource, voting is inherently costly.

This fact alters our previous conclusion that everyone votes if he has any party preference at all. When there are costs to voting, they may outweigh the returns thereof; hence rational abstention becomes possible even for citizens who want a particular party to win. In fact, since the returns from voting are often miniscule, even low voting costs may cause many partisan citizens to abstain.

The importance of their abstention depends on the effects it has upon the distribution of political power. Such effects can stem from two sources: (1) biases in the distribution of ability to bear the costs

---

[6] By *real* returns, we mean those which each citizen would perceive in a perfectly informed world.

of voting, and (2) biases in the distribution of high returns from voting.

The only direct money costs connected with registering to vote and voting are any poll taxes extant and the cost of transportation. Ability to bear these costs varies inversely with income, so upper-income citizens have an advantage. Where poll taxes do not exist, the principal cost of voting is usually the utility income lost by devoting time to it rather than something else. If the time must be taken out of working hours, this cost can be quite high, in which case high-income groups again have an advantage. But if the time comes during leisure hours, there is no reason to suppose any such income-correlated disparity exists.

At first glance, all of these costs may appear trivial, and biases in ability to bear them seem irrelevant. However, the returns from voting are usually so low that tiny variations in its cost may have tremendous effects on the distribution of political power. This fact explains why such simple practices as holding elections on holidays, keeping polls open late, repealing small poll taxes, and providing free rides to the polls may strikingly affect election results.

B. THE NATURE, SIZE, AND IMPACT OF THE RETURNS FROM VOTING

The return a citizen receives from voting is compounded of several factors. The first is the strength of his desire to see one party win instead of the others, i.e., the size of his party differential. As we pointed out in Chapter 3, party policies determine this factor. A second factor is the degree to which he discounts his party differential to allow for the influence of other voters. In the last chapter we showed that this depends upon how close he thinks the election will be. These two factors together constitute his vote value.

The third factor is independent of the other two; it is the value of voting *per se*. Although we discussed it briefly earlier in the chapter, we must examine it more carefully here because of the vital role it plays when voting is costly.

We assume that everyone in our model world derives utility from living in a democracy, as stated previously. When the cost of voting is zero, receipt of this utility is not jeopardized by abstention, because only those who are indifferent abstain. But positive voting costs alter this situation by causing some men who have definite preferences to abstain also. In fact, since each citizen's vote value is usually quite small, any cost at all may threaten the political system with collapse through lack of participation.

Further analysis is complicated by an oligopoly problem similar to that described in Chapter 9. If each partisan voter expects many others to vote, his own vote value is tiny; hence it is outweighed by a very small cost of voting. The more voters there are who feel this way, the smaller is the total vote. But a small total vote raises the probability that any one ballot will be decisive; hence the vote value of each citizen may rise to a point where it outweighs the cost of voting. Therefore citizens who think others expect many to vote will themselves expect few to vote, and they will want to be among those few.

Each citizen is thus trapped in a maze of conjectural variation. The importance of his own vote depends upon how important other people think their votes are, which in turn depends on how important he thinks his vote is. He can conclude either that (1) since so many others are going to vote, his ballot is not worth casting or (2) since most others reason this way, they will abstain and therefore he should vote. If everyone arrives at the first conclusion, no one votes; whereas if everyone arrives at the second conclusion, every citizen votes unless he is indifferent.

Both these outcomes are self-defeating. When no one votes, democracy collapses. Yet if everyone who is not indifferent votes, in the next election each will abstain, since his ballot had so little effect previously (i.e., when everyone voted). Thus if we assume all men think alike, democracy seems unable to function rationally. What rule can we posit within the framework of our model to show how rational men can arrive at different conclusions though viewing the same situation?

The answer consists of two parts:

1. Rational men in a democracy are motivated to some extent by a sense of social responsibility relatively independent of their own short-run gains and losses.

2. If we view such responsibility as one part of the return from voting, it is possible that the cost of voting is outweighed by its returns for some but not all rational men.

Let us examine these propositions in order.

One thing that all citizens in our model have in common is the desire to see democracy work. Yet if voting costs exist, pursuit of short-run rationality can conceivably cause democracy to break down. However improbable this outcome may seem, it is so disastrous that every citizen is willing to bear at least some cost in order to insure himself against it. The more probable it appears, the more cost he is willing to bear.

Since voting is one form of insurance against this catastrophe, every rational citizen receives some return from voting *per se* when voting is costly. Its magnitude (1) is never zero, (2) varies directly with the benefits he gains from democracy, and (3) varies inversely with the number of others he expects to vote. The last of these factors depends upon the cost of voting and the returns he thinks others get from it. Thus we have not completely eliminated the oligopoly problem, but we have introduced another factor which tends to offset its importance.

To show how this factor works, let us approach it from another angle. Implicit throughout our study is the following assumption: rational men accept limitations on their ability to make short-run gains in order to procure greater gains in the long run. This assumption appears in many of the provisions of the constitution stated in Chapter 1, and also in the solution to the indivisibility problem stated in Chapter 10. The limitations men accept are usually "rules of the game" without which no game can be played. Each individual knows he can gain at some moments by violating the rules of the game, but he also knows that consistent violation by many citizens will destroy the game and introduce social chaos. Since he himself would be a loser if chaos prevailed, he resists the momentary temptation to let short-run individual rationality triumph over long-run individual rationality. Surely, such resistance is rational.

However, it is not uniform for three reasons: (1) the connection between a particular violation of the rules and eventual chaos is not equally obvious in all cases, (2) some violations lead to disorders worse than those caused by other violations, and (3) the immediate gains from violation are not always the same. For example, the deleterious effects of universal failure to vote are both clearer and worse than those of universal failure to become well-informed before voting. Similarly, the cost avoided by not paying income tax is much larger than that avoided by not voting. For these reasons, men can rely on each other to abide by the rules voluntarily to different degrees for different rules. In some cases, they have to back up the rules with force in order to insure observance.

Participation in elections is one of the rules of the game in a democracy, because without it democracy cannot work. Since the consequences of universal failure to vote are both obvious and disastrous, and since the cost of voting is small, at least some men can rationally be motivated to vote even when their personal gains in the short run are outweighed by their personal costs. However, this conclusion raises two problems.

The first is the arbitrary nature of assuming that such motivation operates in regard to voting but not in regard to other political actions. Why, for instance, are rational men not willing to find their true preferences before voting, since they will benefit in the long run from doing so? We can only answer by pointing to the factors mentioned previously: (1) the potential ill effects of not voting are worse than those of not becoming informed, (2) the connection between failure to vote and its ill effects is much clearer than that between failure to become informed and its ill effects, and (3) the cost of voting is lower than the cost of becoming informed.[7] Some or all of these arguments apply to all other cases of indivisible benefits where we have assumed short-run rationality dominant (e.g., paying taxes).

A second difficulty is explaining why some men vote and some abstain even though all favor democracy and benefit from its continuance. Solving this problem requires the second proposition men-

---

[7] In this case, another fact is relevant: voting is a discrete and clearly identifiable act; whereas "being well-informed" is a vague state of mind which even the individual himself has a hard time recognizing.

tioned earlier: the returns in fact outweigh the costs for some but not for all.

Although the benefits each citizen derives from living in a democracy actually accrue to him continuously over time, he can view them as a capital sum which pays interest at each election. This procedure is rational because voting is a necessary prerequisite for democracy; hence democracy is in one sense a reward for voting. We call the part of this reward the citizen receives at each election his *long-run participation value*.

Of course, he will actually get this reward even if he himself does not vote as long as a sufficient number of other citizens do. But we have already shown that he is willing to bear certain short-run costs he could avoid in order to do his share in providing long-run benefits. The maximum cost he will bear for this reason in any given election is that which just offsets his long-run participation value.

Thus the total return which a rational citizen receives from voting in a given election consists of his long-run participation value plus his vote value. In other words, the reward a man obtains for voting depends upon (1) how much he values living in a democracy, (2) how much he cares which party wins, (3) how close he thinks the election will be, and (4) how many other citizens he thinks will vote.[8] These four variables insure a relatively wide range of possible returns from voting for different individuals. The range of possible costs is also wide, as we saw before. Therefore a matching of returns and costs can easily result in a mixed outcome—i.e., a large number of voters whose returns exceed their costs and a large number of abstainers whose costs exceed their returns.

Without abandoning our assumption that all men are rational, we can thus explain the following phenomena by means of our model:

1. Some men abstain all the time, others abstain sometimes, and others never abstain.
2. The percentage of the electorate abstaining varies from election to election.

[8] This list shows clearly the reason why the motive for voting is stronger than the motive for becoming well informed. The former encompasses all four factors mentioned, while the latter is comprised of only factors (2) and (3).

3. Many men who vote do not become well-informed before voting.
4. Only a few men who become well-informed do not vote.

Furthermore, our analysis has isolated several factors upon which the incidence of rational abstention depends. Hence it may be useful in designing methods of predicting how many voters will abstain in a given election.[9]

C. A REVISED SUMMARY OF HOW RATIONAL CITIZENS DECIDE HOW TO VOTE

The introduction of voting costs into our model forces us to revise again the behavior rule first formulated in Chapter 3. In an uncertain world, each rational citizen makes his voting decision in the following manner:

1. He makes preliminary estimates of his expected party differential, the cost of voting, his long-run participation value, and the number of other citizens he believes will vote.
2. If his party differential is zero because all party policies and platforms appear identical to him, he weighs his long-run participation value plus the expected value of "change" as opposed to "no change" (or vice versa) against the cost of voting.[10]
   a. If returns outweigh costs and he favors "change," he votes for the opposition party. (In a multiparty system, he chooses one of the opposition parties at random and votes for it.)
   b. If returns outweigh costs and he favors "no change," he votes for the incumbent party. (If a coalition is in power, he votes for one of the parties in it chosen at random.)
   c. If costs outweigh returns, he abstains.
3. If his party differential is zero because he expects identical utility incomes from all parties even though their policies and platforms differ, he weighs only his long-run participation value against the cost of voting.

[9] Needless to say, other authors have pointed out the same factors. For a summary analysis of their views and findings, see V. O. Key Jr., *Politics, Parties, and Pressure Groups* (New York: Thomas Y. Crowell Company, 1953), Chapter Nineteen.

[10] For an explanation of why he considers "change" as opposed to "no change" in this instance, see Chapter 3, part II, c.

   a. If returns outweigh costs, he votes for a party chosen at random.

   b. If costs outweigh returns, he abstains.

4. If his party differential is not zero, he estimates how close the election will be and discounts his party differential accordingly. (In a multiparty system he also must decide whether his favorite party is hopeless, as described in Chapter 3.)

   a. If the discounted party differential plus the long-run participation value exceed the cost of voting, he votes for his favorite party (or some other party in certain cases—see Chapter 3).

   b. If the sum of these quantities is smaller than the cost of voting, he abstains.

5. Throughout the above processes he procures more information about all the entities involved whenever its expected pay-off exceeds its cost. Since this information may alter his estimate of any entity, he may shift from one category to another in the midst of his deliberations. He votes according to the rules applicable to the category he is in on election day.[11]

D. THE RELATION BETWEEN VOTING BEHAVIOR AND THE DISTRIBUTION OF POWER

If we translate the results of the above deliberations into possible types of behavior, we discover that citizens in our model can react to an election by doing the following things:

1. Voting for their favorite party.
2. Voting for some other party chosen for strategic reasons because their favorite party is hopeless.
3. Voting for a party chosen at random.
4. Abstaining.

---

[11] This exceedingly complicated method of deciding how to vote seems to bear little resemblance to how men act in the real world. However, except for one step, the entire process is necessarily implicit in the behavior of any rational voter, even if casual observation fails to confirm this fact. The one step which is not necessary is the use of a random mechanism to "break ties" by citizens who are indifferent but wish to vote, as in 2a, 2b, and 3a above. The implications of this step are discussed in the Appendix to this chapter.

These four types of action do not result in equal influence for the citizens who carry them out. Seen as a group, the citizens who vote by preference determine the immediate outcome of the election and have a strong effect on the long-run development of party policies. Citizens who vote randomly exercise only the latter effect, since their votes cancel in so far as the immediate outcome is concerned. Citizens who abstain also have no influence on who wins the election. Thus voting behavior is a crucial determinant of the distribution of political power.

There are two reasons to suspect that the proportion of low-income citizens who abstain is usually higher than the proportion of high-income citizens who do so. First, the cost of voting is harder for low-income citizens to bear; therefore, even if returns among high- and low-income groups are the same, fewer of the latter vote. Second, the cost of information is harder for low-income citizens to bear; hence more of them are likely to be uncertain because they lack information. Since uncertainty reduces the returns from voting, a lower proportion of low-income groups would vote even if voting costs were equally difficult for everyone to bear.

Because citizens who abstain exercise less influence than those who vote, low-income groups in society are likely to have less political power than their numbers warrant, and high-income groups more. Once again we see that the necessity of bearing economic costs in order to act politically biases the distribution of power against citizens with low incomes. However, we cannot tell *a priori* just how significant this bias really is.

III. SUMMARY

When voting is costless, any return whatsoever makes abstention irrational, so everyone who has even a slight party preference votes. On the other hand, abstention does not harm those who are indifferent because (1) democracy works even if they do not vote and (2) parties still cater to their interests so as to get their votes next time. Thus there is no return from voting *per se*, and all indifferent citizens abstain.

When voting is costly, its costs may outweigh its returns, so abstentation can be rational even for citizens with party preferences. In fact, the returns from voting are usually so low that even small costs may cause many voters to abstain; hence tiny variations in cost can sharply redistribute political power.

One of the returns from voting stems from each citizen's realization that democracy cannot function unless many people vote. This return is independent of his short-run gains and losses, but it is not very large because the benefits of democracy are indivisible. Nevertheless, it helps solve the oligopoly problem voters face, thereby preventing universal abstention from paralyzing democracy.

The total return each citizen receives from voting depends upon (1) the benefits he gets from democracy, (2) how much he wants a particular party to win, (3) how close he thinks the election will be, and (4) how many other citizens he thinks will vote. These variables insure a relatively wide range of possible returns similar to the range of voting costs. Thus when citizens balance their costs and returns, some vote and others abstain.

However, the abstention rate is higher among low-income citizens than among high-income citizens for two reasons. Since the former have a harder time paying the cost of voting, it takes higher returns to get them to vote. And since they can less easily bear the cost of information, they have fewer data and are more uncertain; therefore they discount the returns from voting more heavily.

Appendix: The Possible Existence of Irrationality in the Model

Throughout this study, we have avoided making arbitrary assumptions without presenting at least some reasons why they are plausible. Therefore we offer this appendix as an *apologia* for an assumption made in this chapter which is arbitrary, but for which we have so far given no explanation.

The postulate we are referring to is the following: every citizen who wishes to vote but is indifferent about who wins chooses a party at random and votes for it. From the point of view of the individual, there is no reason why random selection is preferable to certain other methods of choice. Since he cannot distinguish between the parties on the basis of their policies, he might as well use any other basis which pleases him. For instance, he might vote for the party whose leader has the most charming personality, or the one whose historic heroes appeal to him most, or the one his father voted for. Thus a rational man may employ politically irrational mechanisms to decide for whom to vote.

Though use of such devices is individually rational, it is socially irrational. If indifferent voters do not make voting choices randomly, their votes fail to cancel each other; hence men who are indifferent about who wins affect the outcome of each election. Not only is this arrangement inefficient *per se*, but also it may have drastic effects on party behavior. If the number of indifferent voters is large, parties will plan their actions and statements to influence the nonrational mechanisms they think these voters are using. As a result, parties will cease devoting all their energies to carrying out their social function, which is formulating policies relevant to citizens' political desires.

Obviously, we have made the assumption of random selection in order to avoid this outcome. However, we believe that irrationality would not occur to a significant extent in the model even if this assumption were dropped. In our opinion, those citizens who are interested enough in politics to vote at all almost always have some party preference. If this is true, so small a number of rational voters are in a position to be influenced by politically irrational factors that parties do not exert much energy wooing them. Admittedly, this view is merely an opinion.

There are other parts of the analysis where irrational factors might conceivably exercise influence, though none are as unequivocal as the above. For example, if we count the time it takes to go to the polls as a cost of voting, why not count the social prestige received for voting as a return? Clearly, society bestows this prestige upon men in order to get them to vote; is it not therefore rational for men to seek this reward? [11]

[11] Actually, the social prestige connected with voting in the real world is analogous to the long-run participation value in our model. We may reasonably assume that citizens of the real world are not as calculating as those in the model. Therefore the leaders of society arrange to have them perceive social responsibility

As we pointed out in Chapter 1, the difficulty with such arguments is that they rationalize everything. If it is rational to vote for prestige, why is it not rational to vote so as to please one's employer or one's sweetheart? Soon all behavior whatsoever becomes rational because every act is a means to some end the actor values. To avoid this sterile conclusion, we have regarded only actions leading to strictly political or economic ends as rational.

---

in the form of guilt feelings for wrong actions (e.g., not voting) and reward feelings for right actions (e.g., voting). These feelings function on an unconscious level to achieve the same end that the return for voting *per se* achieves consciously in our model. In a certain sense, therefore, we have already accounted for the operation of social prestige in the structure of the model.

Part IV

Derivative Implications and Hypotheses

15

A Comment on Economic Theories of Government Behavior

Introduction

THOUGH few economists have tried to explain government behavior as a part of general equilibrium theory, many have made normative statements that imply a certain conception of government. In this chapter, we examine that conception to see (1) if it is consistent with the basic axioms of economic theory and (2) what implications those axioms have for explicit theories of government like our own.

Objectives

In this chapter we attempt to prove the following propositions:

1. The conception of government implicit in much of traditional economic theory is inconsistent with the axioms that explain how the private sector operates.
2. Any attempt to deal with all forms of government by means of a single economic theory is bound to be either self-contradictory or too general to be meaningful.

3. In order to explain government's role in the economy on either a normative or a positive level, economists must take into account society's political constitution; therefore economics and politics must be merged into a unified theory of social action.

I. THE INCONSISTENCY OF TRADITIONAL ECONOMIC THEORIES OF GOVERNMENT

A. THE VIEW IMPLICIT IN TRADITIONAL THEORY

Attempts to treat government as an endogenous variable in general equilibrium theory are extremely scarce, because most theorists have followed the classical tradition of considering government as a disturbing influence upon the self-regulating private economy.[1] Therefore they regarded it as an exogenous datum rather than an intrinsic part of the division of labor. But the crucial role of government in all fields of economic action has forced economists to make statements about its behavior in spite of the dearth of general theories concerning it. Particularly in the fields of public finance and welfare economics, normative prescriptions abound. If we examine a few of them, we discover they nearly all imply a similar conception of the proper role of government in the economy.[2]

These prescriptions are usually made in one of three forms. The first is a disguised value judgment in the form of an "if" clause positing a goal, and a presumably factual statement describing how to reach it. Thus Professor A. P. Lerner says in *The Economics of Control*:

If it is desired to maximize the total satisfaction in a society, the rational procedure is to divide income on an equalitarian basis.[3]

Lerner qualifies this description of "the rational procedure" later in his analysis, but he retains the idea that some income should be

[1] See Gerhard Colm, *Essays in Public Finance and Fiscal Policy* (New York: Oxford University Press, 1955), pp. 6–8.

[2] This concurrence does not mean all economists agree upon policy recommendations for government action. Rather they agree upon a very broad statement of the object of such action: governments should maximize social welfare. How this objective is best accomplished is a matter of extreme controversy.

[3] Abba P. Lerner, *The Economics of Control* (New York: The Macmillan Company, 1944), p. 32.

redistributed from rich to poor. Since government is the agency which does the redistributing, we may conclude that Lerner believes government's proper function is "to maximize the total satisfaction in a society."

The second type of prescription made about government is an explicit designation of a specific policy goal as "proper" to it. For example, Adolph Wagner regarded redistribution of income as a duty of the state, though he masked this personal opinion as a "demand" recognized by "the modern science of economics." He states that:

> The state, by adopting appropriate policies, should remedy evils which are not due to its previous action in financial or other matters. From this . . . demand it follows that . . . taxation, in addition to serving the purely financial purpose of providing sufficient revenue, should be employed for the purpose of bringing about a different distribution of wealth from that which would result from the working of free competition upon the basis of the present social order.[4]

Another such open value judgment is made by Lerner as follows:

> [It is] a duty of the government—perhaps even the primary duty of the government—to ensure the maintenance of full employment.[5]

Neither of these two kinds of prescription really qualifies as a normative theory of government, since the first is not explicit enough and the second not general enough. But it is difficult to find overt statements of the criteria by which actions proper to government can be differentiated from those proper to private agents. One of the broadest was made by Hugh Dalton in *The Principles of Public Finance*:

> Most of the operations of public finance resolve themselves into a series of transfers of purchasing power . . . from certain individuals to public authorities, and back again from these authorities, by way of public expenditures, to other individuals. . . . As a result of these operations of public finance, changes take place in the amount and in the nature of the wealth which is produced, and in the distribution of that wealth among individuals and classes. Are these changes in their aggregate effects socially advantageous? If so the operations are justified; if not, not. The best

---

[4] Adolph Wagner, *Finanzwissenschaft*, Vol. I, Part 27, as quoted in Elmer D. Fagan and C. Ward Macy, eds., *Public Finance: Selected Readings* (New York: Longmans, Green and Co., 1936), p. 179.

[5] Lerner, *op. cit.*, p. 302.

system of public finance is that which secures the maximum social advantage from the operations which it conducts.[6]

A similar statement occurs in Harvey W. Peck's *Taxation and Welfare:*

If public operation of an enterprise will produce a greater net social utility, the services rendered by this enterprise should belong in the category of public goods.[7]

Peck also cites the formulation advanced by Erik Lindahl:

According to Lindahl . . . the production of public goods should be carried on to the point where utility is just offset by costs, as is the tendency in the private economy, or where the marginal satisfaction is the same from both public and private goods.[8]

These few quotations complete our sample, which, though small, is, in our opinion, fairly typical of non-Marxist economists.

Behind all of the prescriptions quoted lurks a single conception of government: government is that agency in the division of labor which has as its proper function the maximization of social welfare.[9] However, because this conception is almost never formulated quite so explicitly, some of its implications have remained unrecognized. In particular, government is rarely treated as an integral part of the division of labor. The classical tendency to regard it as outside the system being analyzed persists even when the analyst recognizes that government has a specific function in the economy.

B. THE WEAKNESS OF THIS VIEW

As we pointed out in Chapter 2, every agent in the division of labor is assumed to have a private motive as well as a social function. This duality springs from the self-interest axiom, which states that, in general, men undertake economic activity primarily to further their own private aims and only secondarily to provide benefits for

---

[6] Hugh Dalton, *The Principles of Public Finance* (London: George Routledge and Sons, Ltd., 1932), pp. 9–10.

[7] Harvey W. Peck, *Taxation and Welfare* (New York: The Macmillan Company, 1925), pp. 30–36, as quoted in Harold M. Groves (ed.), *Viewpoints in Public Finance* (New York: Henry Holt and Company, 1947), p. 551.

[8] Erik Lindahl, *Die Gerechtigkeit der Besterung*, as cited in Groves, *loc. cit.*

[9] *Social welfare* is here used as a synonym for social utility, satisfaction in a society, social advantage, and all other terms referring to the same general idea.

society (i.e., for other men). From the point of view of society as a whole, the object of each man's action is the discharge of his social function. But from his own point of view, he acts to attain his private ends, which are often unrelated *per se* to that function. Therefore when we theorize about his behavior, we should not limit ourselves to describing his social function; we should also show how he is motivated to carry it out.

Every economist recognizes this state of affairs when he is talking about private economic agents. He does not advise monopolistic corporations to increase social welfare by cutting prices—and thereby reducing their profits. Rather he assumes that the men operating them can be reasonably expected to maximize their own profits because they are human. Similarly, he does not advise a labor union to quit restricting entry because doing so causes inefficient allocation of resources. He might believe that entry should be easier for the good of society, but if he sees that union members benefit from closed entry, he regards them as acting rationally in their own interest.

To remedy such situations, he does not suggest that the men involved stop being selfish. Instead he attempts to devise some social ordering which benefits society through the very leverage of that selfishness. In this sense, the model of perfect competition drawn up by welfare economists is a triumph of selfishness. It demonstrates how, under certain conditions, society actually gains when men attempt to maximize profits and utility.

Economists apply this reasoning to private economic agents not because they are private, but because they are agents. In short, they are human, and the realities of human nature must be accounted for in any economic analysis. *Ipso facto*, the same type of reasoning must be applied to every institution run by men, i.e., to every agency in the division of labor.

However, economic theories of government behavior—in so far as they exist—universally fail to assign any motives to the men in government. In every one of the quotations we cited, and in almost every other similar passage, the theorist discussing government's role in society merely describes its proper function. He says nothing about the incentives which might cause that function to be carried out by the men who run the government. Yet those incentives are vital, because their operation determines in what way the function of government is discharged, just as the degree of competition among firms determines what goods are produced. As Joseph Schumpeter stated in a passage we quoted previously:

> It does not follow that the social meaning of a type of activity will necessarily provide the motive power, hence the explanation of the latter. If it does not, a theory that contents itself with an analysis of the social end or need to be served cannot be accepted as an adequate account of the activities that serve it.[10]

True, the economists who commit this error are rarely guilty of describing reality inaccurately, because most of their statements are normative, not descriptive. Probably not one of them would contend that governments in the real world actually maximize social welfare. Nevertheless, they make policy prescriptions which assume governments should maximize welfare. But there is little point in advising governments to do so, or forming recommendations of action based on the supposition that they might, unless there is some reason to believe that they will. Otherwise the economists' advice may very well be as useless as telling a profit-maximizing monopolist to sell his product at marginal cost so as to benefit society.

C. WHY ECONOMISTS HAVE IGNORED THIS PROBLEM

Most theories in normative economics tacitly assume that government will in fact maximize welfare once it knows how to do so. In our opinion, there are three reasons why economists have ignored the problem of government motivation. The first and most obvious is that this problem lies more in the realm of politics than of economics. As economic theorists shifted emphasis from political economy to purely scientific analysis, they directed less and less attention to the political aspects of economic problems. Instead they tended to leave all quasi-political questions to political scientists and political

[10] Joseph A. Schumpeter, *Capitalism, Socialism, and Democracy* (New York: Harper & Brothers, 1950), p. 282. Schumpeter is one of the few economists who have not ignored this problem.

theorists. Only recently have attempts been made to apply economic concepts to these questions.[11]

Avoidance of political speculation has not prevented many economists from being influenced by the overly abstract conception of government formulated by Jean Jacques Rousseau.[12] In effect, he argued that the government should be merely a device for carrying out the will of the people; therefore in theory it has no existence of its own apart from that will. Acceptance of this view—even on a purely theoretical, normative level—eliminates the need for government motivation, at least on that level. It amounts to assuming that governments are not institutions run by men, but are depersonalized, frictionless machines which operate according to mathematical rules; e.g., they carry out the "will of the majority." [13] Being machines, they have no private motives. Being frictionless, their particular processes of operation do not affect their outputs. Therefore govern-

[11] This study is, of course, such an attempt. An example of other similar attempts is the application of choice theory as developed in economics to political bureaucracies. See Herbert Simon, *Administrative Behavior* (New York: The Macmillan Company, 1947).

[12] See Jean Jacques Rousseau, *The Social Contract*, Hafner Library of Classics Edition (New York: Hafner Publishing Co., 1948). The phrase used by Rousseau is "the general will." He himself was not guilty of applying this conception of government to every political system. In fact, he invented it as an ideal against which to contrast existing governments. Responsibility for erroneously broadening the application of his ideas rests with those economic theorists who followed the reasoning described in the text, though most of them did so unconsciously.

[13] Another possible interpretation of Rousseau's theory is that the government consists solely of hired men who carry out the policies ordered by "the will of the people." This argument explains the private motives of the men in government quite simply: they obey the commands of the people with precision in order to keep their jobs, because the slightest disobedience means immediate dismissal. As our whole study shows, this view is incompatible with uncertainty and the division of labor. It assumes (1) the people as a whole have some will to be carried out on every issue, however trivial, and (2) that they can communicate these myriad wills to their hirelings (the government) without disrupting the performance of their own specialized tasks in the division of labor. In other words, there is perfect information in the world, no Arrow problems are ever encountered, and the minority always submits gracefully to the majority. The unrealistic nature of such reasoning is forcefully demonstrated by Schumpeter, *op. cit.* Admittedly, the assumption that every large corporation maximizes profits rests upon exactly the same type of reasoning, since this assumption does not explain how the motives of the corporation's managers lead them to carry out the desires of its stockholders. But the magnitude of the distortion involved is much greater on a national scale than within a corporation—so much greater that we will not discuss this interpretation of government further.

ments in all societies can be treated by means of the same hypothesis regardless of their constitutional structures. This handy theory not only eliminates the need for explaining how any one government is motivated to perform its function, it also eliminates the need for separate theories to explain different forms of government. How convenient!

Obviously, no economists believe this "machine" theory accurately describes the real world. Nor would many, we presume, accept it as a normative standard. Yet that is a direct implication of many of their statements—some of which we quoted earlier in this chapter. And in so far as such will-of-the-people conceptions of democracy have crept into economists' thinking, their attention has been diverted from the need to explain the operation of government as an institution.

The third reason why economists have not discussed government's incentive to maximize social welfare is that they have been unable to agree either about what social welfare is or about how to determine what it is. Therefore they have concentrated their analysis upon the nature of the social welfare function—i.e., the rule for converting individual preferences into social action. Especially since the new welfare economists rejected cardinal utility and interpersonal utility comparisons, economists have been absorbed by the difficulties of rationally deriving a set of social preferences from a population with diverse tastes. Until these difficulties were overcome, it hardly seemed worthwhile questioning the tacit assumption that government would carry out society's preferences once they were discovered.[14]

II. THE GENERALITY OF THEORIES OF GOVERNMENT BEHAVIOR

A. ATTEMPTS TO APPLY ONE THEORY TO ALL GOVERNMENTS

In our opinion, failure to consider government motivation has led to a false generality in the theory of government decision-making. Even in normative theory, the premise that government acts to maxi-

[14] Kenneth Arrow has proved that the difficulties involved cannot be overcome without some rather restrictive assumptions about individual preferences. See Chapter 4 of this study and Kenneth J. Arrow, *Social Choice and Individual Values* (New York: John Wiley & Sons, Inc., 1951).

mize social welfare means, in essence, that the men who run it are perfect altruists in so far as their productive actions are concerned. They alone, among all the men in society, have no private motives other than discharging their social function. Therefore the nature of that function can be considered apart from the way the division of labor is organized to carry it out.

This disembodiment of government's proper function from its institutional framework means all governments can be looked at from the same point of view, as we mentioned earlier. Since by nature each has general power in its society, its function presumably concerns the general welfare.[15] Therefore we can postulate that the proper function of every government is to maximize social welfare. Such reasoning culminates in the use of a single theory to deal with all governments, whether they are democratic, totalitarian, aristocratic, or monarchist in form. This conclusion seems to be implied by a great many economic theorists who discuss the policies proper to government without reference to the political structure of the society involved.

In some cases, specific arguments are advanced which seemingly justify the view that governments—in democracies, at least—are altruistic even though private citizens are not. For example, E. R. A. Seligman states:

An individual, associated with other individuals in a coöperative group, private or public, becomes at once by the mere fact of association something different from his former self. His special separate wants are transmuted into common wants. . . . The subject of fiscal science . . . consists of the fiscal relations of the members of the state. These fiscal relations are not those of individuals as such, but of individuals in their political or public capacity.[16]

Here Seligman implies that the criteria people apply to choices concerning government action are different from the ones they apply to private choices in the market. But this type of argument is irrelevant to the problem of government motivation. Even if every citizen in a

[15] By *general power*, we mean a unilateral ability to coerce all other men or organizations in society. See Chapter 2 for a more detailed discussion of the nature of government.

[16] E. R. A. Seligman, "The Social Theory of Fiscal Science," *Political Science Quarterly*, XLI (1926), as quoted in Groves, *op. cit.*, p. 4.

democracy sets aside his own special interests when thinking politically, so that decisions arrived at collectively are truly aimed at maximizing social welfare (assuming this process can be defined), there is no reason to assume *a priori* that the men who run the governing apparatus always carry out the policies citizens choose. We must explain why those men discharge this function in terms of their own private interests, as we noted in Chapter 2.

The only alternatives are (1) to assume that the men who run governments are perfectly altruistic in their roles as producers or (2) to treat government as a machine that carries out the will of the people rather than an institution run by men. As we have shown, both of these views are inconsistent with the axioms that explain how all other economic agents in society operate. Therefore we reject them as justifications for using the same theory to explain government action in all societies, even on a normative level.

One other such justification remains. It states that the only way in which various forms of government differ is that each maximizes the welfare of a different portion of society. According to this view, a democratic government and a communist government face the same conceptual problems and handle them in the same way, but individual preferences are weighted differently in their social welfare functions. In a democracy, everyone's preferences receive the same weight; whereas in a communist state, the preferences of Politburo members are weighted much more heavily than those of nonmembers. But the problem of maximizing social welfare, given individual preferences and their weights, is the same in every society and is handled in essentially the same manner.

This type of thinking is exemplified by Abram Bergson's description of the operation of a socialist economy. Bergson says:

Interest has focused recently on the variants of this case [the case of full consumers' sovereignty] that arise where the Board itself undertakes to determine, to a greater or less extent, what is good for consumers and allocates resources on this basis. . . . If the decision is in favor of consumers' sovereignty, . . . the welfare of the community . . . is constant, increases, or decreases, according to whether the utilities of the individual households are constant, increase or decrease. If the decision is against consumers' sovereignty, the welfare function must be expressed by a formula in which the Board's own preference scales are substituted for the utility functions of the individual households.[17]

At another point, Bergson remarks:

> The case where consumers' sovereignty is abandoned or modified . . . is readily disposed of. All that needs to be done is to rephrase the preceding argument to take into account the fact that the pertinent marginal rates of substitution are those decided on by the Board rather than by individual households.[18]

In these passages, Bergson is discussing the problems facing a Central Planning Board which has as its social function the attainment of an optimal allocation of resources in the economy. Behind his reasoning are two tacit assumptions: (1) the Board pursues its social function with equal zeal regardless of whether the preferences it is serving are those of its own members or those of consumers at large, and (2) in the case of consumers' sovereignty, the Board's attempts to maximize the welfare of individual households are equally fervent regardless of the political system extant in the socialist state. In other words, the Planning Board consists of a group of altruists whose only private end is to carry out their social function in the division of labor. Again we encounter the fallacy of a government run by completely unselfish men.

True, Bergson points out that "in the real world the question of comparative efficiency cannot be divorced altogether from questions of politics." [19] But in his analysis, he divorces them. Of course, we cannot expect Bergson or any other economist to specify a complete political theory every time he mentions government action. Nevertheless, it is unreasonable for any economist to set forth a whole theory of government behavior without treating government as a part of the division of labor, i.e., without showing how the private motives of its members influence their actions. Therefore the economic theory of government action—even on a normative level—is simultaneously

---

[17] Abram Bergson (Burk), "Socialist Economics," in A Survey of Contemporary Economics, ed. by Howard Ellis (Philadelphia: The Blakiston Company, 1949), I, 414, 418.

[18] Ibid., pp. 423–424.

[19] Ibid., p. 448.

a political theory, and cannot be based on purely economic considerations.

B. WHY MANY THEORIES ARE NECESSARY

Because every government is run by men, and because all men must be privately motivated to carry out their social functions, the structural relation between the function of government and the motives of those who run it is a crucial determinant of its behavior. This relation is, in essence, the political constitution of society.[20] It determines the effective relationship between the government and the governed (i.e., the rest of society) whether the latter have a direct voice in choosing the former or not. In other words, the constitution specifies the contents of the social welfare function, because it provides a rule for transforming individual preferences into social action.

Since constitutions vary widely, this rule is not the same in every society. The behavior of government in a democracy containing many competing parties is bound to differ from the behavior of a government in a one-party totalitarian state. Nor can this disparity be expressed merely as a different weighting of some general welfare function. In this case, the very processes of social action are so unlike that any theory which tries to encompass both of them must be either self-contradictory or too general to be meaningful.

To avoid this dilemma, economists must formulate a different theory of government behavior for each different institutional structure of government. The need for such diversity in descriptive theory is already recognized. But theorists cannot even make normative prescriptions intelligently unless they take into account the peculiar qualities of the government they are advising. In fact, a normative economist seeking to discover the type of social organization most likely to achieve a given set of goals may have to consider both political and economic arrangements as variables. This is particularly

[20] By *political constitution*, we mean the actual institutional structure of government rather than the documents upon which this structure is based.

likely if the goals in question require specific government action for their fulfillment. Thus on both positive and normative planes, economics and politics merge into a unified theory.

It is important to point out four things this conclusion does not imply. First, it does not mean that economic theories of government can have no common elements. On the contrary, they must all have an identical core of axioms, just as monopoly theory and competitive theory both assume maximization of profits and of utility for producers and consumers respectively. Every economic theory of government must assume that the governors carry out their social function primarily in order to attain their private ends. Furthermore, those ends are probably the same in all societies: power, prestige, income, and the excitement of the political game. Only the particular manner in which government is organized, which partly determines its social function, differs from one society to another.

Second, we do not mean to imply that every economist must also be a political theorist. When discussing a particular society, the economist can take its political structure as given and focus his attention on purely economic issues. However, in doing so, he must not assume—either tacitly or explicitly—that government will automatically carry out whatever function he deems proper for it. If he is dealing with government on a descriptive level, he must take into account the motives of its operators and the nature of its structure. And when he deals with it on a prescriptive plane, he must not assign it a social function inconsistent with those motives and that structure, unless he is deliberately advising a change in society's political constitution.

Third, our insistence on the importance of self-interest in government action precludes neither individual charity and selflessness nor institutionalized efficiency at serving others. As we pointed out in Chapter 2, true altruism is an important force in society and must not be underestimated. But economists from Aristotle to Zeuthen have assumed that men carry out their roles in the division of labor as a means of serving their own self-interests. We are merely requesting that government be recognized as a part of the division of labor.

Furthermore, we do not rule out the possibility that self-interest among the governors may take such forms as competition for the best reputation for service, or striving for professional status by means of excellent work. Thus self-interest may be a far cry from a simple desire for high income or sweeping power; its forms may even be highly beneficial to society. All we ask is that the role of self-interest be illumined so that government may come down from more ethereal—and less realistic—realms and take its place in economic theories as a human agency.

Finally, making government an endogenous variable in economic models does not eliminate the possibility of using government actions as corrective measures in the economy. At present, economists regard the behavior of consumers and producers as determined by their own self-interests and technological conditions. If the results of this behavior are ethically or economically unsatisfactory, then government can be used as a tool to set things right by intervening in the free market. At first glance, this freedom of government to act altruistically upon self-interested private agents seems to be obliterated by making the government self-interested too. If government's own actions are determined by the private motives of the men who run it, then are not all actions in society determined by a set of simultaneous equations based on self-interest? If so, what room is there for policy recommendations at all?

In a democracy, we can see the answer at once from our own model. In the first place, if our hypothesis is correct, the men in government achieve their own goals by carrying out those government actions which most please voters, just as entrepreneurs make profits by producing things people want. Therefore policy recommendations can have results by either (1) changing voters' ideas about what is desirable (i.e., altering their political tastes) or (2) changing the government's views about how best to please voters. Second, uncertainty is so great in the real world that government does not know what voters' goals are or how best to achieve them. Hence its actions are not rigidly determined by a vote function, any more than the actions of oligopolists are precisely determined by a demand function. There is plenty of room for choice, so political parties are willing to listen to policy advice and often adopt it. Voters are similarly confused and open to suggestions. Hence normative recommendations are by no means futile, even though self-interest is the chief motive for all social action.

Exactly how such recommendations might become effective in nondemocratic societies we cannot say. That question must remain unanswered until someone produces a theory explaining the relation between the incentives and the functions of the men who govern each type of nondemocratic society.

III. SUMMARY

Though explicit theories of government behavior are rare in economics, the remarks of several normative theorists reveal a common supposition that government's proper function is the maximization of social welfare. However, these theorists do not explain how the men who run governments are motivated to carry out this function. Thus they fail to apply the self-interest axiom to governments, although it is the foundation of analysis concerning private economic agents.

This inconsistency was probably caused by three factors: (1) economists left the explanation of government's motives to political theorists, (2) Rousseau's ideas fostered the view that governments in a democracy have no real existence apart from the "will of the people," and (3) economists have concentrated their attention upon the problems of defining social welfare.

The result of this failing is an unconscious assumption that all governments are run by altruists; therefore they can be treated by one theory regardless of their political forms. But whether or not the men in government will act so as to maximize the welfare of everyone in society, or of any particular group, depends upon how their motives are related to such maximization institutionally in the division of labor. Therefore the political structure of each society determines how government can be expected to behave therein.

Since such structures differ, several theories are necessary to explain government's economic acts in various systems.

Thus in both normative and positive economics, theorizing about government action requires the use of political axioms. Economists must develop models which unify politics and economics, as we have done in this study.

16

Testable Propositions
Derived from the Theory

Introduction

W<small>E HAVE</small> now completed the main purpose of
our study: to propose a theory of democratic government decision-
making and to explore its major ramifications in a rational but uncertain world. There is no need for us to recapitulate our conclusions,
because we have already highlighted them in the "Objectives" and
"Summary" sections of each chapter. Therefore we devote this final
chapter to a list of empirically testable propositions derived from our
basic hypotheses.

I. THE BASIC HYPOTHESES AND THEIR INTERRELATIONSHIP

Our main thesis is that parties in democratic politics are analogous
to entrepreneurs in a profit-seeking economy. So as to attain their
private ends, they formulate whatever policies they believe will gain
the most votes, just as entrepreneurs produce whatever products they
believe will gain the most profits for the same reason. In order to examine the implications of this thesis, we have also assumed that citi-

zens behave rationally in politics. This premise is itself a second major hypothesis. Therefore two sets of testable propositions emerge from our study—one set derived from each major hypothesis.

Furthermore, these two sets are not entirely independent of each other, because the assumption that citizens behave rationally is implicit in some of the conclusions drawn from the hypothesis about party motivation. As a result, if the evidence contradicts certain propositions it is not possible to tell which basic hypothesis is at fault.

For example, the reasoning in Chapter 7 leads to the following conclusion: if voters behave rationally, vote-maximizing parties will be relatively honest about keeping their promises when elected, and their policies will be relatively consistent over time. Let us assume that the available evidence proves beyond doubt that parties are neither honest nor consistent. Clearly, at least one of the hypotheses is impugned by this outcome, but which one? We cannot tell whether voters are not rational, or parties do not act to maximize votes, or both.

This difficulty frequently arises; hence testing the theory is not as simple as it might at first seem. However, since most of the propositions derived from the rationality hypothesis are independent of the party-motivation thesis, the former can be tested directly without such ambiguous results.

II. SPECIFIC TESTABLE PROPOSITIONS

A. DEDUCTIONS FROM THE PARTY-MOTIVATION HYPOTHESIS

The following testable propositions are derived from the hypothesis that political parties in a democracy plan their policies so as to maximize votes:

Proposition 1: Party members have as their chief motivation the desire to obtain the intrinsic rewards of holding office; therefore they formulate policies as means to holding office rather than seeking office in order to carry out preconceived policies. (Derived from Chapter 2.)

Proposition 2: Both parties in a two-party system agree on any issues that a majority of citizens strongly favor. (Derived from Chapter 4.)

Proposition 3: In a two-party system, party policies are (a) more vague, (b) more similar to those of other parties, and (c) less directly linked to an ideology than in a multiparty system. (Derived from Chapter 8.)

Proposition 4: In a multiparty system governed by a coalition, the government takes less effective action to solve basic social problems, and its policies are less integrated and consistent, than in a two-party system. (Derived from Chapter 9.)

Proposition 5: New parties arise when either (a) a change in suffrage laws sharply alters the distribution of citizens along the political scale, (b) there is a sudden change in the electorate's social outlook because of some upheaval such as war, revolution, inflation, or depression, or (c) in a two-party system, one of the parties takes a moderate stand on an issue and its radical members organize a splinter-party to force it back towards a more extreme position. (Derived from Chapter 8.)

Proposition 6: Democratic governments tend to redistribute income from the rich to the poor.[1] (Derived from Chapter 10.)

Proposition 7: Democratic governments tend to favor producers more than consumers in their actions. (Derived from Chapter 13.)

B. DEDUCTIONS FROM THE CITIZEN-RATIONALITY HYPOTHESIS

The following testable propositions are derived from the hypothesis that every citizen rationally attempts to maximize his utility income, including that portion of it derived from government activity:

---

[1] See R. A. Musgrave, J. J. Carroll, L. D. Cook, and L. Frane, "Distribution of Tax Payments by Income Groups: A Case Study for 1948," *National Tax Journal*, IV (March, 1951), 1–53; and Alan Peacock and P. R. Browning, "The Social Services in Great Britain and the Redistribution of Income," *Income Redistribution and Social Policy* (London: Jonathan Cape, 1954). Since the former study covers only taxation, estimates of expenditure distribution would have to be added to test Proposition 6. The latter study considers both expenditure and taxation and is therefore adequate in itself for testing this corollary. Its findings support our hypothesis.

Proposition 8: Among citizens who decide how to vote on the basis of issues, the records of each party (especially the incumbents) during the election period just ending are more important to their decisions than party promises about the future.[2] (Derived from Chapter 3.)

Proposition 9: Under certain circumstances, a rational man votes for a party other than the one he would most prefer to see in office. (Derived from Chapter 3.)

Proposition 10: Rational men may vote for a hopeless party if (a) they are future oriented and the party's hopelessness is relatively new, or (b) they hope to influence another party's platform by so doing. (Derived from Chapter 3.)

Proposition 11: Many citizens who vote and consider voting important are nevertheless not well-informed on the issues involved in the election.[3] (Derived from Chapters 6 and 13.)

Proposition 12: Because nearly every citizen realizes his vote is not decisive in each election, the incentive of most citizens to acquire information before voting is very small.[4] (Derived from Chapter 13.)

Proposition 13: A large percentage of citizens—including voters— do not become informed to any significant degree on the issues involved in elections, even if they believe the outcomes to be important.[5] (Derived from Chapter 14.)

[2] Not all rational citizens make voting decisions on the basis of issues. As we pointed out earlier, some rational men habitually vote for the same party, others vote by means of ideologies, and still others never vote. On the other hand, not all men who behave thus are rational. See Chapters 6 and 7 for an explanation of when ignoring issues is rational.

[3] The following studies contain material relevant to this proposition and many of the others mentioned later: E. Katz and P. F. Lazarsfeld, *Personal Influence* (Glencoe, Illinois: The Free Press, 1955); Angus Campbell and Robert L. Kahn, *The People Elect a President* (Ann Arbor: Survey Research Center, Institute for Social Research, 1952); Bernard Berelson, "Democratic Theory and Public Opinion," *The Public Opinion Quarterly*, XVI (Fall, 1952), 313–330; P. F. Lazarsfeld, B. Berelson, and H. Gaudet, *The People's Choice* (New York: Columbia University Press, 1948); B. Berelson, P. F. Lazarsfeld, and W. N. McPhee, *Voting* (Chicago: University of Chicago Press, 1954); and Seymour Lipset, P. F. Lazarsfeld, Allen H. Barton, and Juan Linz, "The Psychology of Voting: An Analysis of Political Behavior," *Handbook of Social Psychology*, ed. by Gardner Lindzey (Cambridge, Mass.: Addison-Wesley Publishing Company, Inc., 1954), II, 1124–1175.

[4] See the studies cited in footnote 3 above.

[5] See the studies cited in footnote 3 above.

Proposition 14: The citizens who are best informed on any specific issue are those whose income is directly affected by it, i.e., who earn their incomes in the policy area it concerns. (Derived from Chapter 13.)

Proposition 15: Citizens who are well-informed on issues that affect them as income-earners are probably not equally well-informed on issues that affect them as consumers. (Derived from Chapter 13.)

Proposition 16: Citizens who have definite party preferences are more likely to vote than those who cannot see much net difference between parties.[6] (Derived from Chapters 3 and 6.)

Proposition 17: Many citizens delegate even the evaluative steps in voting to others and follow the advice of those others in casting their ballots.[7] (Derived from Chapter 12.)

Proposition 18: Citizens of a democracy obtain a return from voting *per se* even if they do not care who wins the particular election in question. (Derived from Chapter 14.)

Proposition 19: The percentage of low-income citizens who abstain in elections is higher than the percentage of high-income citizens who abstain, *ceteris paribus.*[8] (Derived from Chapter 14.)

Proposition 20: If proposition 19 is true, the reasons for higher abstention among low-income classes are (a) greater uncertainty caused by the inability to bear information costs and (b) more difficulty bearing voting costs. (Derived from Chapter 14.)

Proposition 21: When voting costs are reduced substantially, participation in elections increases greatly. (Derived from Chapter 14.)

Proposition 22: Citizens who are exposed to information chosen by means of nonhomogeneous selection principles tend to abstain from voting more than those whose information comes from sources with homogeneous principles.[9] (Derived from Chapter 12.)

---

[6] See the studies cited in footnote 3 above.

[7] See the studies cited in footnote 3 above.

[8] See the studies cited in footnote 3 above.

[9] See Lipset, Lazarsfeld, Barton, and Linz, *op. cit.* Actually, since our analysis in Chapter 12 was partly designed to suit the conclusions reached in the study here cited, that study does not constitute a fair test for Proposition 22.

C. DEDUCTIONS FROM BOTH HYPOTHESES

The following testable propositions are derived from both of the hypotheses previously described:

Proposition 23:   Political parties tend to carry out as many of their promises as they can whenever they are elected. (Derived from Chapter 7.)

Proposition 24:   Political parties tend to maintain ideological positions that are consistent over time unless they suffer drastic defeats, in which case they change their ideologies to resemble that of the party which defeated them. (Derived from Chapter 7.)

Proposition 25:   In systems usually governed by coalitions, most citizens do not vote as though elections were government-selection mechanisms. (Derived from Chapter 9.)

III. SUMMARY

Two major hypotheses are explicitly developed in our study: the theory that parties act to maximize votes, and the postulate that citizens behave rationally in politics. Though sometimes the explication of the first is dependent upon the second, each leads to a set of propositions which can be tested empirically. We have listed these propositions and cited any reference we know relevant to testing them.

Bibliography

Aristotle. *Politics*. Jowett Translation, Modern Library Edition. New York: The Modern Library, 1943.

Arrow, Kenneth J. "Alternative Theories of Decision-Making in Risk-Taking Situations," *Econometrica*, XIX (1951), 404–437.

Arrow, Kenneth J. *Social Choice and Individual Values*. New York: John Wiley & Sons, Inc., 1951.

Baumol, William J. *Welfare Economics and the Theory of the State*. London: Longmans, Green and Co., 1952.

Berelson, Bernard. "Democratic Theory and Public Opinion," *The Public Opinion Quarterly*, XVI (Fall, 1952), 313–330.

Berelson, Bernard, Lazarsfeld, Paul F., and McPhee, William N. *Voting*. Chicago: University of Chicago Press, 1954.

Bergson (Burk), Abram. "A Reformulation of Certain Aspects of Welfare Economics," *Quarterly Journal of Economics*, LII (February, 1938), 314–344.

Bergson (Burk), Abram. "Socialist Economics," in A *Survey of Contemporary Economics*, ed. by Howard S. Ellis. Philadelphia: The Blakiston Company, 1949, vol. I.

Boulding, Kenneth. "Welfare Economics," in A *Survey of Contemporary Economics*, ed. by Bernard F. Haley. Homewood, Illinois: Richard D. Irwin Inc., 1952, vol. II.

Bowen, Howard R. "The Interpretation of Voting in the Allocation of Economic Resources," *Quarterly Journal of Economics*, LVIII (November, 1943), 27–48.

Buchanan, James. "The Pure Theory of Government Finance: A Suggested Approach," *Journal of Political Economy*, LVII (December, 1949), 496–505.

Calhoun, John C. "Disquisition on Government," in *Public Opinion and Propaganda*, ed. by Katz, Cartwright, Eldersveld, and Lee. New York; The Dryden Press, 1954.

Campbell, Angus, Gurin, Gerald, and Miller, Warren E. *The Voter Decides*. Evanston, Illinois: Row, Peterson, and Company, 1954.

Campbell, Angus, and Kahn, Robert L. *The People Elect a President*. Ann Arbor: Survey Research Center, Institute for Social Research, 1952.

Colm, Gerhard. *Essays in Public Finance and Fiscal Policy*. New York: Oxford University Press, 1955.

Cort, John C. "The Dice Are Slightly Loaded," *The Commonweal*, LXII (June 24, 1955), 302–303.

Dahl, Robert A. *A Preface to Democratic Theory*. Chicago: University of Chicago Press, 1956.

Dahl, Robert A., and Lindblom, Charles E. *Politics, Economics and Welfare*. New York: Harper & Brothers, 1953.

Dalton, Hugh. *The Principles of Public Finance*. London: George Routledge and Sons, Ltd., 1932.

Durkheim, Emile. "Division of Labor and Social Solidarity," in *The Making of Society*, ed. by V. F. Calverton. New York: Modern Library, 1937, pp. 381–383.

Edwards, Lyford P. *The Natural History of Revolution*. Chicago: University of Chicago Press, 1927.

Fagan, Elmer D., and Macy, C. Ward, eds. *Public Finance: Selected Readings*. New York: Longmans, Green and Co., 1936.

Friedman, Milton. "Choice, Chance, and the Personal Distribution of Income," *Journal of Political Economy*, LXI (August, 1953), 277–290.

Friedman, Milton. *Essays in Positive Economics*. Chicago: University of Chicago Press, 1953.

Groves, Harold M., ed. *Viewpoints on Public Finance*. New York: Henry Holt and Company, 1947.

Hicks, J. R. *Value and Capital*. Oxford: Clarendon Press, 1950, 2nd ed.

Horney, Karen. *The Neurotic Personality of Our Time*. New York: W. W. Norton & Company, Inc., 1937.

Hotelling, Harold. "Stability in Competition," *The Economic Journal*, XXXIX (1929), 41–57.

Katz, E., and Lazarsfeld, Paul F. *Personal Influence*. Glencoe, Illinois: The Free Press, 1955.

Kay, V. O. Jr. *Politics, Parties, and Pressure Groups*. New York: Thomas Y. Crowell Company, 1953.

Keynes, John Maynard. *The General Theory of Employment, Interest, and Money*. New York: Harcourt, Brace and Company, 1936.

Lazarsfeld, Paul F., Berelson, Bernard, and Gaudet, Hazel. *The People's Choice.* New York: Columbia University Press, 1948.

Lerner, Abba P. *The Economics of Control.* New York: The Macmillan Company, 1944.

Lerner, Abba P. "The Essential Properties of Interest and Money," *Quarterly Journal of Economics,* LXVI (1952), 172–193.

Lerner, Abba P., and Singer, H. W. "Some Notes on Duopoly and Spatial Competition," *Journal of Political Economy,* XLV (1937), 145–186.

Lippmann, Walter. *Essays in the Public Philosophy.* Boston: Little, Brown and Company, 1955.

Lippmann, Walter. *The Phantom Public.* New York: Harcourt, Brace and Company, 1925.

Lippmann, Walter. *Public Opinion.* New York: The Macmillan Company, 1922.

Lipset, Seymour, Lazarsfeld, Paul F., Barton, Allen H., and Linz, Juan. "The Psychology of Voting: An Analysis of Political Behavior," in *Handbook of Social Psychology,* ed. by Gardner Lindzey. Cambridge, Mass.: Addison-Wesley Publishing Company, Inc., 1954, II, 1124–1175.

Lösch, August. *The Economics of Location.* New Haven: Yale University Press, 1954.

Mannheim, Karl. *Ideology and Utopia.* Harvest Book Series. New York: Harcourt, Brace and Company, 1955.

Margolis, Julius. "A Comment on the Pure Theory of Public Expenditures," *Review of Economics and Statistics,* XXXVII (November, 1955), 347–349.

Maritain, Jacques. *The Social and Political Philosophy of Jacques Maritain,* ed. by J. Evans and L. R. Ward. New York: Scribner's, 1955.

Marschak, Jacob. "Towards an Economic Theory of Organization and Information," in *Decision Processes,* ed. by R. M. Thrall, C. H. Coombs, and R. L. Davis. New York: John Wiley & Sons, Inc., 1954.

Meyerson, Martin, and Banfield, Edward C. *Politics, Planning, and the Public Interest.* Glencoe, Illinois: The Free Press, 1955.

Musgrave, Richard A. "The Voluntary Exchange Theory of Public Economy," *Quarterly Journal of Economics,* LIII (1939), 213–237.

Musgrave, R. A., Carroll, J. J., Cook, L. D., and Frane, L. "Distribution of Tax Payments by Income Groups: A Case Study for 1948," *National Tax Journal,* IV (March, 1951), 1–53.

Niebuhr, Reinhold. *Faith and History.* New York: Charles Scribner's Sons, 1951.

Peacock, Alan, and Browning, P. R. "The Social Services in Great Britain and the Redistribution of Income," *Income Redistribution and Social Policy*. London: Jonathan Cape, 1954.

Peck, Harvey W. *Taxation and Welfare*. New York: The Macmillan Company, 1925.

Pigou, A. C. *The Economics of Welfare*. London: Macmillan and Company Ltd., 1932, 4th ed.

Plato. *The Republic*. Jowett Translation, Modern Library Edition. New York: The Modern Library, n.d.

Riesman, David. *The Lonely Crowd*. New Haven: Yale University Press, 1950.

Rousseau, Jean Jacques. *The Social Contract*. Hafner Library of Classics Edition. New York: Hafner Publishing Company, 1954.

Samuelson, Paul A. "Diagrammatic Exposition of a Theory of Public Expenditure," *Review of Economics and Statistics*, XXXVII (November, 1955), 350–356.

Samuelson, Paul A. "The Pure Theory of Public Expenditures," *Review of Economics and Statistics*, XXXVI (November, 1954), 387–389.

Schneider, Erich. "Bemerkungen zu Einer Theorie der Raumwirtschaft," *Econometrica*, III (1935), 79–105.

Schumpeter, Joseph A. *Capitalism, Socialism, and Democracy*. New York: Harper & Brothers, 1950.

Scitovsky, Tibor. "The State of Welfare Economics," *American Economic Review*, XLI (1951), 303–315.

Scitovsky, Tibor. "Two Concepts of External Economies," *Journal of Political Economy*, LXII (April, 1954), 143–151.

Seligman, E. R. A. "The Social Theory of Fiscal Science," *Political Science Quarterly*, XLI (1926).

Selznick, Philip. "A Theory of Organizational Commitments," *Reader in Bureaucracy*, ed. by Merton, Gray, Hockey, and Selvin. Glencoe, Illinois: The Free Press, 1952.

Simon, Herbert A., *Administrative Behavior*. New York: The Macmillan Company, 1947.

Simon, Herbert A., "A Behavioral Model of Rational Choice," *Quarterly Journal of Economics*, LXIX (February, 1955).

Simons, Henry C. *Economic Policy for a Free Society*. Chicago: University of Chicago Press, 1948.

Smith, Adam. *The Wealth of Nations*. Modern Library Edition. New York: The Modern Library, 1937.

Smithies, Arthur. "Optimum Location in Spatial Competition," *The Journal of Political Economy*, XLIX (1941), 423–439.

Zeuthen, F. "Theoretical Remarks on Price Policy: Hotelling's Case with Variations," *Quarterly Journal of Economics*, XLVII (1933), 231–253.

Index of Names

305

Index of Subjects

Printer and Binder: The Murray Printing Company
86 87 88 89 90   30 29 28 27 26 25